Sun Over Mountain

A course in
Creative Imagery

Jessica Macbeth

Foreword by Muz Murray

GATEWAY BOOKS, BATH

For Tamara Scott
with much love

Distributors

AcuMedic CENTRE
101-105 CAMDEN HIGH STREET
LONDON NW1 7JN
Tel: 0171-388 5783/6704
Catalogue on Request

First published in 1991
by Gateway Books
The Hollies, Wellow,
Bath BA2 8QJ

Reprinted 1994

Cover design by John Douet
Photograph by Jessica Macbeth
Set 10 on 12 pt Bembo, by
Ann Buchan (Typesetters), Middlesex,
Printed and bound by
Redwood Books of Trowbridge

British Library Cataloguing in Publication Data
Macbeth, Jessica Williams, 1937
Sun over mountain: a course in creative
imagery
1. Meditation
I. Title
158'.12

ISBN 0.946551.67.7

Table of Contents

Foreword — by Muz Murray   vi
Acknowledgements   ix
Introduction   xi

Part I.   I, Mage   1

1. You, the Magician   3
2. The Inner Journey   3
   Light into Darkness   6
3. Keeping Track Of Where You Are   11
4. The Verbal Record   12
5. The Visual Record   14
6. Speaking the Language: Colour   15

Part II.   Discovering the Inner World   19

7. Cultivating Awareness   21
8. Basic Skills for the Guide   22
9. An Exploration   26
   A Walk in the Forest   26
10. Speaking the Language: Line   31

Part III.   Meeting the Natives   33

11. The Natives   35
12. Powers & Shadows   36
    The Wise Old Wo/Man   39
13. Name Magic   43

Part IV.   Where Are We Going?   47

14. Know Thyself   49
15. Destinations   50
    When I Grow Old, Very Old   51
16. Oracles and the Way Ahead   55
17. Where Do You Want to Go?   56

Part V: Recognising the Landmarks   61

18. Speaking the Language: Images   63
19. Seeing a Rose   64

20. Getting the Most from the Journey   67
     21. Observation Skills   68
          Checking It Out   69
     22. Seeing It The Way It Is   71
23. Speaking the Language: Form   74

Part VI.   The Quest for Guidance   77

     24. Forms of the Journey   79
     25. Freeform Journeys   80
          The Journey without a Map 83
     26. Interactive Journeys   84
          The Advisor   85
     27. Speaking the Language: Mood   91

Part VII.   Overcoming Obstacles   95

     28. Tripping over Our Own Feet   97
     29. Co-operation & Compromises   100
          Disarming the Rebel   101

Part VIII.   Down the Wrong Path   109

     30. Who Is in Charge Here?   111
     31. Getting through the Hard Places   112
32. When Not to Go — Cautionary Signs   119

Part IX.   Journey to Healing   125

     33. The Healing Place   127
          Journey to the Waterfall   128
     34. The Wounded Traveller   135
     35. Consulting the Healer   136
          The Healer   136

Part X.   The Maps in Our Minds   143

     36. Travellers' Tales   145
     37. Understanding These Tales   147
     38. The Mental Map   148
     39. Correcting the Map   154
          Creating Affirmations   157

Part XI.   Travel Broadens the Mind   159

     40. The Far Reaches of Space-Time   161
          Pool of Water   161
     41. The Heart of the Matter   170
42. Would You Rather Have Chocolate?   172

Part XII.   The Meeting Place   177
     43. Two Travellers   179
     44. Travelling Together   184
          Round the World in 30 Minutes   184
     45. The Alchemist's Tower   192

46.   Speaking the Language: Puns 194

Part XIII. In the Company of the Gods 195
   47.   The Home of the Gods 197
   48.   Exploring the Unknown 202
         Meta-Mind 204
   49.   Trans-Dimensional Travel 209

Part XIV. Creating New Paths 219
   50.   Choosing a Destination 221
      51.   Landmarks 222
      52.   Signposts 225
      53.   Caravans 226
   54.   Direct & Indirect Routes 228
      55.   Beginnings 229
      56.   Endings 232
   57.   Creating a New Path 232
        The Lake 233
        Emerald City 234

Part XV. Serving as A Guide 237
   58.   Leadership Skills 239
      59.   Group Tours 240
      60.   Individual Journeys 241
   61.   Breakdown or Breakthrough? 242
   62.   The Qualities of a Good Guide 246

Part XVI. Encounter with a Magician 249
   63.   Meet the Magician 251
      The Crystal Cave 251
      64.   Imagic 256

Appendix A: On Working Together 261
Appendix B: For the Teacher 269
Appendix C: Tapes 273
Notes 275
Recommended Reading 276

Foreword

"Inner work often deserves a higher priority than we give it," says Jesa Macbeth. And this book goes a long way to showing us why.

After nearly thirty years of constant spiritual research and psycho-therapeutic practice, I can state categorically that inner work *always* deserves a higher priority than we give it. Yet most people have the tendency to hope that help is always going to come from somewhere outside themselves instead. This naive conception is endemic in India, where many seekers believe that when they find a Guru — a spiritual Master — their work is done and they can rest on their laurels, basking in his glory. They think it is enough to acquiesce to everything; "Yes Guruji, no Guruji, three bags full, Guruji," and thereby imagine that their lives have changed as he is in control of their spiritual benefit from then on and doing all the work for them.

But it does not work that way. A teacher may point out the direction, but we have to walk the road ourselves. Each of us forges our own destiny. Change can only occur from within. It is how we observe, utilise or manipulate our own mindstuff which effects any change in our lives. And I purposely say 'mindstuff' here, rather than 'mind'. Mind — which is a useful abstract concept to indicate all our modes of mental functioning — is not a *thing* in itself, but a fluid process, intermittently functioning at various levels. How we perceive life is determined by which level of consciousness we are operating through at the time.

What we call 'mind' then is — like everything else in this insubstantial universe — actually a form of flowing energy, endlessly upsurging like an unstoppable spring. But left to its own devices, mind-flow is wasteful and unproductive. It tends to run out in all directions, uselessly gathering all kinds of flotsam and piling up log-jams along the way. These log-jams are consciousness blocks which often take a lot of psychological unpicking. But if we were to encourage this mind-flow to run in worthwhile channels, we could water the parched and neglected parts of our being.

However, to the detriment of humanity, our present western world concept of education is to nurture almost exclusively the mind-flow apparently generated through the left (analytic mode) hemisphere of the brain. For the most part it ignores the creative, wholistic, seeing-how-it-all-fits-together mind-flow operating through the right (associative mode) hemisphere of the brain. Were it not for the fantasies of our dreams upsurging via the right-side channel every night, our conscious life might be unbearably sterile.

Dream-flow appears to be an attempt to make amends for the sixteen-or-so waking hours of analytical left-brain logic. It assists us to overcome the imbalance of its exclusive usage. In order to avoid lop-sided living, (each half of the brain is, after all, equal) we need a harmonious co-operation between both the analytical and associative modes of mind-flow in our everyday experience. Brain-fag is a warning of analytical over- exposure. The intensity of our dream images is a counter-balancing activity to bring about equilibrium. Dreams are messages from the heart and soul. But how often do we listen to them? And how much do we miss? We all know the frustration of waking up in the morning and trying to remember scraps of a dream we are sure was trying to tell us something important.

Yet we can call on a similar faculty in our waking life. Guided imagery enables us to access the intuitive insights of the dream-flow channel while in a receptive waking state. Its practice is informative, stimulating, refreshing and freeing. It often brings light to dark corners of the psyche, allowing us to see our hidden motivations. It is like rediscovering a magic land forgotten, for our thoughts create other realities.

"Thoughts are things," says Jesa, affirming what my spiritual mentor, Brahmananda Guru, often maintained. Thoughts are potentised energy patterns of the subtle forces, which have created our universe. Mystics have known this for millennia. Now even scientists are beginning to discover that the whole universe is 'Consciousness Soup'. "More like a great Thought than a great machine," said Sir James Jeans, the eminent physicist. That is, Thought manifesting as the *appearance* of matter.

'Matter' has been found not to be solid in itself, but either visible or not according to different densities of vibratory energy. Therefore if what we see is only energy patterns manifesting or projecting an apparent world from some mysterious seemingly universal Consciousness — what is the real nature of the world? Are we inhabiting a Cosmic Hologramme, appearing according to our capacity of seeing? Evidently everything is made of the same basic scientifically unfindable stuff: Consciousness, say the mystics.

If Consciousness is the base, then mindstuff is the medium through which it operates. The mental pictures our thoughts compose are made up and contained in this mindstuff, which we might visualise as micro-neutrinos or even more infinitesimal subtle particles — rather like the particles which make up the images on the television screen. Just as these picture-bearing particles or waves which appear on our television screen exist everywhere in the atmosphere, but manifest only i the set, so Consciousness is everywhere and manifests through what we think of as individual minds. Thus mindstuff is the individual portion of the living stuff of universal Consciousness: the Mirror of the Divine.

If the universe is only an appearance in Divine Consciousness we are therefore — by virtue of 'individual' consciousness — co-creators with whatever is thinking it into existence. Each of us adds our tithe to creating what the universe is. Or — what it is becoming.

Every sentient being can be likened to a light bulb plugging in to a universal electricity supply, each one adding its brightness to the whole. However we all seem to have our own built-in dimmer-switch which causes us to view the world dimly or brightly according to our lights.

Hence the importance of this book.

Sun Over Mountain is the most fulfilling book of creative visualisation I have encountered. It is inspiring to read and even more inspiring to practice. If I were a neutrino I would be deliriously happy living in the wonder-world of Jesa's imagination. As it is, she stimulates us to awaken our own. We are led warmly and caringly to listen to our hearts, discovering our hidden beliefs about ourselves and our relation to the world along the way. The more we grow and understand, the more our mind-flow influences creation for the better.

If you would enjoy listening to your heart, then lie down on Jesa's magic feathered mattress with utmost confidence. You will journey with a very sensitive and sympathetic guide who well knows the way.

Are you resting comfortably?

Then breathe deeply — for it can take you anywhere!

— Muz Murray

Acknowledgements

Some of the imagery journeys in this book are new, created just for you and me, and others have been adapted from a variety of sources. Although I can create 'new' imagery journeys, they all have their roots in other images, other journeys. For example, I heard an imagery journey several years ago from Elizabeth St. John, who got one version from *Grist for the Mill* by Ram Dass and another version from C. Maxwell Cade, who *may* have obtained his version from the Tantric tradition. She worked with it, blending the two, and adapted it to her own needs. I heard it from her once five or six years ago, liked it, and began working with it myself, again adapting and changing it for my own purposes and calling it *Meta-Mind*. Until she read this manuscript, just before it went to the typesetter, I didn't know her sources for the imagery, and by then there wasn't time to find a copy of *Grist for the Mill* to see how closely mine was like the one in there — so you will have to judge for yourself. I don't even know whether Ram Dass developed his imagery himself, or heard it somewhere. That's how these things travel. Images move from mind to mind, leaving mysterious tracks and strange reactions.

For images and for other reasons, I would like to acknowledge special debts to:

Jonathan and Nadine MacLane for computer conversion so I could see the wretched screen, and for having patience, and for being Really Good Kids,

Joe Bibbey for the elevator, the popsicles, an immortal, and general outrageousness,

Pat Pilkington for trial reading, helping to make this more coherent, and much generosity of spirit,

Canon Christopher Pilkington for healing well above and beyond the call of duty,

Angela Enthoven for living up to her name and generously attempting to create some order out of my chaos,

Rev. Nancy Nelson for loving foresight, clarity, optimism, and being there when needed,

Rev. Judy Dean for loving help in the maintenance of sanity and for spiritual guidance,

Su O'Donnell for generously given healing and interesting discussions,

Elizabeth St. John for trial reading, expert advice, ideas, mind-clearing, and healing — not necessarily in that order,

Eileen Herzberg for making essential connections, for mutual commiseration and support, and for trial reading and a sharp eye — she should have been in the last book too,

Su Fox for trial reading, and constructive, useful suggestions and comments,

Jane Whittle for trial reading with a poet's eye,

John Slade for special assistance in the attempt to create order and increase productivity,

Dr. John Daniel for helpful information and discussions,

Norman King and the west of Scotland for sanctuary and inspiration,

Olga Lawrence and Brockham End for a peaceful nesting place,

Alick Bartholomew for patience with a deranged authoress, helpful suggestions, and good nature against the odds,

Chris Nalder and Ann Buchan for their parts in the production and for being a pleasure to work with,

Sami and Sylvie and the garden for absolutely vital distractions,

The members of the Order of the Ascending Spirit, especially the new U.K. Chapter, for spiritual support and other things,

And very special thanks to the people who wrote to tell me how much they liked and/or benefited from *Moon Over Water*, and the reviewers who said such kind things about it — all of which helped to motivate me through the more difficult bits of this one.

I would like to express special gratitude to Terry Pratchett for writing the Discworld series, *The Colour of Magic, The Light Fantastic, Equal Rites, Wyrd Sisters, Mort, Sourcery, Eric* (with Josh Kirby), *Reaper Man, Moving Pictures, Pyramids, and Guards! Guards!*. Other books include *Good Omens* (with Neil Gaiman) and *The Unadulterated Cat* (with Gray Jolliffe). I'm especially grateful for Granny Weatherwax, whose image strides purposefully through the mountains of my mind. Long may her broomstick soar — or at least get off the ground. These books are definitely recommended reading, and Corgi Books and Victor Gollancz Ltd. are the publishers.

Modern technology is so wonderful. It means I can't blame mistakes on the typesetter or other people — all of the mistakes and misconceptions are my own.

Introduction

This is a book about fantasy, the art of imagination, and the power we have to create our lives, and it is written as a training course. You don't have to use it that way, but I hope you will — partly because I think you will get far more out of it, and also, because I think you will have much more fun with it.

If you are working in a group, using this book for a study guide, I suggest you begin by reading *Appendix A: Working Together*. If everyone reads it before the first meeting, and if you begin your journey together with a discussion of it, you will be able to start with a common frame of reference and mutual understanding. I suggest you also have some discussion about what you each hope to get out of this, your reasons for joining the group.

If you are planning to use the book as the text in a course you are teaching, or if you are using the book by yourself, you may find it useful to read *Appendix B: For the Teacher* before you begin.

Writing a book is, for me, like trying to wrestle an old-fashioned feather mattress into shape. Every time I push one bit into place, it bulges out somewhere else. When I try to pick it up, it slithers in my arms until it has me surrounded. The objective, of course, is to get it smooth and comfortable, with just the right amount of support all over. Although I had a great deal of help with the feathers, in the end the mattress won and assumed its own shape. When I was a child, we had a wonderful, huge, uncontrollable, feather mattress, and it was delightful both for dreaming and for bouncing and playing on. I hope you find this book is like that.

With love,

Jesa

Part I

I, Mage

Scientists have calculated that the chance of anything so patently absurd actually existing are millions to one.

But magicians have calculated that million-to-one chances crop up nine times out of ten.
— *Terry Pratchett*
in Mort

1. You, the Magician

image = i mage = I, mage; I, magician; I imagine

The power to image is the power to create.

You are the seeker, on a quest for wholeness and the holy place within you. You are the wanderer on a pilgrimage to self-knowledge, learning to see and to listen to your inner truth. You are the shaman on a vision quest to find your own power and your natural magic. And as you pursue your quest, you may become the magician who transforms yourself — understanding who you really are and what you can become, transforming 'I can't' to 'I do' as you create a new present and more promising future for yourself, discovering your creativity and inner power, healing your past and yourself, and fulfilling your potential.

Like all magicians, you will need a magic wand and a grimoire, a book of sorcery. This grimoire is something you must create for yourself — it is something no one else can do for you. The grimoire of the seeker-magician is a working notebook — a record of the journeys into the inner worlds, the lessons learned there, and the powers and insights gained. The magic wand is both a pen and a paintbrush. The pen is to transcribe the observations of the linear, verbal, analytic mode of your mind while the paintbrush captures the images of the global, visual, associative mode. This is a momentous journey to take with so little equipment as a pen, a paintbrush, some paints, a notebook, and paper, but it really is all we need.

Are you ready?
Then read on.

2. The Inner Journey

This is a different kind of journey we are embarking upon, a pilgrimage in, instead of out, and rather than starting in the lowlands, as people usually do, we shall start at the top of a mountain at dawn. I'd like you to imagine that your mind is like a mountain, with the top, which we call consciousness, just touched by the light of the rising sun, and the rest, the unconscious mind, still shrouded by night.

Standing on top of the mountain, we can see the tips of other mountains looming up out of the darkness, some nearby, some further in the distance. Each one is another person, another mind, and it seems as if we are all separate islands of light, scattered in darkness. We aren't.

All of these mountains are connected to one another, some nearly and others more distantly. We all have our roots in the same earth. We will be exploring the connections, the illusion of separateness, the valleys and the peaks, the darkness and the light. In fact, we'll be bringing light into the darkness, discovering the monsters and the marvels that lie hidden. The gods don't live just on Mount Olympus; they also live in the depths of our souls and minds.

If the human race as a whole is evolving still (and I know there can be argument about that), it is quite possible that the direction of evolution at present is toward greater balance between Artemis and Apollo, the light of increasing consciousness, and Dionysus and Hekate, the inner wildness, ecstasy, and the mysterious darkness of the archetypal depths. This is a journey both to increasing awareness and to increasing acceptance of the depths and mysteries of the unconscious. This is the journey shared by the shaman and the saint, the alchemist and the healer. We all have within us an untapped natural magic, but we ignore it. We are too busy catching the bus and doing the laundry, filling out forms, forward planning, decision making, remembering to order extra milk — all of the things we think are important, and the things we think are unimportant. They occupy our minds and use up our energy. And all the while, above, behind, and beneath this surface level of consciousness, there are amazing, powerful, magical things going on — obscured from our awareness by the busy activity on the surface. Genius lies beyond this surface, and we are usually too busy to notice it, so we think that we are 'ordinary' people.

Think about this: we actually live on the highland plains and mountain tops of the earth. Most of the earth's surface is underwater. If all the water suddenly disappeared, we would discover that we are all denizens of the heights. The seas are teeming with life, and we know little about the dwellers of the depths. There are giants down there that we never know, and it is always in darkness. We came out of the sea — not from the always dark depths, but from the sunlit surface waters. We have climbed higher and higher, until we reached the highest mountain known, and then went beyond to the moon. And although we have been to the moon, we have still not been to the deepest places of the surface of our earth, although we have sent probes a long way down.

This pretty well describes our relationship with our minds. We have explored some of the well-lit areas, many of us have looked into space, we have even explored some areas of shadow — some of us more than others — but much remains unknown. Such exploration is perilous, yet necessary. Madness is a result of becoming lost in the darkness of the unconscious, but we become lost because we have not learned the territory. Like the depths of the sea, the depths of the mind are the true *terra incognita*. The inhabitants of the depths of our minds influence us, push us, sometimes even compel us. We need to know them.

There are nearly always images rising into our conscious minds. Many of these are messages from the dwellers in the deep. Some of the images are visual, some auditory, some are sensations or emotions. An image is simply a representation in the mind of something we have experienced or imagined, and our minds seem to have an immense, almost infinite store of them.

We use these images to communicate within ourselves, between one level of consciousness and another. A constant exchange goes on between the surface level of our minds (the sunlit top of the mountain, which we call consciousness) and the many deeper levels. The images we carry inside ourselves create the geology and climate of our inner worlds, our inner self. These images determine much of how we interpret the world around us, and this in turn determines how we feel about and respond to it. To a great extent, these inner images determine the quality and direction of our lives.

I chose the title for this book because it *felt* right, and I liked it. It seemed to go well with *Moon Over Water*, my first book, and the title *Sun Over Mountain* indicates that this one is looking at the other side of consciousness, another aspect of the mind. Where the moon is the yielding, reflective image, the sun is the active, life-giving, choice-making principle. Our journey together is about making our choices consciously, creatively, and constructively, through a balanced and integrated blend of analysis and intuition.

Obviously, the title I chose evokes some kind of an image in your mind, as well as in mine. Having chosen the name by 'feel' I immediately became curious, of course, about its symbolism and began to explore what it might mean, not only to myself, but to others as well. There is a well known book of images and interpretations called the *I Ching*. The closest thing to 'sun over mountain' in the *I Ching* is the double trigram 'fire over mountain'. The *I Ching* is a very old book which has been interpreted and re-interpreted, translated and re-translated, in countless versions. In one version[1] 'fire over mountain' is considered to represent the Wanderer or Seeker, about whom it says:

> *The Wanderer: success through smallness. Perseverance brings him blessing. The meaning within is truly great.*

How could I possibly ask for anything more appropriate? We are on a pilgrimage, a vision quest, seeking fulfilment of our own potential, our own wholeness, one small step at a time, with each chapter of the book another stepping stone on the way. To achieve this fulfilment we must, of course, persevere. And the search is within ourselves, where — and only where — we will find our own meaning and purpose and greatness.

For our first imagery exploration, I'd like us to look at the journey we are undertaking together. You may want to put the following imagery journey on a tape (see Appendix C), or you might want to have someone read it to you, slowly enough for you to be able to follow it and to allow your images to have time to arise from the deeper places of your mind. We will be considering the best ways of guiding imagery journeys later on, but for the moment, just see how it goes.

Approximate travel time: 20 minutes. This time is how long it takes me to guide a group through this journey, giving reasonable time for their imagery. Of course, it might be completely different guiding an individual who was responding aloud.

LIGHT INTO DARKNESS

We are going on a journey from light into darkness. Before we begin, I'd like you to be certain that you are seated comfortably and that no one will interrupt you for the next twenty minutes or so.

When you are ready, begin by taking two or three deep breaths and letting go of any tension in your body. Be aware of your head, your neck, your shoulders, your arms, your hands. Notice your chest, your abdomen, your pelvis. Feel your legs and ankles and feet. If there is any part of your body that would like to relax more, just allow it to do so.

Be aware of the movement of your chest and abdomen as you breathe. Notice how it feels as the breath flows in — and out — and in — and out.

Allow your fingers, your hands, your wrists to let go just a little more.

And your forehead to become smoother, more relaxed. Let your tongue and your mouth, your cheeks and your lips relax and become soft.

And again, just observe your breath. Notice how it feels as your chest and abdomen expand — and contract. Breathing in, breathing out in your own time. You are in control at all times. This is your journey and you may leave it at any time you wish, simply by deciding to do so. As you follow the imagery, accept each image as it arises, flowing with it.

You are going to meet the Sun God and the Earth Goddess and receive gifts from them. If at any time during this journey, you wish to come back to ordinary consciousness, you may do so simply by choosing to.

I'd like you to imagine that you are standing in darkness on the crown of a tall mountain, the very highest point. Notice the feel of the stone, the bones of the earth, under your feet. Be aware of the air around you. How does it feel? Is it moving or still, damp or dry, warm or cool?

The sky is filled with the light of the distant stars, but as you watch, it begins to lighten in the east. After a few moments, the first ray of sun touches the crest of your mountain, illuminating the place where you stand. Beneath you, the rest of the mountain is still wrapped in darkness.

As you watch the sun begin to rise, you notice that something is flying toward you from the heart of the sun. As it grows closer it seems at first like a large bird, and then the realisation dawns that it is the figure of a winged man, the god of the sun. He has many names and many guises, but the one in which he comes to you now is that of a red-gold man, with wings and eyes of flame. And he alights gently in front of you, seeming barely to touch the earth.

In one hand, he bears a sword, the blade of fire and light, called *Ru'-in*, and in the other he holds the scabbard, *Cunntachail*.

How do you feel as you look at him, and how does he seem to feel about you?

He asks you if you will accept him as a companion upon your journey, and he promises that, if you do, he will carry a light for you. Do you accept him? If you do, tell him so clearly in your mind.

If you accept him, he places the sword in its sheath, and he belts it around your waist.

If you reject him, he flies away, leaving you in utter darkness, and you may as well go to sleep for the rest of this imagery.

After he has given you the sword, he shows you how to draw it for yourself. If you wish, you may practise drawing it and sheathing it once or twice. The sword seems to weigh hardly anything at all, but the scabbard is heavy.

When you have put the sword back into its scabbard, he reaches into the flames of his aura for another gift, which he then offers to you. When he has placed it in your hands, notice the weight of it. Is it heavy or light? What is the texture of it? Smooth or rough? Soft or hard? What can you tell by touch about this gift? Are there any colours or sounds or scents associated with this gift?

What form does this gift take? This gift is a symbol of something you will receive in this journey to come. Ask the god what the gift symbolises. What does he tell you?

All you need to do to make this gift truly yours is to continue upon your way. For now, the Sun God takes the gift from you and places it in you or on you or around you, wherever it belongs.

You may wish to thank the Sun God for his gifts. If so, go ahead and do that now.

Now, I'd like you to turn around and begin walking or climbing down the mountain a little way, just to the edge of the radiance cast by the Sun God.

There, beside a tall stone, you will find another being, a goddess of the earth. She glows with a numinous light, but you notice that she does not cast light around her. She is as warm and as dark as the heart of the earth. She has many names and many guises, but in this time and place she has the appearance of a gypsy woman, darkly beautiful and vital.

In her hand she holds a silver chain with a dark stone pendant. The stone is named *Eivnus*, and the chain is called *Cuin*. She shows you the dark stone, and in it you seem to see into space and time, into distant galaxies. Then you realise that you are not certain, and you think that what you see may be the sub-atomic particles of the stone — the protons and electrons, neutrons and neutrinos, and the wonderfully named quarks, which are sometimes strange and sometimes charmed. The stone could be either the macrocosm or the microcosm or both, for it is filled with the creative life force that binds the universe together.

How do you feel as you look into her vivid eyes? And how does she seem to feel as she looks at you?

She asks if you will accept her also as your companion upon this journey, and she promises that, if you do, she will guide you in darkness and help you to find meaning in what you encounter there.

If you reject her, she steps away into the night, leaving you in utter darkness, and you may as well go to sleep for the rest of this imagery.

If you accept her, she places the chain around your neck, so that the stone pendant hangs in front of your heart. You may be able to feel the warmth of the stone, first in your heart, and then flowing into the rest of your body, into and through your hands and your feet. If you touch the stone with your finger, you will find that, although it is simply warm against your breast, the longer you touch it with your finger, the hotter your finger becomes, until you draw away from it.

If you have accepted her and her gift of the necklace, she reaches into the darkness behind her and brings forth another gift for you, placing it into your hands. Notice the weight of it. Is it heavy or light? What is its texture like? Smooth or rough? Soft or hard? What can you tell by touch about this gift? Are there any colours or sounds or scents associated with this gift?

What form does this gift take? This gift is a symbol of something you will receive from this journey to come in the company of the Earth Goddess. Ask her what this gift symbolises. What does she tell you?

All you need to do to make this gift truly yours is to continue upon your way. For now, the Earth Goddess takes the gift from you, and she places it in you or on you or around you, wherever it belongs.

You may wish to thank the her for her gifts to you. If so, go ahead and do that now.

When you have finished thanking her, she fades into the shadow. And when you turn around to look up at the Sun God, you find that he, too, has disappeared, leaving you in the soft light of dawn.

When you are ready, I'd like you to take a couple of deep breaths. Be aware of your chest and your abdomen as you breathe. Notice how relaxed and rested your body is.

Allow yourself to become more aware of the chair you are sitting in, and the room around you.

When you're ready, take a couple more deep breaths, flex your fingers and toes, open your eyes, and stretch, feeling relaxed and alert.

The logic of the imagery

The Sun God is the enlightening principle of consciousness. He symbolises your conscious mind, your ability to understand, to be illuminated and to 'cast light upon' ideas, situations, and principles you may encounter. He represents both a danger and a valuable talent — the danger of thinking too much, of believing that everything can be reduced to reason and logic (although the sun gods of an older, more balanced time were also often gods of poetry and music). The talent is, of course, our ability not only to think, to consciously understand, but also make conscious choices — to throw light upon our lives, to extrapolate the future, and to decide upon a course of action.

The sword is *Ru'-in* (original Gaelic spelling: *roghainn*), the meaning of which is *choice*. The scabbard is *Cunntachail*, which means *responsible* and *accountable*. The gift of choice is a two-edged sword. On the one hand it is lovely to have — few of us want to be simply a blind puppet of universal forces or even of our own unconscious forces. But on the other hand, if we have choice, we must also bear responsibility. The sword enables us to cut through to the heart of a matter, to make our choices, but we must bear the consequences of our own choices.

The goddess of earth and shadow is the symbol of the unconscious, in all its complexity and depth. She has dominion over our a-rational emotions, our ability to feel ecstasy, to create something never before seen or thought of, to experience genius. She, too, is both perilous and desirable. There is the danger of becoming lost in our feelings, without capacity for reason, and yet, what would life be without love and hate, fear and courage, joy and sorrow? She gives our lives meaning and creativity.

The gift she gives us marks this. The stone, *Eivnus* (Gaelic *eibhneas*) is the capacity for ecstasy or rapture, for the highest joy and deep sorrow. It carries us to the edge of madness and the edge of divinity — and sometimes over. The chain, *Cuin* (Gaelic *caoin*, as a verb means *weep, lament, mourn*, but as an adjective it means *kind* or *tender* or *seasoned*, as hay is seasoned by drying in the sun. How do you think these meanings might bind and connect with ecstasy?

What you have been doing in this imagery journey is to make a commitment to the greater journey of exploring your inner world, and to invoke your own inner god and goddess, the light of reason and the capacity for depth of experience, to aid you on your way.

The interpretation

The second gift of the Sun God represents something that you will receive from working with this book, following the exploratory trail through your own inner world, using your capacity to illumine, to understand that world. Were you able to understand the meaning of the gift? If not, don't worry — it will become evident in time.

Like the second gift of the Sun God, the second gift of the Earth Goddess symbolises something you will receive from working with this book. In this case, however, it will be the result of experiencing the feelings, knowing the reality, the passion, the creative power of your own inner world. Were you able to understand the symbolic meaning of the gift? Again, if not, don't worry — it, too, will become evident in time.

I suggest you write down what the Sun God and the Earth Goddess were like, a description of the gifts they gave you, and anything else about this journey that especially stands out in your mind.

3. Keeping Track Of Where You Are

Keeping a verbal and visual journal, a personal magical grimoire, helps us to clarify our thoughts and feelings, to interpret our inner images more clearly, and to improve the communication and enhance the integration between the linear, verbal, analytical mode of mental processing and the metaphoric, imaging, associative mode. This journal does not need to be a literary masterpiece or a great work of art. In fact, it will probably be more honest if it is neither of those things.

Words are used by the analytical part of our minds, the part that does not understand images until we have given them names. There are three ways of processing information and ideas. The *analytic mode* uses words and follows — or tries to follow — certain logical rules. The *associative mode* processes information primarily through feeling (both sensation and emotion) and images. The third mode, *holistic*, is an integrated function of the *analytical* and *associative* modes.

The associative mode is the kind of thinking we usually are doing when we say we have a hunch or an intuition. What we are actually doing is non-verbal thinking, arriving at a conclusion without the use of words. This kind of thinking is often considered to be unconscious, partly because it does not use words (which we usually believe to be 'real' thinking) and partly because it functions most clearly in a different kind of consciousness. We will come back to this subject later on.

Working with images in certain ways encourages us to communicate more freely between the analytic and associative modes, enhancing creativity and self-understanding.[2] As these two modes become more integrated into a holistic mode, we become better able to heal ourselves of old trauma and present illness, and to fulfil our creative potential. Working with a journal that is both verbal and visual will help you to integrate the two modes into a powerful whole. It will also provide you with a record of your process and progress. This will be very useful to you to refer back to later on, but the most important

use of the journal is probably in the present moment, helping you to
see and understand what is happening now.

4. The Verbal Record

Writing things out helps us both to clarify our thoughts and to find
greater depth of meaning in our journeys. The associative mode
largely communicates in images — images which are in themselves a
vocabulary, a complete language. We have one vocabulary of words
and another of images, and to truly understand either one we need to
understand both — and to be able to translate, insofar as this is
possible, between one and the other. As we go on our journeys into
the depths of ourselves, we will be learning the verbal equivalents of
the images we find within.

There are many books that offer to tell us about our inner images,
especially those seen in dreams. Unfortunately, the image vocabular-
ies defined in these books, although they may be related to ours, do
not quite speak the same language — like the difference between an
American biscuit (which is an English scone, more or less) and an
English biscuit (which is an American cookie, more or less). Some of
these books can be useful by suggesting ideas we might not readily
have considered. On the other hand, books that say things like
dreaming of one sheep is lucky, dreaming of two sheep means you are
going to confront a danger, and dreaming of three sheep means that
money is coming into your life are quite useless for this kind of work.
So is the sort of obsessive interpretation that insists that *every* tall,
slender object is a phallic symbol.

The inner language of images varies from person to person, and the
only way to learn our own is to work with it. Writing down
descriptions of our images and what we think they may mean is one of
the obvious ways to do this, and it has the advantage of enabling us to
refer back to an old image when we encounter it in a new situation.

Including your dreams in this record is also helpful. When you
work with imagery, your dreams often begin to assume a different
character. They may become more vivid, more coherent, more
creative, more understandable. It is as if, through consciously working with imagery, the unconscious begins to learn how to communicate more clearly with the conscious mind, as well as the conscious
mind learning to understand the unconscious more easily. Dreams *are*
imagery journeys, but they are unrestricted, free of the constraints and

intentions of the conscious mind. They can be interpreted in the same way, using the same verbal and visual techniques.

We'll be looking at many tricks and techniques for interpreting and translating our images into words, but the important thing just now is to begin by forming the habit of writing things down — even if you are not a 'writer' (whatever that is). It doesn't need to be immortal prose; it only needs to be clear enough for you to remember what you meant when you wrote it.

Whenever you write something in your journal, date it, label it with the subject, and if it is an exercise given here, give the page number from this book which relates to it . This no doubt seems obvious to many of you, but it's the sort of thing I forget to do myself.

The image dictionary

In a separate part of your journal, begin keeping an image dictionary. Each time you work with interpreting a particular image or symbol, enter the information that you get in this personal dictionary.

You can begin this dictionary by making a practice of translating some of the more important people and things in your life into symbolic images. First, make a list of the important people and situations in your life. This might include your spouse or lover, mother and father, each of your children, job, boss, and your favourite activity. Make certain your list includes all the people and things that are really important to you.

Begin by letting yourself relax. If you meditate, a few minutes of meditation is the best way to begin. If you don't meditate, start by spending five minutes just noticing and counting your breath. Count your breath up to ten, then start again. Repeat this for five minutes. If that doesn't seem enough, continue until you feel relaxed and peaceful.

If counting your breath does not help you relax, you might want to use another technique. Choose a two or three syllable sound which has no meaning to you but falls pleasantly upon your inner ear. Repeat the sound over and over for five minutes or longer. You may say it aloud or silently, or alternating between silently and aloud (obviously, you would use it silently when working in a group).[3]

Once you have reached that calm, centered feeling, allow the first person or thing on your list to come into your mind, and ask for an image that represents that thing for you. What is the *first* thing that comes into your mind? It may be a thought, a picture, a scent, a sound or word — all of these are images, each a symbol of your subject. Hold that image and your subject in your mind, and ask for the image to be clarified and expanded. Just sit quietly until the image seems as complete as it is going to get at this time.

An important thing to realise here is that the image doesn't need to make 'sense' — that is, you may not be able to make conscious, verbal, analytic mode connections between these spontaneous images and your subject. The associative mode has its own logic, and these symbolic representations make sense to it. We just need to know who is represented by which symbol. One of my images for money is a cactus. This may be partly because it seems to be so hard to hold on to, and I can think of other possibilities, but the important thing is that money may be involved when a cactus appears in my dreams or imagery journeys.

When you find an image for a particular subject, enter the image and the subject it relates to in your image dictionary. Make an impressionistic painting (as described in the following chapter) of it. Hereafter, when you encounter this symbol in your dreams or imagery, you will understand that this particular, specific image is likely to have some bearing on your feelings about and relationship with that subject. An image can hold much of the complexity of the subject and your relationship with it in one compact thought, when words might require pages and pages.

A given subject may have more than one primary image, and several secondary ones. For now, ask for at least one, but no more than three for each subject.

Give yourself time with each subject. Don't rush on to the next one. Pause and explore each one. It may take you several sessions to go through your list, but it is time well spent. It is also worth repeating the process later on, noticing how the images alter as your feelings and experience of the subject change. You can learn a lot about what is going on in your life, as well as about your images, in this way.

5. The Visual Record

Would you be interested in buying a travel book if there were no pictures? Or would you feel that such a book could not give you the completeness of information you would want? Words would not enough to describe our imagery journeys, even to ourselves.

Use your paints to make a picture of the second gifts you were given by the Sun God and Earth Goddess in *Light Into Darkness* — not the sword and necklace, but the other, personal gifts. Do not try to make a detailed drawing, even if you can, but try to convey the feeling, energy, and meaning of those gifts as well as you can.

Many people will groan here and say, 'But I can't draw!' We are not talking about Great Art — we are *expressing* ourselves. Children can't draw like Rembrandt, but they can express themselves in paint. What we will be doing is to paint, like children, from the heart, rather than from the head. Technique is unimportant; thinking and planning are forbidden. We are more interested in conveying the *energy* and *feeling* of our imagery than in trying to attempt photographic reproduction — which would kill it. We want to bring it into life. The very exaggerations and distortions of a child's painting convey things no precise rendering could ever delineate.

Have fun with your painting. Don't take it seriously. Make it splashy and colourful. It *should* look like a child's. Forget everything you learned about painting after you were five. This can be very difficult for trained artists. In each of us, trained or untrained, there is a part of the mind that is filled with rules, but it should not be allowed to dictate or judge the painting. This kind of fun/work is none of its business. Let the painting come from your feelings rather than your mind.

This drawing also goes into your journal, dated and labelled on the back, next to the written interpretation. It might also be fun (and a good idea) to make an impressionistic painting of the Sun God and Earth Goddess.

As we explore our inner world, we will be looking at a variety of ways to discover the obvious, the subtle, and the hidden meanings in our paintings, but for these first ones, let's just think about the colours you have used.

6. Speaking the Language: Colour

Are the colours in your paintings muddy or bright? Is the overall effect of the colours cheerful or sinister? Clear or confused? Optimistic or depressing? Or perhaps neutral, with not much emphasis either way? Are the colours simple (a few distinct colours) or complex (many colours blended in unusual ways)? Remember, we are looking at feelings and moods, not at technique.

Have you used mostly primary colours — red, yellow, and blue — or have you used blends? Primary colours tend to be more direct, to hit us in the eye. They are definite and emphatic. The secondary colours — orange, green, and purple — can also be very vivid, but the other, more complex blends convey more complicated, mixed feelings — perhaps more subtle, perhaps more ambivalent.

Have you used more warm or hot colours (reds and oranges) or cool or cold ones (blues and greens)? Warm colours tend to indicate a more active approach. They may also indicate the warmer feelings — love and affection (pink and rose), appetite (orange), passion (red — note that passion can be either anger or desire). In our society red is used to indicate something inflammatory or forbidden and orange as a caution or a warning. This reflects a Western cultural pattern of holding ourselves in, not allowing ourselves to feel/express strong emotion and desires. We are supposed to 'keep cool' and to stay under the control of our rational, linear thinking.

The cooler blues and greens tend to indicate a more detached, calm experience. They are less exciting and more peaceful, more passive, perhaps more mental than emotional.

Purple and yellow stand between the warm and cool colours. An orange-yellow is, of course, warm, and a greenish-yellow is cool. The so-called neutral colours of brown and gray can also be shaded in either direction.

What have you painted/seen in warm, active colours and what in cool, calm colours? Is anything painted in cool colours that you thought you had warm feelings toward? Or vice versa? Did your choice of coolness/warmth for anything in the painting surprise you?

Pale, pastel, ethereal colours can indicate subtlety, sensitivity, fatigue, avoidance. Vivid colours may speak of strong feelings or energies, directness, emphasis, intensity.

Looking at the pictures overall, do the colours of all the elements in a picture seem to be expressing the same feeling/mood, or do some of them differ, perhaps even seem contradictory? If there are differences or contradictions, can you relate them to your conscious feelings about the subject?

Is there much space left white on the paper? This could indicate a variety of things. Is anything in the painting separated from other things by white space, perhaps indicating something in you that is cut off from everything else? Or perhaps the white space is a positive expression of a sense of spaciousness in yourself. White may suggest peacefulness or serenity, or it might represent isolation or emptiness. What do you think it might indicate in each of your drawings?

We'll be looking at other attributes of your paintings in later chapters, but you might want to begin to apply what you have just learned to more than your painting. What colours are you wearing right now? What kind of colours do you usually wear? What colours are missing in your wardrobe? What does all of this say about the kind of person you are and the kind of impression you want to make on others?

Part II

Discovering the Inner World

Mort tapped the stallholder in the small of the back.
"Can you see me?" he demanded.
The stallholder squinted critically at him.
"I reckon so," he said, "or someone very much like you."
"Thank you," said Mort, immensely relieved.

- Terry Pratchett
in Mort

7. Cultivating Awareness

Before we begin the next guided imagery journey, exploring around the edge of the light on the mountain crest, I'd like to offer a few suggestions about doing these excursions. First, I really recommend that you *do* the imagery exercises, the paintings, and the interpretations as you go along. Many of them will give you more revealing information about yourself, your own growth processes, and your needs on the first attempt if you have not yet biased or inhibited yourself by reading the explanatory material that follows them.

The sequence of the exercises is important as well and, while you can do the later ones without having done the earlier, you will not get quite what I hope you might from doing them. There is a definite pattern here which takes the stages of psychological and spiritual growth into account. So, doing first things first is important.

I also especially ask you to remember that the very things that we see the least point in doing, that we like the least, *that we have the most resistance to* are probably the things that we most need to do. Please remember this as you do (or don't do) the imagery journeys, the visual and verbal journal keeping, and the other exercises in this book.

Listen instead of directing

When doing any of the guided imagery exercises, take the first thing that comes into your mind when you are asked for an image of something. Don't argue with it. If your sky is green with pink polka dots, let it be as it is. It is trying to tell you something by being like that — though I can't think what. As soon as you start directing or arguing with your images, you begin consciously making up the imagery instead of seeing what the unconscious has to offer — which defeats the whole purpose of many of the exercises. We may not always like what we find in our own minds, but if we look at it honestly we probably will learn something of value. If, instead of listening, we change the imagery to suit our conscious ideas, we are only playing with a sort of mental echo, and such echoes have nothing new to offer us. They are only blurred 'yes men' of the psyche.

Be aware of all your images

In addition to accepting things as they are instead of insisting on some
idea of what they 'ought' to be, let them come in the form they prefer.
We will discuss this more thoroughly later on, but for now do bear in
mind that some people see pictures, but many of us image better in
other senses — touch, scent, hearing. And some of us image in pure
thought — we just *know* what is there. If you visualise, fine — but
don't ignore the other senses. And if you are one of the very many
people who don't visualise well, that's all right too — just listen and
feel and sense, and your images will be quite as clear and creative as
those of people who do visualise.

Posture

I haven't said much about posture. I said a great deal about its
importance in *Moon Over Water*, so I'll just briefly mention it here. It is
best to sit with your spine erect and relaxed, but properly aligned. If
you are seated on the floor with your legs crossed, place your hands
on your legs. If you are seated on a chair, please place your feet flat on
the floor and allow your hands to rest comfortably on your thighs.
Your palms may be turned up or down, whichever is easiest. Let your
shoulders and neck relax, but keep your head erect during the exercise
so that your entire spine remains in proper alignment. Allow yourself
to relax into this position, your body balanced in an effortlessly
relaxed yet erect posture.

Good posture is always important in order to receive the full
benefit of any meditation or imagery exercises. A slumped, half-asleep
body gives the wrong kind of messages to the mind. If you try the
above journey both ways — slumped and erect — you will see what I
mean.

8. Basic Skills For The Guide

Once we step out of the light on the mountain top, it is helpful to have
a guide. In fact, we often have two guides, one in the outer world, and
another in the inner world, who act as interpreter and helper. Because
we are moving from our ordinary state of consciousness into a more
relaxed, dreamlike state, we need our outer guide to help us to
remember why we are there and what we are intending to do.

Whether you are acting as an outer guide for yourself or others, leading imagery journeys is simple in theory, but rather more complex in practice. Here are a couple of things that will help you to get started.

Tone of voice

Perhaps the most obvious, yet most often misused factor in helping others through guided imagery is the tone of the voice the guide uses. There are two common mistakes that people make. One is to use a 'dramatic' voice, as if we were reciting Shakespeare on an Elizabethan stage. The other, at the opposite extreme, is to speak in a monotone in the mistaken belief that this is 'hypnotic'.

When you are guiding others, it helps them if you sound calm, keeping your voice smooth, relaxed, and quiet. You want the imagers to be relaxed and to feel secure, and they are much more apt to feel this way if you seem calm, at ease, and give the impression that you know what you're doing. The guide's voice should flow like a peaceful river — gently, softly, and soothingly. It should sound quietly natural. Some of us have a naturally soothing voice, but others need to cultivate one. Listen to the people you know and to speakers on the radio and television. Notice how an actor changes his voice when he wishes to sound gentle or comforting. Think how people speak to babies when they want them to go to sleep. It's almost like singing a lullaby.

Avoid sudden changes in pitch and volume. You need to speak loudly enough for people to hear you clearly, but in a conversational tone. Even when something dramatic is happening in the imagery, describe it in a gentle, natural, calm way. As you practise with some of the imagery journeys in this book, play with your voice. If your voice is especially high pitched try to lower it a bit. Exaggerate it in different ways. If you can, record yourself on tape and see what works best for your own imagery journeys — it will probably work best for other people as well.

The pitch and smoothness of the guide's voice can greatly contribute to lulling the imager into a deeply relaxed state where the imagery flows freely. Another important factor is the speed at which we travel.

Rhythm and pace

Like the tone of voice, the pace should flow smoothly. Avoid alternating between rapid and slow speech. A good masseur knows that the client's mind tends to move at the pace of his hands, so when he wants the client to relax deeply, he starts at a medium speed and gradually moves more and more slowly. He avoids making any sudden or unexpected moves. The same principle applies to using our voices to create the deep relaxation in which imagery most easily arises. And again, like the masseur, the rhythm we work with is important.

As an imager relaxes and moves more deeply into a relaxed state of consciousness, we need to slow down our questions and suggestions in guiding their imagery. We do not do this by making our words longer in an exaggerated way. 'Nnnoooow looooook foooor theeeeee doooooooor toooo yoooouuuuurr leeeffffffft' sounds silly and is irritating. Give the imager time by inserting pauses. Generally speaking, many small pauses are more effective then occasional long ones, which tend to allow the imager time to wander off or to fall asleep.

If you can, make the pauses rhythmic. This facilitates the deepening of the relaxed, receptive state. Sometimes it is helpful to use your own body as a metronome, rocking back and forth slightly to keep the rhythm.

The following example will give you some idea of what I mean. Comments on the ideas we have been discussing are in italics, and pauses are indicated by / for a very brief pause and // for a longer one. Read it through to get the comments and sense of the passage, and then try reading the second copy (without the comments) aloud, inserting the pauses. You may want to try it several times at different speeds, until you are satisfied that you have a workable pace and rhythm for someone in a very relaxed state of consciousness.

As you walk along // *(allow time for the imager to begin to develop a sense or feeling of movement)* notice the ground / under your feet. // Is it hard / *(brief pause for recognition or rejection)* or soft, // rough / or smooth? // What is the surface made of? //

What is the air like around you? // Is it warm / or cool? // Moving / or still? // Damp / or dry? // If it's damp, / where is the moisture coming from? //

And as you feel the air around you, // notice the thing closest to you. // If you were to reach out and touch it // *(pause for the imaginary action)* how would it feel to your fingers? // What is the texture like? // Are there any colours / or sounds / or scents // that you especially notice / about this object?

Now practise the following aloud:

As you walk along // notice the ground / under your feet. // Is it hard / or soft, // rough / or smooth? // What is the surface made of? //

What is the air like around you? // Is it warm / or cool? // Moving / or still? // Damp / or dry? // If it's damp, / where is the moisture coming from? //

And as you feel the air around you, // notice the thing closest to you. // If you were to reach out and touch it // how would it feel to your fingers? // What is the texture like? // Are there any colours / or sounds / or scents // that you especially notice / about this object?

If you are working individually with someone and she is answering you aloud, the speed with which she is speaking will give you clues about the length of pauses she needs. Try to keep your pace as slow as (or just a little slower than) hers. You don't want too much difference between the speed with which you are speaking and her speed of thought processing. This is almost always slower than we, in our fully awake and alert state, would expect.

If you are working with a group, leading them all through the same journey simultaneously, you will probably find that some people will feel rushed, and others will feel you are too slow. If there are some of each, you're probably about right. If a group continues to work together, they tend to fall into a rhythm and pace that is comfortable for everyone, but in the beginning, you may as well resign yourself to never getting it quite right for everyone.

Practical tips

If you want to tape the imagery so that you won't have to try to follow the directions and do the imagery at the same time, you may want to read Appendix C before you make the tape.

Before you actually start the imagery, be that sure you are seated comfortably, that the telephone will not disturb you, and that you have arranged to be left uninterrupted. It is helpful for both the guide and the imager to be seated in a comfortable, relaxed position.

9. An Exploration

For our next imagery journey, we'll explore some of the territory close to the mountain top. This is an opportunity to give your unconscious a chance to tell you, in symbolic form, what it feels about certain aspects of your being. In order for this to work well, all you need to do is to acknowledge and accept the very *first* image that comes into your mind, without trying to analyse it during the journey.

Approximate travel time: 20 minutes.

A WALK IN THE FOREST

We are going on a walk in the forest. Before we begin, take a couple of deep breaths. As you inhale, imagine that you are breathing in peace. As you exhale, imagine that you are breathing out the tension in your forehead, in your neck, and in your shoulders.

As you inhale the next breath, clench your fists, and as you exhale, allow them to relax. And two more slow, deep breaths.

As you inhale, flex your toes. As you exhale, let them relax again, and as you do, allow any tension in your feet and ankles and legs to flow away. Take your time and let yourself become relaxed, a little more deeply with each breath.

As you continue breathing gently, naturally, you may feel some sort of sensations in your body. Perhaps it is feeling lighter or heavier or tingly — or perhaps you feel only a sense of calmness as your body begins to soften and loosen in a delightful way. Perhaps you need to move a bit to become more relaxed. Just allow your body to find the position in which it can truly let go, as you continue to breathe gently, naturally.

You are in control of this journey at all times. If you should wish to leave the forest, you may do so just by willing it. However, as long as you remain in the forest, allow the images to present themselves to you as they wish, just following my voice as I guide you.

I'd like you to imagine that you are standing on a path in a forest. Notice the path under your feet. Is it earth or rock or something else?

And how does the air feel to you? Is it warm or cool, moving or still, dry or damp?

Please begin walking along the path, noticing the forest around you. What kind of trees are there? What season is it? And what time of the day or night? Is anything growing beneath the trees? How do you feel about being in this forest?

What colours or sounds or scents do you particularly notice in your forest? And what stands out most as you look at and feel the forest around you?

After you have been walking a while, you come to a clearing on your left. In the clearing there is some kind of a building or a structure. What is the first image that comes into your mind? How big is it? And what is it made of? What colours or sounds or scents do you notice around it? Is it accessible to the path or far away? Does it have an open aspect or is there a wall around it? How do you feel about it?

After you have finished looking at the building, continue walking along the path, noticing the path and the forest as you go.

And as you walk, you come to a container of some kind just to the right of the path. How big is it? And what is it made of? If you touch it, how does it feel to your fingers? Is it open or closed? Can you tell if there is anything in it? What colours or sounds or scents do you particularly notice about it? What do you feel in yourself as you look at or sense it?

After you have finished looking at the container, you continue walking along the path, noticing the forest and the path as you go.

And as you walk, you come to some water. It may be a pool or a spring or a fountain; it may be a lake or a river or the sea. What is the first image that comes to your mind? What is the water like — warm or cool, salt or fresh, clear or muddy? If you would like to drink the water or get in it, go ahead.

And then continue on along your path through the forest, noticing the path, noticing the forest as you go.

And as you walk, you come to another clearing in the trees. In this clearing is the most amazing, fantastic thing you ever saw — the first image that comes into your mind. What is it? And how big is it? What colours or sounds or scents are associated with it? How do you feel about it?

After you have finished looking at this astonishing thing, you continue walking along, noticing the path and the forest as you go. You soon come to a place where the path forks. One of the paths goes uphill, and the other goes straight ahead, continuing on the same level. I'd like you to take the uphill path first.

When you have climbed upward a short while, you come to the end of the trees and the top of the hill at the same time. From here you can see a long, long way. What do you see? What is the landscape like? Is it inhabited or uninhabited? Are there roads or paths through it? What colours or sounds or scents do you especially notice out there?

After you have finished looking out from the top of the hill, I'd like you to go back down to the main path and continue in the direction that you were travelling. Notice the path once more. Has it changed in any way? Is the forest still the same or has it changed? What colours or sounds or scents do you especially notice now?

As you continue to walk, much to your surprise, you see the place where you started ahead of you, and you realise that you have been walking in a big circle, and you are now back at the beginning.

When you have reached the place where you started, I'd like you to take a couple of deep breaths.

Become aware of the room around you.

Flex your fingers and toes.

Take another deep breath. And another. Open your eyes and stretch, feeling relaxed and alert.

Write a brief description of your journey for your journal, and make a quick, free impression-painting of the thing that stood out most for you in your *Walk in the Forest*. It would be best to do both of these things before you begin to think about the interpretation of the symbols encountered in the journey.

The logic of the imagery

The symbols you encountered on the walk represent particular aspects of yourself, *as seen by your unconscious mind*. This is an important distinction. Your conscious view of these aspects of yourself may be quite different. Think about these symbols with an open mind, not judging them by whether or not they agree with your conscious views. They are not 'right' or 'wrong' — they just are. Your liking or disliking, approving or disapproving of them does not alter the fact that they are what they are. If it's any comfort, they are all subject to change without notice.

In doing an imagery expedition like this, without knowing in advance what the symbols represent, we have to rely on more or less 'universal' dream/imagery symbols. One symbol may have several different interpretations — *and all of them are valid*. At the moment, however, we are only concerned with the simple interpretations below.

The interpretation

We will be going more deeply into the interpretation of symbolism in general later on, but let's take a brief look at the elements of this particular imagery journey.

Path: this is a symbol of how you are making your way through life at the present time. Is it rough or smooth, easy or difficult, clear or indistinct? Do you trip over things or do you progress smoothly? Do you need to pay a little or a lot of attention to where you are going? What else do you notice about it?

Forest: this represents your inner feeling state at the time of beginning the journey. How did you feel about being there? Did it feel crowded (harassed or overstressed — or perhaps just busy) or spacious (relaxed — or perhaps empty)? Was it light or dark? Easy to tell what was going on or difficult? What did you like best about it? What did you like least? Think about how the attributes of the forest relate to and symbolise the way you have generally been feeling lately. Are the adjectives you use to describe the forest also words you might use to describe the way you feel?

Building or structure: this symbolises your presence in the world, both your physical presence and your beingness. How solid is it? Does it seem strong or weak? A 'good place' or not? Is it beautiful or utilitarian — or worse? What is it for? How did you feel about it? What does it tell you about how you unconsciously feel you are? How much does this agree or disagree with your conscious view of yourself?

Container: this is a representation of how you unconsciously feel that others see you. It is NOT how they actually see you, which is something you cannot know, but only how you unconsciously feel you are seen. What does the container tell you about this? How open/accessible are you? Are you the sort of person who accumulates other people's rubbish? Or are you perhaps full of your own rubbish? Or do you perhaps contain something refreshing or nourishing? Or are you empty? Is the container beautiful or is it plain and utilitarian? Or is it even worse than that? Is it something with value? Is it noticeable or insignificant? Does it blend with the surroundings or does it stand out?

What is the relationship between this image and the image of how you feel that you actually are (the building)? Are they reasonably harmonious, or is there a significant dichotomy between how you unconsciously feel about yourself and how you unconsciously feel others see you? If there is a such a split, what do you think is the cause of this? Are your feeling about yourself realistic? Do you feel you present a 'false front' to others?

Remember, this is not how you are and it is not how you are really seen — it is only how you unconsciously believe that you are — or should be — seen. Many people find rubbish containers here (perhaps because they let other people 'dump' their emotions on them, and perhaps for other reasons). I remember someone, who lived on a diet of junk food, whose container was a rusty barrel with 'toxic waste' stencilled on it.

Water: this symbolises your energy. Is there a little or a lot? Is it clear (healthy) or muddy (distressed, stressed, not healthy)? Is it sparkling (filled with vitality) or stagnant (depressed)? Is it still (calm) or flowing (active)? Is it free or contained or blocked?

Amazing thing: this represents your spiritual nature and does not 'interpret' in the usual way, but just Is. How did you feel about it? How do you feel about it now that you know what it is? Does it surprise you or is it something you might have expected?

Path up and view beyond: upward is a symbol of movement into the future. This view represents your unconscious view of the near future. Is it a place that appeals to you or would you like to change it? Is there an obvious symbol of a goal, a destination, in your view? If so, is there a clear road or path to it, or are you going to need to find or invent a path?

Upward paths can also be paths to goals or ambitions or to spiritual aspirations. These things may be found on the heights of our inner worlds. However, in this journey you are not actually looking up, but simply reaching a place from which you have an overview and can get a look at what is ahead of you, both literally in the journey and metaphorically in your life.

There are, of course, many other possibilities in this particular journey, which is very adaptable to different needs. We will look at how it could be altered to examine other aspects of ourselves much later on, when we reach the point of creating journeys.

We must always remember that nothing is absolute in interpreting symbolism. The suggestions here are just that — suggestions. They may give you some ideas to help find more insight in your imagery, but they cannot tell you what is there. You are the only one that knows what is in your mind, and much of that information is locked up in your unconscious. If you use these suggestions as carefully and sensitively as a locksmith uses a pick, you may be able to gently open the door.

10. Speaking the Language: Line

Now let's look at your painting of whatever seemed most outstanding to you in your *Walk In The Forest*. In looking at it, what do you feel? What feelings did you have about this special thing when you first encountered it in the imagery? What do the qualities of the colours you have used in it tell you?

Another clue to reading a picture for its emotional contents is to look at the qualities of the lines in it. Before we begin with that, I'd like you to try a little experiment. Take three pieces of paper and divide each paper into four more or less equal parts. Label each square (or rectangle) with one of the following qualities, putting the word in small letters in one corner of the square so that most of the square is blank. The qualities to be drawn are: Power, Peace, Femininity, Masculinity, Growth, Anger, Defeat, Love, Triumph, Fear, Doubt, Awe.

In each square make a few lines that are an abstract expression of that quality. You are not making a picture of any recognisable thing, but just simple lines that convey your feeling. Before you start each square, let yourself experience the feeling. Remind yourself of times you have felt that way and recapture them. Take all the time you need for this, and allow yourself to really let go of one feeling before you go on to the next.

Use a pen or paintbrush, whichever you prefer, and keep it very simple — just a few lines that express the feeling. Let your lines flow freely.

If there are other emotions or feelings you would like to look at, do them now as well.

I suggest you do this exercise before you read any further.

These little abstract sketches can tell you something about the qualities of the lines and shapes in your drawings. Look at all the paintings you have done so far. How do the lines relate to the drawings you have just done? Do any of them express conflicting energies? For example, you might find lines indicative of peace and of anger in the same painting. Do the colours reinforce or conflict with the lines?

Are the lines distinct and crisp or are they blurred into one another? Clear definition of lines might indicate clarity or emphasis of feeling, while blurred, indistinct lines might show less definite feelings.

Are different types of lines separated or do they flow into each other? Does this suggest that the feelings represented are distinct from one another, or are they hooked into each other, perhaps making it difficult to distinguish what you really feel?

Remember, these paintings are an expression of feelings, and one of the things we are looking at here is whether or not our feelings on a particular image are harmonious or conflicting. It is quite possible to love someone, and at the same time, to be angry with something they are doing. It is also possible both to desire and fear something (or someone). We tend to go into a kind of emotional paralysis when our feelings are in conflict with themselves. The way we regain our power of choice and action is to find a way to identify the opposing impulses so that we can see them clearly. *Then* we can decide what we want to do.

What does each of your paintings tell you now?

Each of us makes these lines a bit differently, but the similarities in any group of people are often quite remarkable. If you are working with a group, compare your drawings. If several on the same subject are similar and yours is different, this *does not* mean that yours is wrong. It just means that the images in your mind are different — and different is neither better nor worse — it is simply not alike.

Part III

Meeting the Natives

"I just think the world ought to be more sort of organised."

"That's just fantasy," said Twoflower.

"I know. That's the trouble." Rincewind sighed again. It was all very well going on about pure logic and how the universe was ruled by logic and the harmony of numbers, but the plain fact of the matter was that the disc was manifestly traversing space on the back of a giant turtle and the gods had a habit of going round to atheists' houses and smashing their windows.

– Terry Pratchett
in The Colour of Magic

11. The Natives

In the inner world we create our own realities. As we stand on our mountain peaks, calling ourselves conscious, reasoning beings, our inner images, ectypes and archetypes, our past conditioning, our present situation, our thoughts, and our hopes and fears for the future all combine in our psyches to create our experience of each moment as it passes. Reality (or at least the part of it that actually matters to us) is not 'out there' — it is the way we feel about and respond to what happens in our lives. External reality is seen through and judged by an inner reality, individual to each of us. So it is the inner reality that, in a way, matters most. It determines how we feel about ourselves and about our lives. It determines our emotions and our choices, decides our actions and reactions, and affects our health.

In the well lit part of our inner world, we find our thoughts, conscious feelings, and some of our beliefs. In the dark, there is our hidden reality of unconscious beliefs, archetypes, self-imposed limitations, hidden fears, and unconscious assumptions. This hidden reality largely decides the path we take through life. We make our choices unconsciously and then we rationalise them by finding reasons for doing what we have already decided, deeply within ourselves, to do. This is a form of sleepwalking. We are often unaware of our true motivations — and all too often unable to see and hear each other as well.

When I look at you, I don't see you — I see what I can understand about you and what I believe about you. Because of this, you will surprise me from time to time. Just when I think I can predict your next move, you may well move in some (to me) entirely unexpected direction. Even more confusing, I sometimes will surprise myself, because I can only see what I believe and am able to understand about myself. This may be a pleasant surprise — or it may not. How often have you said things like 'I didn't mean it that way' or 'I can't think why I did that'?

In the same way that looking out through a stained glass window colours what we see, looking out through our prejudices, preconceptions, hopes, and fears distorts our vision. It's really all a matter of interpretation. If I fear dogs, I will interpret a wagging tail as a threatening gesture. If I believe all dogs are softies and refuse to accept that this may not be the whole truth, I may interpret a hostile growl as an invitation to play — and be badly bitten. We often do this sort of thing, failing to see what really *is* and seeing our coloured, distorted view instead.

This may be a little (or perhaps even very) disturbing.

But . . .

But, have you really understood this?

We create much of our own reality because, out of the materials and experiences available to us, *we create ourselves*. And we continue, every moment, creating who we are to become. Many of us sleepwalk through this process, waking only fitfully, if at all. However, it is possible to travel through life differently, consciously.

So here we are, having embarked on a journey together to discover who we are, to see glimpses of who we might become, and to find the paths that lead to fulfilling some of that potential. This is the journey of the Seeker, the Magician, the Shaman, the Alchemist. Like the mountain at dawn, the lower regions of the unconscious are still deeply shadowed, unknown and mysterious, filled with potency and potential. We shall be bringing light into the darkness, discovering the hidden treasures, and perhaps even domesticating some of the lurking monsters. We all know that things in the dark are usually much more frightening than the same things seen in broad daylight. Most of our childhood monsters under the bed faded to nothing when mother or father turned on the light. We'll be turning on the light within ourselves in a multiplicity of ways.

As in all true communication systems, information flows both ways. In dreams and daydreams and conscious imagery, information encoded in symbols moves from the darkness on the lower slopes of the mountain into the light of consciousness. And everything we see, hear, feel, or think flows into the unconscious for storage and processing. Some things disappear like fallen leaves into the earth, becoming an undifferentiated part of the compost out of which we grow. Other images may make a much bigger stir, resonating with the dwellers in the shadowy depths, the momentary gods of the mind.

12. Powers & Shadows

Our inner images have great power. They push us from the past and pull us toward a future, which they embody. They are charged with emotion. The advertising industry knows this very well, and uses outer, visual and verbal images that relate to our inner images to manipulate us. The impact, especially the emotional impact, of an advertisement depends largely on how closely the outer image reflects the inner one. We have an entire rich world of images within us — and mostly we ignore it, even though it influences all that we think and do.

These inner images are complex. They have a life of their own, partly visible to our conscious minds and partly hidden. At the sunlit top of the mountain of consciousness, the figures are familiar to us — rocks and trees, squirrels and bluebirds and other wild creatures, flowers and plants. We have power and choice and clarity on the top of the mountain — unless we are enveloped in the clouds of emotion. Further down, where the rising sun does not yet reach, the creatures and the trees are larger, more mysterious, hidden in the twilight. At the very bottom of the mountain, archetypal figures stride through the valleys, from mountain to mountain, sending waves of joy and terror, exaltation and fury rising through the other creatures higher up, even affecting the sunlit creatures at the top. 'I can't think why I did/said/thought that' we say, as one of these deep surges of feeling-thought-imagery takes momentary charge.

We need to remember that we have motivations and impulses coming into consciousness from two directions. One direction is the outer world as it puts various pressures upon us to form and shape us to suit it. Our parents, family, friends, society, and even the situations in which we find ourselves all do this. The other direction is from the archetypal energies in the depths of our inner world — the Great Mother, the Wise Elder, the Hero, the Trickster, and all of the others that humanity shares. An *archetype*, according to the dictionary, is 'the original pattern from which copies are made' — a prototype. These archetypes are primary aspects of being, the basic drives and possibilities of being shared by all humans. They are, in a sense, one-dimensional, but like a fanatic, their very singleness of purpose gives them power. I want to differentiate here between archetypes and archetypal images or *ectypes*.

In working with imagery we almost never directly contact an archetype. We communicate with that archetypal energy through an intermediary, an archetypal image, the ectype. The primary definition of *ectype* is 'an impression of a seal or medal', but ectypal has come to mean 'of the nature of a copy' as well. Our ectypes are formed by the meeting between the fundamental archetypes and our experience of life, the conditioning, shaping forces of our family and society. They are a combination of these inner forces and our personal experience. An archetype is an energy, a power, but an ectype has a face. An ectype is the way we personalise and give human dimensions to the archetypal energies.

One of the differences between archetypes and ectypes is that we can bargain with ectypes. We can influence ectypes. We can transform them, changing some of their more destructive habits and characteristics. Archetypes, on the other hand, just *are*. They deal with and influence us. They have a special numinous power; they glow in the dark. Archetypes are the 'first cause' — the one-pointed driving force, the primal power. Ectypes are the way we have adapted, limited, and defined that energy in our lives. Both archetypes and their manifestations, ectypes, also try to shape us into their image.

To realise more of our creative potential, we need to integrate these archetypal energies and ectypal figures and their creative powers into consciousness, without being overwhelmed and dominated by them. This process, the bringing of these hidden powers into the light, raising them from darkness to the summit of consciousness, is part of the process we call 'enlightenment' and I believe we need to become more and more enlightened if we are to grow beyond the unconscious destructiveness of our wounded, repressed, angry, neglected inner aspects. Humanity is in trouble because our creative energy is too often used by our damaged selves, rather than coming from the light within, and our trouble is harming the earth and the other beings who share it with us.

In our imagery work we very rarely encounter one of our larger-than-life archetypal energies, but we frequently meet the ectypes, who live on the slopes of the mountain, sometimes wandering into the light, more usually striding through the twilight and the darkness. The archetypes themselves are like invisible, elemental powers that we will never meet face to face because they have no faces, but the ectypes, humanised and personalised comprehensible images of the universal archetypes or prototypes of human possibilities, will be encountered often.

Some of these personal ectypal figures are so close to the archetypes that they can become the living myths of a social group or culture. Who in the Western world doesn't have an image of Superman flying through the air with his cape streaming out behind him, fighting Evil and defending Good? Superman is a good example of someone's simple, childlike picture, their personal ectype, of the Hero archetype which we share. Because this ectype is simple, direct, and unambivalent, it is something that the child in most of us can relate to as the inner Hero. Superman is just one of a long line of hero/godling figures, extending back into the most ancient myths of humankind — and doubtless beyond. Each of us carries an ectype of the Hero inside of us *and it tells us what to do*.

We don't, of course, always do it, but many of us feel a bit (or perhaps very) inadequate when we don't live up to our ectypal vision of the Hero. The reason we don't do it is that we have more sense — or we have important conflicting pressures from our society and environment — or we have been conditioned to believe that we can't — or we have other powerful archetypes and ectypes within us issuing conflicting instructions.

To begin learning something about our personal ectypes, let's take a look at the one for archetypal wisdom.

THE WISE OLD WO/MAN

Do a ten minute (or less) impressionistic painting of the Wise Old Man or the Wise Old Woman — your choice which. Start by choosing a colour that best represents wisdom in your mind and begin your painting with that colour. Never mind if it isn't *logical* to do it that way. If a red tree more accurately conveys your feeling about it than a green one, paint it red. Perhaps some things in the painting need to be upside-down or sideways from the way they are usually seen. Allow your painting to step outside of the rules of realism, ought, and should. The less you get bogged down in realism and detail, the more information your painting will reveal to you and the more insight you will gain from it. Make your drawing impression-istic — childlike and wise. You are drawing both a feeling and an abstract idea, not an object.

If you are not satisfied with the first painting, do one or two more to try to catch your Wise Old Wo/Man from different points of view. Don't spend more than ten minutes on each painting. Less is better.

Now do another painting. In it just put symbols of wisdom. Paint whatever symbols and colours come to mind, even if they don't make 'sense' to the logical-verbal part of your mind. It will have its turn next.

When the drawings are finished (and labelled on the back), make a list of the qualities a Wise Old Wo/Man would have. Use that list to help you to describe his/her personality.

Now look at the list and description and the paintings together. Do the paintings suggest any qualities or attributes that the list doesn't include? Does the list contain anything that you can't see in the pictures?

The Big Question: How do you suppose this person, who lives within you, affects your life and the choices you make?

You may want to try this same exercise with some of the other ectypes. Can you think of any that may have special influence upon you at this time? A few of the possibilities are:

The hero: This is the soul of courage and bravery, usually also of integrity. This one would *always* attempt to rescue the endangered child, no matter what the danger to itself — and would nearly always succeed.

The saint: The drive for spiritual perfection. Conscience or the superconscious are a part of this. In a sense, this is what we unconsciously believe we would be if we behaved perfectly in accordance with spiritual law.

The nature spirit: We are familiar with many ectypes for this archetype — fairies, elves, dwarves, Pan, fauns, dryads and naiads, and many others. Some are sinister, some benign, some simply uninterested in humanity. One form they take in our modern world is that of space people, aliens — a modern version of an ancient denizen of the psyche. This is not to say that there are not *real* aliens and fairies — just that, when there are not, we must invent something to fill their place.

A few of the many others are: the Noble Savage, the Hunter or Huntress, Death, Lord or Lady of the Otherworld (or Underworld), the Great Mother, the Sun Father, the Protector (or guardian angel), the Magician, the Wicked Witch or Evil Necromancer. I'm sure you must have the idea now.

These are just a few of the possible universal archetypes for which we each have our own ectypes. As you may have noticed, myth and fantasy are full of them. Some people feel that, in an ideal world, people would be entirely rational and would not have any interest in mythological figures or in fantasy, but such people want to live in a world that limits all of us to the use of only one mode of thinking — the one that does not include mystery and power and magic and meaning. We would only be half-human machines, but we would be much more predictable and controllable.

If we are going to make conscious choices in the present to create the future we want for ourselves, we must know two things. First, we must know who and what we are. We began to look at that in *The Walk in the Forest* in Chapter 9. Understanding who we are is a tricky process, not only because we find it difficult to acknowledge certain things about ourselves, but also because we are not so much a *thing* as a *process*. We are constantly growing, even when we don't think we are, and even when we are growing in a direction that we will have a hard time growing through. Several of the imagery journeys we are going to do are about recognising and understanding our process and direction of growth — and perhaps doing a little judicious pruning and redirecting.

Second, we must know what we want to become, which is part of what we were looking at in the exercise above. We will consider it in another way when we do the *When I Grow Old* imagery journey. If we don't know our destination, our chance of taking the 'right' path is just that — pure chance. If we know what we are trying to become, we have a convenient measuring device — the question simply is 'will doing this make me more or less like the person I want to become?' This doesn't tell us everything about making choices, but it is surprising how much it does answer.

Our ectypes and other images are a part, but not all, of what we are in the present moment, as well as contributing greatly to our vision of our possible selves. They have been and are being greatly influenced by our experience of the world around us. There are the beliefs we acquire from our parents, from our society, and there are the things that happen to us in infancy and childhood. Many people go through life never questioning these early impressions. In the book *Magical Child*, Joseph Chilton Pearce[4] notes that many of us had a first experience of the world which was quite unpleasant. Immediately after birth we were taken from our mothers, washed, weighed on an unsteady and insecure-feeling scale, drops were probably put in our eyes, and other uncomfortable things were done to us.

After all this, we were finally wrapped up snugly in a blanket, put in our beds, and left alone. Our first impressions of people were that they were a source of stress and discomfort, and our blanket became our first learned image of comfort. Pearce goes on to wonder if this has something to do with our attachment to material things. I would also wonder if it has something to do with our increasingly fragmented family relationships, the rising divorce rate, and the difficulties we have in forming lasting bonds with others.

How would our perceptions, our fundamental images of the world differ if we had all been born gently, in soft light, handled lovingly, and immediately comforted and nursed by our mothers? There are a number of people who have a deeply ingrained belief that the world is a hostile place. How much of that do you suppose might originate from that all too typical experience of birth in a hospital? For some years now, people have been trying to change that first experience of the world in a variety of ways, but many in the Western world (and those other countries that have been heavily influenced by Western culture) still have the same kind of experience. Maybe some people enjoyed their birth, but most of us cried and cried.

So what does this tell us about our images? For one thing, it shows us that they can be deeply buried, hidden under the layers of years of experiences and forgotten by the conscious mind, and yet they can continue to affect us profoundly.

For another thing, it reminds us that words do not have to be a part of the formation of images. In fact, the experience/image probably always comes first and then we may add the words to it — words which may explain, interpret, modify, strengthen or weaken, but nearly always *limit* and *change* our perception of the image. (This is one reason why we are working with both words and paintings to try to come closer to the totality of our images and their meaning.)

For yet another thing, it tells us that the idea of 'universal symbols' has difficulties. Yes, we all have a set of images about birth, but yours will differ from mine, perhaps subtly, perhaps radically. Even something as 'universal' as the sun will be experienced/felt/imaged very differently by someone raised in an equatorial desert and a person from the north of Norway. If they each described their images of the sun, an alien could be forgiven for thinking they came from different solar systems.

So everyone's images are different, individual. We all know what I mean when I say, 'He just stood there like a tree stump', but if we all drew a picture of that tree stump, each one would be different. Words may be symbols of real things, but they are also symbols of images we hold, which are themselves symbols of our impressions of reality. Words, then, can be symbols of symbols. It is no wonder that we so often experience difficulty in communication.

As we go through life, we keep adding to our store of images and modifying our ectypal figures. Our old ones are pushed back into the corners and shadows of our minds, but they remain active, popping unbidden into consciousness, sometimes to our delight and sometimes to our dismay. Just about every ninety seconds a bubble of imagery, containing concept/thought and feeling, comes up into the light of consciousness, like a wild creature hidden in the shadow suddenly stepping into the sunlight. These are a part of the inner communication between one part of ourselves (which we think of as our conscious minds) and the many other aspects of our being.

If we are busy, concentrating on something, we may dismiss these images without noticing them. If, on the other hand, we are doing something we dislike or aren't that interested in or if we are not doing much of anything at all, our consciousness gladly seizes on these little thought bubbles and turns them into full-fledged daydreams or chains of thought. These thought bubbles may be just the bare bones of an idea, but often they are more than that. Usually the image is a gestalt, a wholeness, of thought and feeling. This feeling is the 'emotional charge' on the idea and does much to determine what we do with the image — whether it becomes something that cheers us, depresses us, frightens us, comforts us, makes us feel better or worse about ourselves, or starts us off on a creative new tack.

These communications are the way that the deeper levels of mind/feeling has of suggesting, nudging, sometimes even driving us in a particular direction. Through images, our conscious minds may be hearing from our old programming, our unconscious hopes and dreams, our hidden inner fears and insecurities, our archetypes and ectypes, our superconscious or higher self, or our mysterious creative process that ferments in the darkness and bursts forth in a blaze of genius.

These are *our* own expressions of these energies, the forces in us that create our realities.

13. Name Magic

Words are simple. They have definitions in the dictionary, and if we get into an argument about what a particular word means, we can look it up. Words have hard edges. Images are complex and multi-layered, and they have soft edges. Did you ever read stories when you were a child which used pictures in the text? The first sentence in such a story might begin with the picture of a boy's head (which we will represent with @ to avoid driving the typesetter mad). The story would begin with something like: The @ is named Sam. @ likes to run and to climb trees. @ does not like to go to school. @ has a friend named Jane, who looks like this %. % does well at school, and she also likes to run and to climb trees.

When we read a story like this aloud, we tend to say Sam when we see @ and Jane at the % — but we could just as easily have read @ as

the-boy-who-likes-to-run-climb-doesn't-like-school-named-Sam,
because the image carries all that information more vividly than just
the name Sam.

Images carry information, in a way that words seem to lose. I
remember reading a fantasy years ago, and as best I recall, one scene
went something like this:

Three young men were standing one night in the parking lot of a
coffee house in California. One of them was playing a recorder,
tootling happily, while the other two were discussing something. As
they stood there, a huge black object floated over the trees and paused
above them. It was making strange sounds and flashing unearthly
lights over the scene. All three of the men looked up at it in stunned
silence, as well they might.

'What is it?' whispered one.

After a pause, one of the others said, 'Hey, man, that's a flying
saucer!'

'Oh, yeah. Of course,' said the third, and he went back to playing
his recorder while the other two went on with their discussion.

I call this *name magic*, and it demonstrates the unspoken belief we
hold that, if we have a name for something, we understand it, and we
can dismiss it — we needn't really pay attention to it. We don't need
to know any more; we can file it in a neat little pigeonhole in our
minds.

Think for a moment of how it would change our thinking about
each other if we did not have names. Suppose that, each time we
wanted to mention someone, we had to describe them well enough
for the listener to recognise whom we were talking about. Would you
have to describe the same person in varying ways to different people?
If you couldn't use the label 'father' or his name, how would you
identify your father to your mother? To a stranger? To a close friend?
We would need to actually *think* about the person we were describing,
their relationship with us, and their relationship with the person to
whom we were speaking. We would also constantly need to reassess
our view of this person, keeping up to date with who they are, rather
than maintaining an old, unchanging image of them in our minds.

The important thing to remember about this is that we react to the
image in our minds rather than to the real person. For example, if the
mother *in your mind* is dictatorial, violent, and demanding, and if the
real woman in the real world is aged, rather feeble, and tries to
appease others (a change that often happens to bullies as they lose their
strength), how are you likely to respond to her? Would a stranger,

seeing only what *is* in the present, view that response as somewhat weird? We often do respond inappropriately to people, because we are responding to what *we thought they were* when we formed an image, gave it a label, and filed it in our minds. These labelled and frozen images keep us from seeing what is real.

An image without a name holds volumes of mystery and information. The unconscious speaks in images, with huge quantities of abstract concepts, thoughts, feelings, and experience distilled into each one. The conscious mind tends to use words much more, and each word tries to place an image in a neat little box. In our attempts to expand our consciousness, to bring light further down the slopes of the mountain, and to begin to explore in the dark, we must remember that an image is much more than a single word, or even several words. It may have layers and layers of meaning as we explore more deeply into ourselves.

Part IV

Where Are We Going?

Alone of all the creatures in the world, trolls believe that all living things go through Time backwards. If the past is visible and the future is hidden, they say, then it means you must be facing the wrong way. Everything alive is going through life back to front. And this is a very interesting idea, considering it was invented by a race who spend most of their time hitting one another on the head with rocks.

          – *Terry Pratchett*
          in Reaper Man

14. Know Thyself

The words KNOW THYSELF were inscribed in letters of gold over the portico of the temple at Delphi, and Cicero speaks of this as a precept of Apollo, the god of light and consciousness. And millennia later we still have not got the message.

Our inner worlds are mostly dark, unconscious, unknown. Feelings, memories, thoughts, and physiological processes carry on out of the sunlight, on the slopes of the mountain and in the valleys and lakes below. Many of our hopes and dreams live in shadow, unarticulated and unknown, only occasionally glimpsed at the edges of the light. Some things have hidden in the darkness, afraid of being hurt if they can be seen, and other are there, like the sprouting seedling underground, because they have not yet grown strong enough to face the light of consciousness.

Many of the people who seek counselling or therapy or attend psychic and spiritual growth courses do so because they are trying to find a sense of meaning and purpose in their lives. Unfortunately, they are usually going about it in the wrong way. They ask, 'What am I *meant* to be doing?' The implication is that it is written in letters of gold on the walls of the heavens, divinely preordained, that this person is meant to be a hairdresser, this one is meant to be an executive, this one a plumber, a model, priest, writer, dancer, guru, tramp. As far as I can tell, it really isn't like that. But . . .

If they are told something like, 'You're meant to be growing and learning and fulfilling your potential, and if you do this, everything you do along the way will be meaningful and satisfying' — well, they don't seem to be able to hear that as an answer. They are so focused on *doing something* that they cannot imagine that anything else is relevant. Yet, we cannot know what we need to *do* until we begin to understand something about who we *are* and what we want to *be*.

If I know what I am and if I am true to that knowledge of myself, everything I do will be appropriate to the time and situation in which I find myself. I can't possibly know what I ought to do until I know who I am, what I need, and — this is very important — what my goals are.

It's simple really — at least in theory. Understanding who/what I want/need to become will have implicit in it much of the knowledge of what I must to do to get there from here.

If I set out in the car with the idea of getting somewhere that is meaningful and important to me, I must know where I am and what the destination is before I can begin to work out the route. Just frantically driving as fast as I can up one road and down another will probably not get me anything but lost.

Staying with the same analogy, if I find that I am in London and my destination is Los Angeles, I could rush about in the car until it collapsed around me and I still wouldn't be anywhere near Los Angeles. Thus, if I am an actress and I want to be a contemplative nun, better parts in better plays will not get me any closer. Or if I'm a contemplative nun and I want to be an actress, prayer and contemplation alone, however devoted, will not get me there. Appropriate action is required.

What I am 'meant' to do *absolutely and totally* depends on who I am and what I want to become. We have had a brief look at ourselves in the *Walk in the Forest*, and much of what we will do in later chapters will be concerned with learning to know ourselves better and with making choices. Before we go any further with that, this seems a good time to give some thought to our goals.

15. Destinations

Many of us have a general plan for our lives, not only for our working life, but also for our retirement years. But is it what we really need and want to do? We have our ideas, but do our unconscious needs agree with this? Do our ambitions and our potentials mate happily?

One way to look at our future possibilities is through the following imagery experience. In it we take a look at your future as it might be, glimpsing what you have the potential to become — *if you make good choices between now and then*. In this journey you will have the opportunity to ask your potential Elder Self a question about your present life — or you may just want to ask the Elder to tell you what you most need to know at the present time. You may want to think about this a moment or two before you begin.

Because there is complex dialogue in this imagery journey, I have put the more complex questions at the ends of paragraphs to help you to remember to give such questions more time. It often takes longer to get and clarify the answer to a question asked of a character in the imagery that it does to get simple images and information about your surroundings. If you are taping the journey or reading it for others, remember to allow longer time for such questions.

Are you comfortable? Phone switched off? Ready to go?

Approximate travel time: 25 minutes.

WHEN I GROW OLD, VERY OLD

This imagery journey is to visit the self you might become, when you are very, very old, if you follow the most creative and constructive growth path available to you in the rest of your life. I'd like you to start by taking a couple of deep breaths, just breathing out any tension you may notice in your body.

As you breathe, remember that you are in control of this journey at all times. If you want to stop, you may do so, just by willing it. As long as you remain in the journey, allow the images to arise in their own way, accepting them as you find them.

Let your breath be relaxed and normal. Some breaths will be longer, some shorter, some deeper and some more shallow. As you breathe in this relaxing way, I'd like you to begin to notice the point at which the inhalation becomes the exhalation and the point at which the exhalation becomes the inhalation. Notice the point at which the breath turns around.

Let yourself make just a tiny pause at the point of change in your breath. Don't try to make the breath itself longer or shorter. Just add that little pause.

As you continue to breathe in this way, making a small pause as the ebb and flow of your breath changes, I'd like you to imagine that there is a light switch, an ordinary light switch on the top of your right foot. This switch is on. Please, imagine reaching down and turning it off. Please, imagine that there is another switch on your right knee. It also is on. Please, imagine turning it off. There is another switch on your right hip. It also is on. Please, turn it off.

As you turn off these switches, please continue to notice and make the small pause as your breath turns around.

There is another switch on top of your left foot. It is on. Please, turn it off. There is another switch on your left knee. It, too, is on. Please, turn it off. There is another switch on your left hip. It's on. Please, turn it off.

For a moment just be aware of the pauses in the ebb and flow of your breath.

There is another switch on the back of your right hand. It's on. Please, imagine reaching over with your left hand and turning it off. There is another switch on your right elbow. It's on. Please, turn it off. There is another switch on your right shoulder. It's on. Please, turn it off.

As you continue to be aware of the pauses in your breath, we move now to the left arm.

There is another switch on the back of your left hand. It's on. Please, imagine reaching over with your right hand and turning it off. There is another switch on your left elbow. It's on. Please, turn it off. There is another switch on your left shoulder. It's on. Please, turn it off.

Once again, notice your breath. Your breathing may have changed in some way as you have become more relaxed. It may be deeper, it may be shallower, it might be longer or shorter. Your body will be finding just the right way for it to breathe in a deeply restful state. You may be beginning to find it quite easy to notice the pauses as your breath turns and begins to flow the other way.

There is another switch at the base of your spine. It's on. Please, turn it off. There is another switch at the base of your neck. It's on. Please, turn it off. Observe the whole of your body. If there is any place that you particularly notice, find the switch in that area and turn it off.

Still noticing the pauses in your breath, find the large switch, the master switch on your forehead. It is on. Please, switch it off.

Now, I'd like you to imagine that you are standing in front of an elevator door. This is the elevator that will take you to your potential self in very, very old age. This person you will meet is one of the possible selves that you might become, if you live your life creatively and consciously. I'd like you to step into the elevator, and turn around to face the door. Beside the door there will be a control panel. The highest button on the panel will take you to the home of your potential self. Please, push the button.

When the elevator comes to a halt, the door will open and you will find yourself stepping into your potential home, the home of your Elder Self. Pause for a moment, and notice what is under your feet. What is the floor made of? Is it covered with anything? What are the walls like? And what is above your head? What colours or sounds or scents do you especially notice? Do you like this place?

As you look around, you notice your Elder Self. What kind of clothes is the Elder wearing? Imagine yourself holding out your hand and letting the Elder take it. What one word best describes your feelings as the Elder holds your hand?

Look into the Elder's eyes. What one word best describes the expression you see in those eyes?

And now, ask the Elder to show you something of special interest in the house. What are you shown? Does the Elder have any particular comments to make about it?

Is there anything you would like to ask about what you have been shown? If there is, go ahead and ask.

What is the reply?

Now you may ask the Elder for some information. You may either ask about the best way to handle a particular situation or question, or you may simply ask the Elder what you most need to know at this time in your life. What do you ask?

What does the Elder answer?

If you are not quite clear about the answer, ask the Elder to clarify it for you.

If you have any questions about the answer you have been given, ask them now.

When you have understood the information the Elder has to give you about your present situation, ask if there is anything else that the Elder would especially like to tell you. What does the Elder say?

If you don't fully understand, ask the Elder to explain it to you more clearly.

If you have any questions about what you have just been told, you may ask them now.

Is there anything else the Elder would like to show you in the house? If so, what is it?

Does the Elder have anything to say about this?

Do you have any questions or comments you wish to make to the Elder at this time? If so, go ahead.

When you have finished speaking with the Elder, say goodbye for now and go back into the elevator. When you get there, push the button to take you back to the ground floor.

When you reach the ground floor, again imagine the master switch on your forehead. As you turn it on, all of the other switches flip on at the same time.

Let yourself become aware of the chair you are sitting in, while you take a couple of deep breaths.

Flex your fingers and toes, and when you're ready, open your eyes and stretch.

The logic of the imagery

We know things we don't know we know, and the unconscious has access to information we don't know we have. This journey does not *predict* the future, but it shows us a *possible* future — and then we have to do the work to get there, or not get there, as the case may be.

This imagery journey can give us an expanded view of our possibilities and potential, which is sometimes very helpful — even inspiring. I find that it helps to act as a touchstone. If we like this future view of ourselves, the Elder can act as a guide, whom we may consult whenever we wish. When we have a decision to make or an action to take, we can ask ourselves whether or not any given choice will bring us closer to being that kind of person or take us farther from it. It is surprising how often this helps us to make our choices — both the small day-to-day ones and the bigger changes.

The interpretation

First, write down the dialogue between you and the Elder, and make a note of what the Elder showed you. Then do a quick impressionistic painting of the Elder. When these are completed, write a description of this potential self.

Did you like this person?

Did you find that the Elder, his or her actions and comments, and his or her environment suggested possibilities you had not considered before? Is any of this useful or helpful to you at present?

Was there anything about the Elder — attitudes, habits, appearance — that you would like to change? If so, *now is the time to start*.

Possibilities for expansion

When you have an important choice to make, you might want to use this imagery journey to explore who you might become if you make the choice one way, and who you might be if you choose the other path. This would mean doing the imagery two separate times. This is easy enough to do — you simply state your intention to yourself at the beginning of the imagery, changing the wording of the first sentence to suit your intention. For example, one journey might begin with 'going to visit the self I will become if I take the job in Spain' and the other 'if I do not take the job in Spain'.

When we have made a major choice or change in our lives, or if we have been working persistently at making small changes, it may be interesting to go back to visit the Elder and to see what changes there are in him or her. The unconscious can use this vehicle to tell us what it sees as possible long-term outcomes to current choices. This is not infallible, but it can be thought-provoking and stimulating.

16. Oracles and the Way Ahead

We know much more than we consciously realise. We have information that we have forgotten on the conscious level — perhaps even information that we never consciously knew we had. I don't know how much looking into the future is simply unconscious associative reasoning, which is so much more wide-ranging and powerful than conscious analytical logic. I do know that we can see much more of the probable future than we usually allow ourselves to glimpse. It can be very useful to give our Elder Selves an opportunity to make comments and suggestions about our plans. This gives us a chance to look ahead without quite so much conscious censorship.

Cautions

If we are going to consult our Elder Self (or any other aspect of ourselves) about the future, we need to be very grounded and clear. Both fear and desire can interfere with foresight. We need to be really willing to hear the truth, without distortion.

Another thing that makes consultations about the future difficult is that we are considering possibility, probability, and potential, not fate. There is no fate. If you believe in fate, there is really no point in doing this kind of work because it is ultimately about making conscious choices — and if there is fate we don't have choice.

What we are looking at here are *possibilities*, perhaps even probabilities, as seen by the unconscious at this time. We can learn something about what will happen *if everyone involved goes on behaving the way they normally behave*. If anyone makes a sharp turn, an unlikely choice, all bets are off — and because we have choice, we can do just that. However, the predictions of the Elder Self are still useful because they *are* probabilities, and we may want to do whatever we can either to reinforce or change them.

When consulting the Elder Self or any other inhabitant of the inner world, whether about the present or the future, it is not good practice to ask the same question again just because you do not like or do not understand the first answer! Think about the response you have been given for a while. These inner guides do not promise that you will be pleased with their answers. They are here to help you — not to stroke your ego or tell you what you want to hear. Anyone who simply tells you what you want to hear is completely useless — so it all depends on your willingness to be honest with yourself. I would be very suspicious indeed of anyone who always told me what I wanted or expected to hear.

One last thing about this: don't rush back again and again. Give yourself time to contemplate the images and answers before you go on to more questions. Questioning the Elder Self and other aspects of ourselves is a way of helping us to think, not a way of avoiding thinking.

Information gained through imagery cannot tell us what to do. It can only suggest possible courses of action. Like an oracle, its proper use is to help us to see hitherto unseen possibilities, to think more deeply about things we may have skipped over or not noticed, to see things from another point of view, and to draw upon the wisdom of aspects of ourselves other than our conscious minds.

Sometimes the guidance we receive through imagery is quite clear, but more often it requires some thought and interpretation. *The true value of imagery guidance is its ability to stimulate thought and intuition in the Seeker.*

Remember: No imagery journey can accurately foretell the future. The future is not fixed. We have choice. The unconscious can make some amazingly good guesses about it, because we know things on the unconscious levels that we don't know we know, and also because the unconscious has ways of processing information that the conscious mind does not have. This is where much of inspiration and intuition come from. However, it can only deal with potential, possibilities, and improbabilities. Do not kid yourself — there are no guarantees.

17. Where Do You Want To Go?

Now that you have seen what your unconscious feels you might become, write a description and paint a quick impression (or more than one, if you like) of who and what you consciously wish to be when you become very, very old. If you live to be ninety or more, what kind of a person would you like to be? How would you prefer to be living? What would you want to be able to tell your great-grandchildren, if any, about your life?

Now look at this description and these paintings together. Do the paintings suggest any qualities or attributes that the description doesn't include? Does the list contain anything that you can't see in the pictures? What does it tell you about what you want to become? Can you see anything there that you hadn't been consciously aware of?

You may want to write your description in the ordinary way, or you might like to try poetry for a change. Poetry sometimes allows us to discover and say things we find it difficult or even impossible to say in prose. It also is easier for the associative mode of thinking to join in with poetry, perhaps because it doesn't have to be so remorselessly linear and logical. Poetry allows us to be outrageous. Have fun with this — it doesn't have to be Great Literature — for example:

I GIVE YOU FAIR WARNING . . .

When I grow old, *really* old,
I shall be eccentrik.
I shall wear long silken skirts
that sweep in the dust
and keep Abyssinian cats.

I shall speak clearly to the cats, of course,
but to other people I shall speak
only in symbols, codes, and cryptograms,
and let them think
that they understand.

I shan't knit.

My garden will be wild and rich.
I shall plant tall stones
in suitable places, and I shall make potions
of flowers and light. I shall be
a healing presence
in the world.

With my knobby old knees
and sagging breasts, I shall dance
naked under the full moon,
and I shall sing to the moon
with the cats.

I shall keep bees.

I shall carry a blackthorn stick,
and frighten small boys away
from my apples. They will like that.

And I'll tell tales of the Goddess
to little girls so they will know
who they are.

I shall say outrageous true things
to people, and make waterfalls
and small pools
in wild places. My hands
will create beauty.

I shall have a deep, deep well
of silence
in myself, and it will fill
with the love flowing through me
like a wild underground river. My hair
will be very white and unmanageable —
rather like a dandelion. My roots
shall rest in Earth's heart,
and the god
will be
a *personal* friend of mine.

What are the similarities and dissimilarities between your vision of the Wise Old Wo/Man and your vision of yourself in old age? For example, was your image of a wise person the same sex as you are? Why do you suppose that it was or wasn't? How do you feel about the nature of wisdom in the opposite sex? In your own? Write down notes about any observations you make about this and other factors in your concept of wisdom and your vision of yourself. Don't take this too seriously — remember that humour and playfulness are attributes of wisdom.

Review

From time to time, I shall be making a few suggestions for review. Most of the imagery journeys and exercises in this book are intended to be used repeatedly and to become an integral part of our personal growth processes and daily life. The use of these journeys encourages us to live consciously, instead of sleepwalking through life, as we have a tendency to do.

For example, I find it useful to take a *Walk In The Forest* once a month or so, just to check on what I'm doing — and to discover when I'm headed into trouble before it becomes all too obvious.

Is your imagery dictionary up to date? This might be a good time to read back through it to see if you have anything to add to it — either to the definitions already listed or other subjects/images to add.

Although *Light Into Darkness* was meant to be done just once at the beginning of this course, you may want to take the time to look back over the images, especially of the gifts, and see if they mean more to you now than they did when you originally did the journey. If you had difficulty with the journey at that time and didn't receive your symbolic gifts, this may be a good time to try it again.

Part V

Recognising the Landmarks

*"Granny is taking me to Unseen University," said Esk.
Hilta raised her eyebrows. "Do you know where it is?"
Granny frowned. "Not in so many words," she admitted.
"I was hoping you could give me more explicit directions."*

*"They say it has many doors, but the ones in this world are
in the city of Ankh-Morpork," said Hilta. Granny looked
blank. "On the Circle Sea," Hilta added. Granny's look of
polite inquiry persisted. "Five hundred miles away," said
Hilta.*

"Oh," said Granny.

*She stood up and brushed an imaginary speck of dust of her
dress.*

"We'd better be going, then," she added.
      — Terry Pratchett
      in Equal Rites

18. Speaking the Language: Images

The trickiest thing about travelling is usually trying to keep track of where we are and what that means in relation to where we want to go. People say things like, 'turn right at the hill' — but there are five hills and three of them have roads going off to the right. *They* know which one they mean; it seems obvious to them. We have similar problems in the inner world. The unconscious is quite clear about what it wants to convey with a particular image, and it just can't understand why the conscious mind is so slow and dim-witted. And I must admit that when we do finally get it right, it often does seem pretty obvious.

Our symbolic images are the landmarks and road signs of the inner world. They are perfectly plain to the unconscious mind, but we need some tools or techniques to help us understand them. When working with the verbal interpretation of a symbolic image, there are many techniques for extending the image into words. One of the simplest involves a free-association technique to help us form word-concepts about the meaning of an image.

Image association

The first step is to place the image (either the word for it or, better yet, a simple pictorial representation of it) in a small circle in the centre of a piece of blank paper. Let yourself relax a few moments. A simple technique for relaxing and focusing on the here-and-now is to close your eyes and count your breaths, until you feel you have become centered and still. If you lose count, just start again, and continue until you feel relaxed and quiet. Don't rush; give yourself the time you need for this.

Now, look at the image and focus your attention upon it.

As you relax, other images, words, and feelings will begin to arise in your mind. Write each word or the name of the image or feeling in the space surrounding the central image. Scatter these words at random over the paper; don't make a neat list. Lists tend to move linearly, from one idea to the next in a chain, and we don't want that. We want each word to relate back to the central image rather than to the preceding word, forming a part of the whole of that image.

If you get stuck, just focus on your breath again, letting your eyes rest on the central image until another word or feeling or image arises.

Remember: you are not trying to 'think' of words, but just allowing them to float to the surface of your mind. *Write all of the words that come up,* whether there is any obvious relationship or not. Do not censor them because you feel they are too silly or don't make sense. If it comes into your mind, it should go onto the paper. Often quite unexpected things emerge if we stay centered on the primary image and continue with the process until it feels fully complete.

If the paper becomes crowded and the concepts are still coming, start a second sheet.

Next, take another page and begin to make columns of words that seem to be related to one another by a single central concept. Put all of the words that seem connected into one column. Make as many columns as you need for the various concepts that you find. For example, there might need to be a column for positive feelings, one for negative feelings, another for physical qualities, one for spiritual qualities, and others for still other attributes of the image.

The number of columns needed depends partly on the nature of the image and partly on the variety of individual words that are evoked by the image. Each column may have any number of words in it, from one upwards. Individual words can go in more than one column if they seem related to more than one idea or quality.

When you have completed making the lists, are there any concepts or qualities you are surprised to find?

What this process does is to give us a set of concepts, each list focusing on one of those concepts. The individual words in the list define and refine and establish the boundaries of that concept. This is a good technique for use when we feel that we are somehow blocking interpretation or when we are dealing with an image which we have not encountered before and for which we have no frame of reference. It is also worth doing if we feel that a thorough understanding of one image is particularly important to us. As you can see, it is a bit cumbersome to use for every image in every journey, but it can be extremely helpful in special cases.

19. Seeing a Rose

Perhaps this associative technique will seem easier if you see an example from my own notes. In this case, I needed to understand more about the red rose offered to me by an ectype in one of the

imagery journeys. The words that came up scattered about the page
(in no particular order) were:

falling petals, ecstasy, potpourri, mother, ring, green, admiration,
heartbreak, dewdrop, generosity, love, message, grief, gift, wild,
seed-bearer, spring, softness, decay, linkage, rejoice, remembrance, sun heart, sharp, exposing the centre, bare in winter, life,
prayer, touching, honour, yellow, intoxicating, pain, honey,
hybrid, remembrance, velvet, loss, garden, sweetness, last rose of
summer, red, crystal, bud, defence, cut back, open, heart, fear,
abundance, summer, death, beauty, hospital, carving, thorn.

Then I listed them by categories/concepts as:

Feelings	*Time/Cycle*	*Qualities*
love	falling petals	generosity
grief	seed-bearer	wild
ecstasy	spring	softness
admiration	decay	sun heart
heartbreak	remembrance	exposing the centre
generosity	bare in winter	bare in winter
rejoice	remembrance	touching
touching	last rose of summer	honour
fear	bud	intoxicating
pain	cut back	defence
loss	open	hybrid
	summer	beauty
	death	abundance

Physical Characteristics	*Associations*	*Mother*
falling petals	potpourri	love
green	mother	grief
seed-bearer	ring	decay
softness	dewdrop	remembrance
decay	message	exposing the centre
exposing the centre	gift	prayer
bare in winter	linkage	life
yellow	carving	death
hybrid	life	pain
bud	prayer	loss
death	honey	garden
beauty	sweetness	hospital
thorn	heart	death

crystal   seed-bearer

Places	*Romance*	*Of the Spirit*
wild	ecstasy	ecstasy
garden	ring	love
hospital	admiration	message
	heartbreak	gift
	love	wild
	message	seed-bearer
	grief	rejoice
	gift	sun heart
	rejoice	exposing the centre
	remembrance	prayer
	exposing the centre	intoxicating
	sweetness	open
	heart	abundance
	fear	beauty
	thorn	

Sorrows	*Joys*	*Beauties*
falling petals	ecstasy	falling petals
heartbreak	admiration	green
grief	generosity	dewdrop
decay	love	generosity
sharp	gift	wild
bare in winter	seed-bearer	seed-bearer
pain	spring	spring
loss	softness	softness
last rose of summer	rejoice	sun heart
cut back	remembrance	crystal
defence	sun heart	bud
fear	exposing the centre	open
death	life	heart
	touching	abundance
	abundance	summer
	summer	carving
	beauty	thorn

As you can see from the above lists, the associations are partly held in
common with many people, and partly personal. Love and beauty are
usual associations, and so is the idea of the thorn for sorrow and pain.
The rose is often used in both romantic and spiritual symbolism. If we
think about it, the cyclic nature of life is pretty obvious, although

perhaps a bit less obvious is the concept of sometimes needing to be 'cut back' in order to grow and bloom more richly.

On a more personal level, the rose symbolising 'mother' comes from my experience of having a mother with a very green thumb and also from having used a red rose (her favourite flower) as a key or trigger into a hypnotic state to distance her from the pain she felt while dying from cancer.

Looking over the lists, I suppose the things that surprise me are the strength of the connection with my mother's death, and the repeated importance to me of the rose as a symbol for 'exposing the centre' — the heart. The word 'remembrance' occurs more often than I would have expected. And I quite fail to understand how the word 'linkage' crept in and what it is about. I might someday do a whole exercise around that word to clarify it.

In the particular imagery where the rose was presented to me, it seemed that the idea of accepting the need of cutting back in order to give myself room to grow was the most important concept, closely followed by the concepts of the repeating cycle of life and the inextricable nature of joy and sorrow, flower and thorn.

Using this technique of image association, I'd like you to choose the symbol from your *Walk in the Forest* that you found most difficult to understand and work with. (You can either use one from the original walk, or you can repeat the exercise and use a more up-to-date image.) When you have finished the last of the lists, ask yourself, what does the most important meaning of the symbol in this particular imagery journey seem to be? What are the other most relevant meanings? Have you learned anything from this that you did not already know about yourself?

20. Getting the Most from the Journey

First of all, practise the imagery exercises. Use them a lot. As you use them, the symbols will become more clear, more vivid, and more helpful.

Secondly, apply the information and insight you got from the imagery to your daily life. Everyone likes to be listened to, even your own unconscious mind. As you use the information and insight gained from the imagery to make beneficial changes in your life, your unconscious will also learn to use this as a powerful tool for self-improvement, and it may even decrease its resistance to change.

This will allow you to experience change more joyfully and less painfully. The pain we experience with change does not come from the change itself, but from our resistance to it. Contrary to popular belief, change can be a joyful experience.

Thirdly, write up the imagery as soon as possible after experiencing it. This will help you to get much more out of it because images tend to fade or distort as we examine them in the bright light of consciousness. It will also be useful and informative to periodically review your old imagery journeys and to note any changes that have been made, times that requests have had to be repeated or information duplicated by the unconscious, and so on. I suggest that you take notes immediately after doing any journey and use them to help you write it up more completely as soon as possible. This will help immeasurably in your quest for guidance and transformation.

Fourth, do the paintings to get the input from the more feeling, visual self, the associative mode of thinking. The analytic mode of words helps us to take something to pieces and think about those pieces, but the associative mode adds significance and depth to those thoughts, and helps us to see the meaning of the whole.

21. Observation Skills

You may notice that I use the words 'imagine' and 'image' a great deal, but hardly use the words 'visualise' or 'visualisation' at all. An image can take many forms — a sound, an emotion, a memory, a physical sensation, or an inner vision. Some people find it easy to form visual images, seeing with the mind's eye, while others may find that difficult or impossible.

This need not be a handicap to working with imagery.

An image is a representation in the mind. Such a representation may use any of the senses — or any combination of them. Sight, hearing, touch, taste, and scent are all equally useful in guided imagery. There is also the 'kinesthetic sense' — the feel of the body and its position in space and in relationship to its surroundings. For example, can you imagine the feeling of walking, of moving your arms, of standing on the ceiling with your head hanging down?

Another way of sensing images is to perceive them as if we were remembering something that once had happened. This kind of 'knowing' can provide a richness of detail and depth of experience that a simple visual picture may lack.

The problem for some of us is that, if we can't *see* something, we find it difficult to trust our other perceptions of it. This is like our desire to turn on the light in order to cross a darkened room even though we are so familiar with it that we could easily cross it blindfolded — and possibly backwards as well. In ordinary life, most of us take in about 80% of our conscious information about the world through our eyes. We are so accustomed to depending on that one sense that we tend to undervalue the rest. One of the ways in which imagery can expand our consciousness and enhance our capacity to be fully in the world is by helping us to learn to consciously observe through *all* our senses.

Let's try a small imagery journey just to check out which senses we can easily use and which we need to learn to pay more attention to.

Approximate travel time: 15 minutes.

CHECKING IT OUT

Please begin by taking a couple of deep breaths. Notice each breath as you inhale, as you exhale. As you release the next breath, allow any tension in your shoulders to release with the outgoing breath. As you inhale the next breath, breathe in calmness, and breathe out anything in yourself that you don't need or want. As you inhale, just say to yourself, 'I am breathing in calmness' and as you exhale, just let go. Just continue for a few minutes to breathe in calmness and breathe out anything in yourself that you don't need or want.

As you take the next breath, begin to imagine that you are standing barefoot on grass. Imagine the grass — its softness, its coolness, its greenness. You may even be able to smell the grass. Imagine yourself wiggling your toes in the grass, and as you wiggle your toes, feel the breeze with your fingers. The air around you is warm and soft, moving gently over your face, your hands, over all of your skin that is exposed.

As you begin to sense what is around you, you notice some rose bushes to your left. Imagine yourself reaching out with your left hand and touching one of the deep, deep red roses. The rich scent of the roses floats on the air, and the texture of the petals is soft and smooth, like a baby's skin. If you touch the tip of a thorn, you will find that it is very sharp, sharp and piercing.

As you turn away from the roses, you find a marble column to your right. It is just about the height of your chest, and resting on top of it there is a sculpture. At first you may think it is made of glass, but you realise that you can feel the cold coming from it, and it is extremely cold ice. It seems very strange that the ice doesn't melt, and you touch it to be certain that it really is ice. You can feel the coldness and slickness and wetness with your fingers as you stroke it.

While you are touching the ice, you realise you can hear voices singing. You look around you but there are no people in sight. This is puzzling, but after a bit, you tilt your head back and look up. Just about fifty feet above you a balloon is floating past, and the people in the balloon basket are singing a familiar song. The music floats down upon you like gentle warmth.

As you watch, one of the children looks over the side and sees you. She waves a green silk scarf at you, and then ducks out of sight for a moment. When she reappears she is holding an apple, and she tosses the apple down to you. It seems to fall and fall and fall with dream-like slowness, but as you catch it in your hand, it smacks hard against your palm.

The apple is a Golden Delicious, and it has a wonderful aroma. You sniff the smooth, scented skin, and bite into it. It is so juicy that the juice runs down your chin. The taste is surprisingly tart, sweet and tart at the same time.

To your surprise, the apple disappears from your hand just as you start to take another bite. You look up again, but the balloon, too, has vanished. You look around you, but the rose bush and the marble pillar have also gone. The ice sculpture is suspended in the air, but it is melting, melting, melting — and as you watch, it evaporates into the air.

Even the earth beneath your feet is gone and you are floating in a soft, misty void.

You take a deep breath and find yourself back in this room. Be aware of the surface you are sitting on.

Take another two or three deep breaths, and then flex your fingers and toes.

And another deep breath.

When you are ready, open your eyes and stretch.

Was your imagery primarily visual, or were you also able to imagine the other senses? Which of the senses (sight, hearing, touch, taste, scent, kinesthetic) are the clearest for you? Do your images feel like physical sensations or are they an inner knowing? Or perhaps some of each?

The way we improve the kinds of images that are less clear is by paying more attention to them in our daily life. If vision is the dominant sense (as it is for most people), we could benefit by paying more attention to the textures, the scents, and the sounds we encounter in our everyday activities. One reason for the dominance of vision is that it gives us warning of things while they are still at a distance. We have more time between becoming aware of something and actually encountering it, more time to prepare ourselves. Hearing is the next most dominant sense, for the same reason. Yet the interesting thing is that we tend to react much more emotionally, more intimately and immediately to touch, taste, and scent. A small child explores with all the senses, worrying its parents by putting everything in its mouth, and if possible, swallowing it. As we grow older we distance ourselves from our environment by concentrating on vision and hearing. Practising awareness of our other senses helps us to be more present in the here-and-now.

The necessity of actually seeing pictures in an imagery journey is overrated by people who do it well. All you need to do is to accept whatever you do get from your unconscious in whatever form it comes. Your images may come in the form of thought impressions, physical sensations, or emotional feelings. These may be vivid or very subtle. The important thing is to flow with whatever you do get — don't argue with it or try to change it. Arguing with the images or trying to control them pushes you out of that receptive, relaxed state of consciousness in which you best perceive your inner images.

Most people don't have really vivid impressions, visual or other-wise, at first unless they have had quite a bit of practice in some related mental discipline. However, for nearly everyone, the imagery experience becomes much more vivid and 'real' with practice. Simply accept what you get, allow yourself to follow along.

When you don't get an immediate response to a request for an image, just allow yourself to skip over it — without criticizing yourself for not having the response. It is best to stay in the flow of the imagery than to become bogged down over one recalcitrant image. Let yourself be a part of the flow, a free-wheeling part of the process.

22. Seeing It The Way It Is

One of the primary aspects of working with imagery is learning to allow ourselves to flow with the images. We have a tendency to 'improve' our images, especially when we find them frightening or when they seem to be expressing something about ourselves that we do not approve of or don't understand.

Resistance expresses itself in many forms, and one of the most frequently encountered is resistance to the images themselves. We 'decide' that our images are too weird or too common, that they are 'only' our imagination or 'only' associations from the past. You can't win, can you? If it's strange, it's unacceptable, but if it's ordinary, it's also unacceptable. If it comes from inside us, it isn't good enough, and if it is something we have seen in the outer world, it also isn't good enough. People even try to deny an image if someone else in the group has a similar one, saying that they must have 'picked it up' from the other. This is all rubbish. An image is an image is an image.

The images that come up — whatever they are — are the ones that we need.

What we are really saying with all this denial is that we are embarrassed or frightened about revealing ourselves in this way. We are afraid of being 'seen' through our own inner eyes, either by ourselves or by others. We feel vulnerable and as if we were about to be judged and found wanting — so we judge ourselves first, before anyone else does it.

When we were small children, most of us learned that 'truth' (reality as seen by the adults around us) was good and that 'imagination' (our creative inner reality) was lies — and lies were bad. In order to please the adults, we often had to deny and suppress our creativeness and inner life. If we drew pictures, they often were judged by and valued for how much they were like the outer world. We were made to feel guilty and ashamed of daydreaming and imagining things. The only permissible use of the imagination was to relive someone else's imagination through stories, books, and films, and often, those too were censored and limited to suit the current adult ideology. It is all part of the efforts of any society to see to it that no one rocks the boat, and that we are all good little people who will do as we are told. It is undesirable (to authority) for us to trust and perhaps even act upon our own inner knowing in preference to the Voice of Authority — even when authority is blatantly wrong. This socialisation process doesn't happen to everyone with the same degree of oppression, but it happens to most of us to a greater or lesser extent.

What we learned from this process was to censor and reject our own inner world — in effect, to disown our creativity and our feelings. The way that we disown our images is to *judge* that they are meaningless or that they are flawed — trite, foolish, boring, bizarre, silly, made up, frivolous, copied. Whenever we hear ourselves disowning an image in any way, we need to acknowledge that this is our resistance speaking. It is the voices of the people who taught us that what is inside us is without value. It is also our fear — fear of having our inner reality denied and devalued yet again.

So what can we do about this? Well, the first thing is to *stop judging* the images as if they were in some kind of a contest for Best Image of the Year. Whenever we hear ourselves making a value judgment about an image — good, bad, or whatever — we need to apologise to the image itself. I'm serious about this. The image is a part of ourselves, which we have rudely rejected, and it deserves to be treated with loving respect, *even if we don't like what it represents.*

We also need to respect our images during the imagery journey itself. If we try to change them, we move from *listening* to the unconscious to *directing* our mental scenes. This may be fun, it may be creative, but it will not give us the information that we went on this journey to find. We cancel the value of the imagery when we begin to change it. If the grass is made of feathers, if the aspect of yourself is a pumpkin, if the animals are straight out of a Disney film, if it is unbelievable, outrageous, or absurd (our resistance's judgments), it is what it is, and that is what it is meant to be. The instant we start to push it into something else is the moment it loses its value as communication from the unconscious, and we begin suppressing our unconscious creativity. This is resistance on the conscious level, but there can be unconscious resistance as well.

Unconscious resistance can take various forms. There may be physical distractions (itches and aches are common), or simply an inability to concentrate, with every little sound or movement in our environment a distraction. We may fall asleep or simply blank out on parts (or all) of the imagery. There may be no image at all, it may be so vague and indistinct as to be useless, or there may be a kind of double image.

When an image starts to form and is replaced by another without the imager willing that to happen, it may be unconscious censorship. If an image comes up quickly and is immediately replaced by another image, it may be resistance. This does not mean that the second image is invalid; it only means that there is something still hidden. This is different from double images that express ambivalence or more than one thing. If there are two (or perhaps more) images, either side by side or alternating back and forth, this may be the unconscious trying to express something too complex to be embodied in a single image. In such a case, all of the images are the answer.

We need to form the habit of making a mental note of conscious or unconscious censorship when it may be occurring. These images are the symbols around which our resistance is coiled, like a serpent around its egg. There will be more later on about working with resistance, but the important thing now is that you allow yourself to experience the images and feelings as they come from the unconscious mind in response to the statements made and questions asked by the person guiding you through them. Save the evaluations and judgments for later, if you must make judgments — although I do hope that you will learn to stop judging your personal inner world by the limitations of the outer world and of your upbringing.

The phrase 'being non-judgmental' is bandied about a great deal. It is extremely difficult to do, but well worth striving for, both in our relationships with ourselves and with others. It enables us to see clearly as we travel the path of self-exploration.

23. Speaking the Language: Form

I could have called this chapter 'Seeing It As It Is Not' — but I'll restrain myself. Do you remember lying on the grass as a child, looking up at the clouds and seeing sailing ships and whales and bears and castles and faces? I want you to do something like that with your paintings. Take all of the paintings you have done so far, and look at them in soft focus in the same way you once looked at the clouds. Turn them upside down, and find all the hidden shapes that you can. Now, look at the paintings from each side so that you are looking at all of the possibilities.

This way of looking at these paintings may seem to be just nonsense, but if we are truly painting freely, things will reveal themselves without our conscious intention. Symbols and images will appear in the drawing that are relevant to the subject of the drawing and to the present state of the painter. One of the students in a class complained that her picture was 'just scribbles' and that it didn't and couldn't mean anything. I had already seen it from another angle and held it up sideways for the class to see. They all immediately saw a figure standing in a doorway. It was quite clear and very relevant to what was going on for her. She was standing at a metaphorical open door in her life and was unable to decide whether to go through or not. Once she realised what she had painted, she began to think about the colours and the kinds of lines she had used. She found, not too surprisingly, that she not only clarified her dilemma, but also could see what she really wanted to do.

Sometimes, as in these two cases, there is a complete hidden painting within the painting, but more often there are just single images, perhaps scattered in different places. Such images may overlap, and some images may form parts of other images.

Look at your paintings closely and then prop them up somewhere so that you can go across the room to look at them. If you are working with others, look at each other's paintings and see what you can see. Don't try to interpret one another's paintings, but do mention the images that you see.

Make a list of the hidden images and symbols you have found in each painting. How many of these symbols can you readily relate to the primary subject of the painting in which they are found? How many relate to other subjects? For example, if a bent pine tree is one of your symbols for your job, and there is a bent pine tree shape in your painting, you might consider how the subject of the painting may be relevant to your job.

Such hidden forms can also give us information from the unconscious in our everyday life. Recently I had a nasty virus, and on my first day back out of bed, I went to Glastonbury to run some errands. While there I thought I'd get a card for a special occasion. As I walked past the postcards I noticed, out of the corner of my eye, one with a modernistic pink elephant against a dark background. Intrigued by this, I went back to look more closely at the elephant — only to discover that the card was actually a photograph of Glastonbury Abbey and the 'pink elephant' was a sunrise sky outlined by the ruins. I suddenly realised that I was exhausted, that I was not well enough to be trotting all over the place doing things, and that it was definitely time to go home when I started seeing pink elephants in Glastonbury Abbey. A very clear and simple message.

Review

How are you coming along with getting to know some of your more powerful ectypes? Using the Wise Old Wo/Man exercise in Chapter 12, I suggest that you work with some more of them — your choice which. If you are working in a group, it might be interesting for everyone to do the same ones. That would give you a wider range of experience with the same archetype and different ectypes.

If you are working with a group, this is a good time to review *Appendix A: Working Together.* How would you assess your group's performance on the various points? Is there room for improvement?

And if so, what commitment do each of you, as individuals, need to make to enhancing the functioning of the group?

This is also an appropriate time for anyone who is acting as group leader to review *Appendix B: For The Teacher*. If several or all of the group share the task, you may want to have a discussion about the way that leadership is functioning for you. What can each of you do, both as individuals and collectively, to improve?

Part VI

The Quest for Guidance

As Magrat plunged down towards the forest roof in a long shallow dive she reflected that there was possibly something complimentary in the way Granny Weatherwax resolutely refused to consider other people's problems. It implied that, in her considerable opinion, they were quite capable of sorting them out by themselves.

— *Terry Pratchett*
in Wyrd Sisters

24. Forms of the Journey

There are three basic types of guided imagery — freeform, interactive, and structured. In the first, freeform imagery, the guide provides a seed, but the imager provides all the rest. For example, the guide might ask that the imager imagine an animal which symbolised his father. The guide then would ask questions about the animal, its environment, its actions and interactions with the imager. The answers to these questions, when carefully interpreted, would reveal things about the imager's relationship with his father — including things that may have been unacknowledged or even unsuspected.

In this type of imagery work, each question naturally leads on from the preceding answers until the desired information is obtained or until the imager blocks. Freeform imagery usually works best when the imager is not heavily blocked on the issue, and when he is fairly fluent in imagery work. We will consider this type of imagery more in the next chapter.

The second type, interactive imagery, is a mixture of structure and questions. The guide has a predetermined sequence that he wishes to take the imager through, with a set intention, but discovering the imager's responses to the situations and the beings encountered in the journey is the primary purpose of the imagery. To a limited extent the imager may make choices that partially determine the course of the journey, but overall the pattern is set. The imagery itself is designed to elicit the imager's responses, together with the information and guidance they contain. Both the *Walk in the Forest* and *When I Grow Old* are examples of this kind of imagery. We will be doing additional interactive journeys, beginning with *The Advisor* in Chapter 26.

In the third type, fully structured imagery, the process is the opposite of freeform imagery. Here, both the path and the things that are experienced along the way are predetermined. The guide directs and does not ask questions. These structured imagery journeys are intended to produce a particular desired effect, such as relaxation, development of mental skills and awareness, specific kinds of transformation, and the expansion of consciousness. Structured imagery journeys are exercises that develop certain mental/psychic 'muscles' and they are practice in doing particular things. We will not encounter any structured journeys until we reach *Journey to the Waterfall* in Chapter 33 — and even it has interactive elements.

Nothing to do with the human mind is ever as neat and orderly as this tidy division into three types of imagery. As we travel together, you will find that there are often structured elements within an interactive journey. Freeform imagery might turn up unexpectedly when you are working one-to-one. Notice these elements in the journeys as we go along and see how they fit together.

Let's take a look at what we can do with freeform imagery.

25. Freeform Journeys

Perhaps the simplest — though not necessarily the easiest — form of imagery journey is an unstructured, freeform exploration that centers around a concept or a question and uses whatever images arise to look at it. This freeform imagery is especially helpful when we feel blocked or frustrated on the conscious level, knowing that we have a problem, but perhaps not even able to see clearly what it is.

For example, a woman was having difficulty in finishing a project, and she seemed unable to get on with it even though she knew what needed to be done. We decided to use freeform imagery to see if we could find out what was holding her back. The exercise went something like this:

I'd like you to begin by taking a couple of deep breaths, allowing the tension to flow out of your body as you exhale. Be aware of your forehead and allow it to relax. Let your eyelids become soft, and your throat — soft and at ease. Allow this ease to flow down from your throat, through your shoulders and down your arms to your fingertips. It's a feeling of softness, of peacefulness, with your face, your throat, your neck and shoulders and arms an hands at ease, at peace. And this feeling of peace flows down through your body, through your chest, your abdomen, through your pelvis and hips, down through your legs, your feet, your toes.

You have a question in your mind about something you want to do and in another part of your mind you have the answer tucked away out of sight. The hidden part of your mind would like to give you this information in the next few minutes. All you need to do is to allow this to happen.

Imagine that you see your project in a symbolic form in front of you — what form does it take?

A fountain.

Please describe the fountain for me.

The water springs out of mid-air and showers back down into a large, gray stone basin.

How close are you to the fountain?

It's about fifty feet away.

Do you want to come closer to it?

Yes. I'm thirsty and the water looks lovely and cool, but it's surrounded by a pack of horrible little dogs and they are yapping at me. They won't let me near it.

Try calling one of the dogs to you. Does it come?

Yes, but it won't stop yapping.

Ask the dog what it wants. Why is it barking at you?

It says it wants me to straighten up my house. It won't let me near the fountain until my house is tidy.

Call another one and ask what it wants.

It says I must answer a lot of letters and organise my desk. Now another one comes and it makes noises like the telephone ringing.

Are there others?

Yes. One of them is dragging a big basket of other unfinished projects I have started. One of them is yapping in my next-door neighbour's voice, and another is dragging garden tools behind it. More and more of them are appearing and they are all milling around between the fountain and me. They are yapping louder and louder. I'm trying to chase them away, but there are too many and they won't go.

All right. I want you to forget about the dogs for a moment and concentrate on your breath. Take a couple of deep breaths, and as you do, become more aware of the room around you, of the sounds you hear in addition to my voice, of your total environment. Be aware of your body, and flex your fingers and toes. When you are ready, open your eyes, and if you like, stretch.

This unstructured, freeform imagery gives us the beginning of an understanding of how images can help us to see what we unconsciously need or want to do. Because it bypasses the logical part of the mind, it is especially helpful when our logic breaks down or becomes confused.

When we discussed the images in the exercise above, it was immediately clear to the imager that she felt overwhelmed by all the things that she *unconsciously* felt needed to be done before she could work on her project. Although she *consciously* wanted to do this project, it was yet another burden in an already overburdened life. She

decided that the best solution was to work out a schedule that would
enable her to gradually catch up on the things that needed to be done
and also allow a regular time to work on this project.

The trick to facilitating this kind of freeform imagery for someone
else is simply to ask the right questions. The questions should be
open-ended. That is, they should never imply an answer, even if
(perhaps *especially* if) you are quite certain you know what it ought to
be. The questions asked should leave the answer entirely to the
creative imagery of the imager.

The important imagery doesn't always come up right away, but
open-ended questions about the scene and what is going on in it
usually will point, eventually, to the problem — and often to the
solution as well.

It is important for the facilitator to follow the imagery carefully as
it comes up. Listen to the imager's tone of voice and listen for emotive
words. In the example above, it immediately seemed likely that the
'horrible' dogs, who were blocking her from her fountain/project,
were the symbolic representation of the source of her difficulty. An
early encouraging sign was that they were all little, yappy dogs. It
would have been much more worrying if they had been wolves or
fierce guard dogs.

As we began to investigate the dogs, the problem quickly became
clear, needing little following up. It was also significant that more
dogs kept appearing, and the situation became progressively more
difficult. At this point it seemed time to terminate the imagery because
it's best, if we can, to avoid letting the imager become bogged down
in an untenable situation.

As you become more proficient with imagery work, you will find
that freeform imagery is a magical source, from which answers and
solutions, information, and creative inspiration may flow. It can be as
simple or as complex as it needs to be at any time. All that is required
is a willingness on the part of the imager to explore honestly the
images that arise, remembering always to accept and use the first
image that comes into the mind. We can do these explorations by
ourselves, but it usually takes a fair bit of cxperience with this kind of
work. Working with an alert and open-minded guide is usually much
more productive.

Freeform imagery is probably the trickiest kind of work to do,
requiring by far the most attentive awareness and quick thinking from
the guide. It works best on information that is fairly attainable — the
sort of thing about which we tend to say 'but that's obvious now that

I think about it!' It also works best when the imager is well practised in the use of imagery. In the example above, the problem was relatively simple and straightforward and the imager found it easy to flow with the images.

THE JOURNEY WITHOUT A MAP

First, the imager chooses a subject on which he would like more information. It need not be a question — it might simply be a wish to understand his relationship with a particular person, an aspect of himself, or a situation better. For example, he might use this technique to gain insight about his relationship with one of his parents, with a friend, with his migraine headaches, with his work. Anything that can be named can be symbolised in this way.

For this to work best, the imager should choose a subject or a question that he is really interested in learning more about, but not one that has him all stirred up emotionally.

You begin by doing something to help the imager to relax. There are examples, which you could use, of various relaxation inductions at the beginning of each of the imagery journeys in this book. If the imager is experienced, he may have his own preferred relaxation technique which you can use. Once he is relaxed, you are ready to begin.

You might begin by saying something like, 'We are interested in learning more about . . . You have information and insight within you that you need at this time. I'd like you to ask your unconscious mind to give you a symbolic image relating to . . . What is the first image that comes to your mind?'

From here on, it's up to you and the imager. Just continue asking open-ended, non-judgmental questions until you feel you have the information needed — or until the imager wants to stop or shows signs of getting bogged down. At this point, bring the imager gently back to ordinary consciousness, perhaps using one of the endings from one of the other imagery journeys.

Have the imager paint and interpret the primary image.

Discuss the journey and the painting with him, including any suggestions he has that might help you to act as guide more proficiently in the future.

Obviously, these freeform journeys need to be done on a one-to-one or individual basis. They couldn't work in a group because the facilitator would not have any idea what needed to be explored next.

For work in a group, work where the block is more serious or the information more deeply hidden, or where the imager does not find it easy to flow with the images, interactive guided imagery may offer a more suitable path.

26. Interactive Journeys

We can use interactive imagery to explore unfamiliar territory, to get guidance of various kinds, and to transform ourselves. We took a *A Walk In The Forest* to learn more about how we unconsciously saw certain aspects of ourselves. *When I Grow Old* gave us a glimpse at some of our potential. We also have many other aspects of ourselves. We are each like a diamond — what an outsider sees depends on which facet they are looking at, and what we see outside ourselves depends on which facet we are looking through. Within us there are the happy child, the wounded child, the angry child, the idealist, the rebel, the wise one, the fool, the victim, the martyr, the trickster, the bully, the hero, the coward, the destroyer, the creator, and many others. They are our ectypes, our personalised versions of human archetypes. These parts-of-ourselves are not all equally strong; various ones have more or less power in different people. And we shift emphasis from one to another at various times.

Many of us would like to find someone, who absolutely *knows* what is best for us so that they can tell us what to do next. Humans have searched for centuries, millennia perhaps, for Someone Who Knows. This is not to say that we would follow this super-excellent advice if we had it, but it would be comforting to be told. And yet, we have much of the information we need within us. Hidden on the dark slopes of the mountain of consciousness there is someone who has a pretty clear understanding of what is happening and what we need to do next.

Each of us has an Advisor, our own personal counsellor, teacher, and guide, within us. The value and effectiveness of our advisors, guides, and teachers in the outer world depend, in part, upon how well they resonate with that inner Advisor. In a sense, the inner Advisor is who we would be if only we could put into practice all of the things that we know — including those we don't even know we know. Such an Advisor is tricky to find, hidden as it is behind a maze of self-delusion, unacknowledged motivations, conflicting desires, and general disbelief — but not impossible.

As our first example of an interactive imagery journey, I have chosen *The Advisor*. It is one of the most useful imagery exercises I know, and it can be adapted to many purposes, some of which we will consider later.

Just a word before we begin — you may find that some of your personal images don't quite fit the journey below as it is written. For example, your Advisor might take the form of a tree and you would not be able to hold its hand or look into its eyes. Just do what you can and go on to the next thing. You might, for instance, touch a branch of the tree and notice how you feel while you are holding it. Instead of looking into its eyes, you might simply look at the tree and notice what feeling, if any, it seems to express and how you feel toward it. Another example of this is that we may sometimes find ourselves floating in outer space or in another dimension rather than in a realistic or a fantastic world. Several of the questions below become immediately irrelevant in such a case.

If you are using a tape or being guided as a member of a group who are all doing the journey, you will simply need to adapt the questions within your own mind to make them relevant to your personal experience. If you are working one-to-one so that you can tell your guide what is going on as it happens, it is up to your guide to adapt the journey to your inner world. Whatever you do and however you are working, *don't* try to change your initial impression to fit some predetermined idea of what you think you 'ought' to find. Your inner world is the important thing in this journey, and you want to discover it and its wonders. You don't want to change it to fit someone else's ideas. As you go through this journey, you will meet wondrous beings, do and be extraordinary things, and make fascinating discoveries — but only if you remember to co-operate with the images that come up as they really are.

Approximate travel time: 25 minutes.

THE ADVISOR

We are going on a journey to meet your Advisor. Please begin by taking a deep breath. And now another. Be certain you are seated comfortably, and take still another deep breath. As you exhale, allow your fingers to relax, and then allow any tension in your arms, to flow down and out through your fingertips.

On the next exhalation, allow your shoulders to relax, anything you don't want or need flowing down and out through your fingertips. And on the next exhalation, allow anything you don't want or need in your neck to flow down and out through your fingertips.

Take another deep breath, and as you exhale, allow any tension in your body and your legs to flow down and out through your toes.

Breath in stillness, and as you exhale, breathe out anything in your mind that you don't need or want at this moment. And again, breathe in stillness, and as you exhale, breathe out anything remaining in your body that you don't want or need at this moment.

We are going to visit your personal Advisor, the wise person who can counsel and guide you. Remember that you are in charge of this journey. If, at any time, you wish to leave the inner world, you may do so. All you need to do is to choose to leave, and you will be out.

I'd like you to imagine that you are standing in front of the entrance to a room or a cave. Please walk a few steps into the cave or room and pause there.

What is under your feet? Is the surface hard or soft? Rough or smooth? What is it made of?

What does the air feel like? Is it warm or cool? Moving or still? Is it damp or is it dry? If it is damp, where is the moisture coming from?

If you were to reach out and touch the nearest wall, how would it feel to your fingers? What is it made of?

How big is this space? How high up is the ceiling and how far away is the farthest wall?

What colours or sounds or scents do you particularly notice here?

Is there anything special or unusual about this space?

As you consider the space around you, notice where the light is coming from.

Now walk on into your space, until you come to a door or passage to your left. You can go through this door or passage to your inner world. If there is a door and the door is locked, the key will be hanging on a hook to the right of the door. You may open it and go through. Your inner world may be an extension of the cave or room, or it may be some other kind of space altogether. Let it be the first thing that comes into your mind.

When you reach the inner world, stand still for a moment and notice what is under your feet here. Is the surface hard or soft? Rough or smooth? What is it made of?

Is the air warm or cool? Moving or still? Damp or dry? If it's damp, where is moisture coming from?

If you were to reach out and touch the thing nearest you, what would you touch, and how would it feel to your fingers?

And what do you see or sense in the distance?

What is above your head, and where is the light coming from?

What time of the day or night is it? What season of the year?

What sounds or scents or colours do you especially notice? Is there anything that particularly stands out? As you begin walking and exploring this place, notice your surroundings.

After you have been walking a short while, you meet a person, your wise Advisor. What is this person doing as you approach?

The Advisor

When you reach your Advisor, imagine yourself closing your eyes and reaching out with your hand, letting your Advisor take it. What does your Advisor's hand feel like? Does it feel strong or delicate? Hard or soft? Large or small?

What one word best describes the way you feel as your Advisor holds your hand?

What are your Advisor's eyes like — the first impression that comes to your mind? What color are they? What one word best describes the expression you see or sense in your Advisor's eyes?

What else do you notice about this person? Is it male or female? Large or small or in between? How is the Advisor dressed?

What is your Advisor's name?

At this moment, I'd like you to give your Advisor permission to tell you the truth always, even if it is something you don't want to hear.

The Agreement

And now I'd like you to ask your Advisor what he or she needs from you or needs you to do in order for the two of you to work together in your best interests.

If the answer you receive is not clear, ask your Advisor to clarify it. The answer should give you clear guidance about what is needed from you.

Is this something you feel you can agree to and actually do? If it is not, discuss it with your Advisor until you reach an agreement on something you can do to improve your working relationship with your Advisor.

When you have reached an agreement, state clearly in your mind exactly what it is that you are agreeing to do.

Do you need any suggestions or advice from your Advisor about what practical steps you need to take in order to fulfil this agreement? If so, ask your Advisor for this now.

The Gift

When you have the information you need, I'd like you to imagine that you are holding your hands out in front of you. Your Advisor will place a symbolic gift in your hands. This is a symbol of the gift you will receive for keeping your agreement.

What does this gift feel like in your hands? Is it light or heavy? What is the texture like? What colours or sounds or scents do you associate with this gift? What is it?

Ask your Advisor what this gift symbolises.

Is this gift something you want to accept? If you are not certain, discuss it with your Advisor.

If you don't want the gift, give it back, and if you like, ask if there is another gift that might be more acceptable to you. If you do want it, give it back to your Advisor and ask him or her to place it on you or in you or around you, wherever it belongs.

If you have accepted the gift, what does your Advisor do with it?

Ask your Advisor if there is anything you need to know about using your gift. Is it for use in the inner world? The outer world? Or both worlds? How are you to use it in your everyday life?

Completion

When you have all of the information you need, I'd like you to thank your Advisor for being with you and helping you, and to say goodbye to your Advisor for now.

When you are ready, go back to the place where you entered this inner world. As you go, notice if there have been any changes in your inner world. Is anything any different or is it just the same?

When you reach the door or passage through which you entered this world, come back through the cave or room to this world.

When you reach this world, take a couple of deep breaths. And another. Be aware of the seat you are sitting in. Flex your toes and your fingers as you take another deep breath.

As you begin to pay attention to the sounds of the room around you, notice how your body feels.

When you are ready, open your eyes, take another deep breath, and stretch, feeling rested, relaxed, and alert.

The logic of the imagery

As in the *Walk In The Forest* there is a general interpretation of certain elements in the journey, as well as any personal meaning they may have for you. These are as follows:

Cave or Room — represents how you feel about looking within yourself, and/or the state of your mind, especially in relationship to your Advisor.

Door or Passage — a symbol of the willingness or resistance you have to honestly confronting and communicating with your unconscious at this moment.

Inner World — how you feel within yourself, especially in relationship to your inner Advisor at this moment. Also perhaps how you feel within yourself in a general way at this time.

Journey to the Advisor — eagerness or resistance to meeting your Advisor. Also perhaps a symbolic perception of obstacles to a solution of the problem you are bringing to your Advisor.

The Advisor — He is as he is, but how does he (or she or it) present himself to you? What does this indicate about the kind of support that you need and/or find acceptable? Your Advisor may present itself to you in different forms at different times.

The Gift — since you were told what the gift symbolised in the imagery itself, you do not need to interpret it, but especially note colors, textures, attractiveness, and feelings associated with the gift. How did you feel when it was incorporated into you and your energy? The gift is a natural consequence of keeping your agreement — although perhaps not one you would have thought of. Can you see the relationship between the promise you made and the gift you received?

The interpretation

Whether you are working with a group or another person or by yourself, the first thing to do is to write down a brief account of the imagery for your journal. You may want to include the following:

When you are the imager:
1. The name of the person who guided you and the date.
2. A description of the imagery. Be certain to include promise(s) made and gift(s) received.
3. An interpretation of the imagery, especially those symbolic aspects listed above.
4. What difficulties did you have with the journey, if any?
5. What could the person guiding the imagery have done to make it easier or more effective for you?

6. What thoughts, feelings, or reactions do you now have about the agreement you made with yourself?
7. If you did the section on penetrating blocks, discuss your feelings about what happened.

When you are the guide:
1. The name of the imager and the date.
2. A summary of the imagery.
3. Your perceptions of the journey, especially:
   resistance, if any, encountered and how it was dealt with, apparent insight gained by the imager, and apparent effectiveness.
4. How would you change the imagery or your part in guiding it if you were to do the same journey over again with the same person?
5. What have you learned from this about guiding imagery in general?

The next thing is to make a quick painting of the image that stood out most for you in the entire journey. This painting should be abstract or childlike. You are not (as you must know by now) trying to make a realistic painting. Paint your impressions of and feelings about that special image.

Once the painting and the journal entries are done, if you are working in a group or with another person, I suggest that you discuss the journey you have just completed. You may want to let each person simply tell the story of their experience in the inner world without interruption, and then other members of the group can ask questions that they feel will help clarify the meaning of the imagery. These questions should be open-ended and non-judgmental. If you have not already read *Appendix A: On Working Together*, I suggest that you do so before beginning your discussion.

If you are working alone, simply interpret the various symbolic elements of your imagery and your painting, using the suggestions above and the techniques you have already learned.

Possibilities for expansion

In this journey we asked how we could work better with our Advisor, and this is the first thing we need to know. It is also something that should be reviewed from time to time. However, once we have that information, there is much more we can do with our Advisor. We can seek information and guidance on virtually any problem we might have.

In addition to that, our Advisor can assist us in meeting and working with another part of ourselves. We will be using an adapted version of this journey when we meet our inner Rebel and again to contact our inner Healer. There are many other aspects of ourselves that we might wish to meet and communicate with — and we will be able to see how this might be done later on.

If you would like to do so, you may give yourself extra time at the end to get better acquainted with your guide, to wander around and explore your inner world, or just to stay there and rest. If you do any of these things, it usually is best to give yourself a specific amount of time in which to do them. Otherwise, we tend to drift off to sleep and forget the entire journey.

The importance of contracts

Before we finish this chapter, there is just one more thing I want to mention. In this particular exercise, you made an agreement with your Advisor, which is an important part of yourself. Never make a promise to yourself unless you are reasonably certain that you can and will keep it. One of the long-term benefits of this kind of inner work is to give you more confidence and trust in yourself. Making promises to yourself and then failing to keep them will have exactly the opposite effect, decreasing your self-confidence and self-trust. Break your promises to others, if you absolutely must, but at least keep the ones you make to yourself.

If you later find that you have made a promise that you cannot fulfil, go back into your inner world and talk to your Advisor again. Explain why you cannot keep your promise to it, and ask for something else you can do instead. If you make another promise, be sure to keep it.

27. Speaking the Language: Mood

In *The Advisor* and many other imagery journeys, there are questions asked about the general environment. This 'background' to the central focus of the imagery sets the mood and tone of the journey, and also has information and insight to offer us if we care to consider it. Although you must, of course, work out your own interpretation of the various elements, the following general ideas may suggest some possibilities.

Water may indicate fluidity, the emotions, energy, sexuality, the free-flowing unconscious mind. It may indicate purity, confusion, or many things. Is the water moving or still? Clear or muddy? Salt (like blood or amniotic fluid) or fresh? Steam may indicate overheated or overcharged emotions, fog may indicate confused or obscured emotions, and ice may indicate repressed or 'frozen' emotions.

Ask yourself:

if my primary feeling about X (someone you know) were water, what would that water be like? What is the first image that comes into your mind, and what does it tell you about your unconscious feelings?

Plants and trees may indicate growth, fertility, creativity. Are the plants beautiful or not? Nurturing or poison or neutral? Are they things you would like to touch or not? Is the world of the imagery primarily symbolic of growth and movement or is it stagnant or sterile, dormant or dying? How alive is it?

Ask yourself:

if my relationship with my mother (or father) were a plant, what would it be and how would it look? What is the first image that comes into your mind, and what does it tell you about your unconscious feelings about your relationship with that parent?

Buildings and other artificial structures may indicate images of our own emotional and mental constructions and/or a symbolic representation of our own bodies or perhaps the body of someone else represented in the imagery. This symbol was used in *The Walk In The Forest*.

Ask yourself:

if I were a house, what kind of a house would I be? What is the first image that comes into your mind, and what does this tell you about your unconscious image of yourself?

Mountains and hills may indicate spiritual aspirations, emotional or physical challenges, ambitions, or they might be symbolic of obstacles or barriers to be overcome. Do they look unscalable or insurmountable? Volcanoes may indicate dangerously repressed emotions or the breakthrough of energy or emotion. Are they erupting or quiescent? Steaming? Are there earthquakes? Noise?

Gentle, rolling hills may indicate the nurturing aspects of the earth/mother. Are they fertile (covered with plant life) or sterile (bare, rocky, or covered with dead plants)?

Ask yourself:

if my ambitions about my work were a mountain or hill, what would it be like? What is the first image that comes into your mind, and what does it tell you about your unconscious ambitions?

Weather may indicate the unconscious emotional state. This is obvious when you think about how often we use weather terms to describe emotions — stormy, sunny, face like a thundercloud, under the weather, and all the other weather metaphors for feelings. In a sense, it is the kind of emotional energy present within us.

Ask yourself:

if the weather were reflecting my feelings at this moment, what would be happening? What is the first image that comes to your mind, and what does it tell you?

Each time you analyse one of your guided imagery journeys, you will learn more about your attitude to and relationship with the central focus of that journey if you also consider the background. For example, did any of the above symbols appear in *The Advisor?* If so, do these symbols suggest anything you didn't already understand about your feeling and attitude towards the Advisor and the information you were given?

When using any of the suggestions above, always remember that interpretation must be highly individualised. You may find it useful to look for these and other related ideas in interpreting your imagery, but it is important to remember that these are only general suggestions. In the final analysis we must each make our own interpretations, find our own meanings. The more we practise interpreting these images (and our dreams) the richer our interpretations, the deeper the insights, and the more meaningful the experience becomes.

If you are helping someone else to interpret their imagery, they *must* make the final interpretation — although you may offer suggestions and insights which may perhaps enrich their understanding of themselves. Remember, every individual is different, and we each speak a different symbolic language, so your own image interpretations may suggest ideas to other people but **cannot** define their images.

Review

This might be a good time to go back over all the paintings you have done, using all the interpretive techniques you have learned: colour, line, image association, and finding hidden forms. You could also consider the background in the paintings, if any, analysing the environment with the suggestions given in the preceding chapter. What do they tell you that you hadn't noticed before?

When you need insight on a subject, you can make an impressionistic painting of the symbols that represent it for you. Ask yourself, how do these symbols relate to one another in the painting? The painting can help to clarify your thoughts and emotions about the subject.

Is your image directory up to date?

Are you using the tools you have for interpreting imagery to work with your dreams? If you are not already keeping your dreams in your journal, perhaps it is time to start.

Part VII

Overcoming Obstacles

Granny Weatherwax walked quickly through the darkness with the frank stride of someone who was at least certain that the forest, on this damp and windy night, contained strange and terrible things and she was it.
— *Terry Pratchett*
in Wyrd Sisters

28. Tripping Over Our Own Feet

So here we are, trundling down the path, learning all sorts of interesting things, and we suddenly find ourselves facing a brick wall or lost in the fog. Perhaps that hasn't happened to you yet, but it probably will, sooner or later. C. G. Jung wrote, "It is towards oneself that one has the strongest resistances."[5]

There is a part of us that always says NO to any change in ourselves or in our lives. We can call it reasonable caution, we can call it cowardice or stupidity — it all depends on how we are feeling about the situation and ourselves at the moment. And there is another part of us that always wants to leap forward into new experiences and new ways of being. We can call this bravery or foolhardiness or stupidity, again depending on how we feel about what is happening.

The tension between these two opposing energies in ourselves keeps us wavering between *I will* and *I won't*. We have free will and we have free won't. Anyone who has ever owned a cat probably understands this principle thoroughly. The cat goes to the door, and after waiting very patiently for at least two seconds, lets you know unmistakably that it wants to go out. When you open the door, the cat puts one paw outside and pauses to look around. It may, if allowed, stand there for quite a while. Sometimes a gentle nudge is enough to get the cat moving, but at other times it simply causes the cat to become stuck to the carpet, immovable. At this point we have choices.

We can pick it up and toss it though the door, but if we do it will either nip smartly back between our legs or rush around to a window and howl pathetically to be let in. Or it will be gone for hours, returning muddy or dishevelled, shivering with terror, and generally letting us know that our unfeeling behaviour sent it out, unprepared, into a dangerous, hard, cruel world.

Alternatively, we can wait patiently (much longer than two seconds), while it decides whether or not it is safe to go out. And the colder and wetter the weather is, the longer the cat will take to decide. Will I get my fur wet? Will my hairstyle be ruined by the wind? Are there any dogs out there? Where's that tough old tom from down the road? Will they laugh at my new collar? Any rogue motorcycles? Dragons? Nearly every cat has an attack of paranoia on the doorstep. A cat who doesn't is not in touch with the real world of cats.

And then, if the answer is that it's not safe to go out this door, the cat will turn back into the house, and with its tail straight up, head for another door to see if things are any better out there. Some of this is simple, sensible caution, and some of it is over the top and into paranoia. We are like this, too. We need time. We need not to be rushed. Sometimes a gentle nudge is enough to get us moving, but sometimes it just makes us resist more.

The proper purpose of resistance is to give us a chance to look cautiously at where we are going — and to decide not to go if it really is dangerous. This is a useful and important function.

However, resistance sometimes gets carried away with itself and keeps us from moving at all. It is always our choice, but the question is, which part of us is making the choice? We have met the Advisor and begun to get a glimpse of the possibilities for self-transformation in working with our inner images, but we, unknowingly, may also have encountered the Rebel, who often insists on travelling in a direction other than the one we have consciously chosen. The Rebel cannot adjust to the world, and it tries to enforce an order in which it feels more comfortable and powerful. The current of events is against it, so it often resorts to violence.

There is a part of us, an old and cunning part, which regards all new experiences and new ideas with extreme doubt. It says, 'I survived yesterday just the way I am. If I were to change now, I might not survive. Why go looking for trouble?' This part of us also collects experiences, and then forms judgments based on very simplistic assessments of those experiences. It creates and then really believes simple programmes like:

> You can't trust men/women;
> You never get what you want, so there is no point in really trying;
> People laugh at me when I show my feelings;
> If I love you, you'll hurt me;
> People will hurt you if you give them a chance;
> I'm only safe when I behave submissively;
> If I attack first I'll be safe;
> . . . and so on.

These programmes are the Dragon's hoard, its treasures, and like all dragons, it defends its hoard with vigour. This underlying dragon energy belongs to all of us (like an archetype), but the programmes it devises are individual and based on our personal experiences (like an ectype).

This part of us does not believe in 'if' or 'potential' or 'possible' or any hypothetical alternative to actual experience. It cannot even see that something we have done before and survived might menace us in the future. In *Moon over Water* I called this part of ourselves the Dragon in the Depths, the creature that lives in the deep chasms and the abyss of the sea of the unconscious. The really important thing we need to remember about this rebellious Dragon is that *it is trying to keep us safe*.

It doesn't want us to rush foolishly into things that might cause us pain or harm. The proper purpose of this Dragon in the Depths is to get us to take a second look, to think before we act. It urges us to remember what happened before, to value and to learn from our past experiences. It is a useful and important denizen of our inner world. The only problem is that it cannot see anything but the past, and it bases all its choices upon the past. In a sense it is quite mechanical. And it is certainly not equipped to be in charge of our future.

One of the questions we need to ask ourselves when we encounter resistance is, 'does this resistance protect *me* or is it protecting one of my faulty programmes?' The rebellious Dragon can't tell the difference. This is important, because every time we base our actions upon one of the programmes, tacitly accepting and reinforcing it, we make it stronger. On the other hand, every time we recognise it as a faulty programme and refuse to allow it to make our choices for us, we make it weaker.

We all know people who are ruled by their rebellious Dragon. They talk about security and safety and the good old days, as if these things were real and in some way absolute. Being alive is, by its very nature, an insecure process. It won't last. It won't even stay the way it is at this moment for more than a minute or two. Change happens around us all the time, carrying us — will we, nil we — with it. If we, ruled by the Dragon in the Depths, dig in our heels and say *no, no, no,* we will just get our heels worn down to the bone very quickly. You know people who do that, don't you? So do I — and sometimes I do it myself.

The other side of this is the part of us that always wants to do the new thing, is willing to take any risk, delights in leaping empty-handed into the void — the Dragon that Soars. It says, 'Come *on!* Let's *go!*' It never asks if this is safe or sensible or practical. It says 'why not?' and doesn't wait for the answer. It is completely ungrounded. You can probably think of several people like that as well, can't you? I can too — and sometimes I am one myself.

This is a tension, a permanent conflict, a constant stress within ourselves, as we try to find a working balance between these two extremes. Sometimes we tip one way, sometimes the other. The problem is that whenever we tip too far in one direction, the other Dragon gets worried or upset and tries to take action. The Dragon in the Depths has access to the codes that run our bodies, and if it feels we are outrunning — or outflying — our safe limits of known territory, it rebels and quite literally trips us up. We become ill, or we become accident-prone, or we find ourselves inexplicably just not doing what we intend to do — we have forgotten or become distracted. We have stopped ourselves. There is mutiny in the ranks and civil disorder.

If it is the Dragon that Soars who feels its wings have been clipped too far back, we begin to feel depressed. We bore others and we bore ourselves. Life seems not to have any point — and indeed, life truly has no point without growth. If we are not growing, we are decaying — mentally, emotionally, spiritually, and physically.

So here we are, standing on the top of our sunlit mountain. From the depths we hear the terrifying roar of the Dragon of Resistance, and from the sky above us, we hear the alluring song of the Winged Dragon. This is the real conflict — do we want safety or growth? Security or adventure? How about growth with reasonable attention to safety? Is this possible? And if it is, how would we find it?

29. Co-operation & Compromises

We need to listen to our resistance, our Dragon in the Depths, our Rebel. If we have listened to it and taken its experience and knowledge into account, it is much less apt to trip us up when we try to change our habits and patterns. Our Advisor suggests ways in which we might grow, and our resistance, if not attended to, will become the Rebel who waylays us. We can use an adapted form of the imagery journey we used earlier, *The Advisor*, to engage in three-way discussions with our Rebels and our Advisors. There are other ways to achieve the same purpose, of course, but this also gives you an example of how you might adapt *The Advisor* to other purposes.

We may often find resistance in ourselves to doing what we have promised ourselves or others, even when we know that it would be a good thing for us to do. We must remember that our habit patterns and conditioned responses were developed because they worked better for us in a given type of situation than anything else we could find. In order to transform our resistance into co-operation (or at least, to neutrality), it is important to the Rebel, that we take whatever steps are necessary to protect ourselves from harm (whether real or imagined) while we try to change.

When you are trying to keep a promise you have made to your Advisor (or another part of yourself) and you find yourself experiencing a mutiny, the following imagery journey can be very useful. In this first discussion with the Rebel, I suggest that you ask it what you need to do to enable it to co-operate with you as you keep the agreement you made with your Advisor.

Approximate travel time: 30 minutes.

DISARMING THE REBEL

We are going to speak to the Rebel within. Before we begin, please be seated comfortably, with your spine erect and your head upright. Take a couple of deep breaths. And now another. And take still another slow, deep breath. As you exhale, allow your fingers to relax, and then allow any tension in your arms, your shoulders, and your neck, to flow down and out through your fingertips. Take another deep breath, and as you exhale, allow any tension in your body and your legs to flow down and out through your toes.

Breathe in peace, and as you exhale, breathe out anything in your mind that you don't need or want at this moment. And again, breathe in peace, and as you exhale, breathe out anything in your body that you don't want or need at this moment. Please remember that you are in charge of this journey and you may withdraw from it at any time simply by wishing to do so. However, while you continue with the imagery, all the images are to present themselves in their own way and in their own time, simply following with my voice as I serve as your guide.

Now, I'd like you to imagine that you are standing in front of the entrance of a room or a cave. This entrance is big enough to walk into.

Please walk a few steps into the cave or room and pause there.

What is under your feet? Is the floor hard or soft? Rough or smooth? What is the surface made of?

How does the air feel to you? Is it warm or cool? Moving or still? Is it damp or is it dry? If it is damp, where is the moisture coming from?

If you were to reach out and touch the nearest wall, what does it feel like to your fingers? What is it made of?

How big is this space? How high up is the ceiling and how far away is the farthest wall?

What colours or sounds or scents do you particularly notice here?

Is there anything special or unusual about this space?

And where is the light coming from?

Now walk on in, until you come to a door or passage to your left. You can go through this door or passage to your inner world. If it is a door and the door is locked, the key will be hanging on a hook to the right of the door. Go through the door or passage into the inner world. Your inner world may be an extension of the cave or room, or it may be some other kind of space altogether.

When you reach the inner world, stand still for a moment and notice what is under your feet here. Is the surface hard or soft? Rough or smooth? What is it made of?

Is the air warm or cool? Moving or still? Damp or dry? If it's damp, where is moisture coming from?

If you were to reach out and touch the thing nearest you, what would you touch, and how would it feel to your fingers?

And what do you see or sense in the distance?

What is above your head, and where is the light coming from? What time of the day or night is it? What time of the year?

What sounds or scents or colours do you especially notice? Is there anything that particularly stands out? As you begin to walk ahead and explore this place, you may notice your surroundings.

When you have been walking a short time, you meet a person, your wise Advisor. Your Advisor may take the same form that it took before or it may take another form, more appropriate for this moment. What is this person doing as you approach?

The Advisor

When you reach your Advisor, imagine yourself closing your eyes and reaching out with your hand, letting your Advisor take it. What does your Advisor's hand feel like? Does it feel strong or delicate? Hard or soft? Large or small?

What one word best describes the way you feel as your Advisor holds your hand?

What are your Advisor's eyes like — the first impression that comes to your mind? What color are they? What one word best describes the expression you see or sense in your Advisor's eyes?

What else do you notice about this person? Is it male or female? Large or small or in between?

What is your Advisor's name?

The Rebel

Ask your Advisor to bring before you, in its symbolic form, the Rebel within you.

As the Rebel appears, what form does it take? Is it a person, a creature, or some more abstract form? What colours or sounds or scents do you sense or associate with it? How big is it?

How do you feel as you look at the Rebel? And how does it seem to feel as it looks at you?

At this moment, I'd like you to give both your Advisor and the Rebel permission to tell you the truth always, even if it is something you don't want to hear.

The Agreement

Explain to the Rebel what you are planning to do or to change. If you have made a promise or an agreement, tell the Rebel what the agreement is and why you want to do it.

And now I'd like you to ask the Rebel what it needs from you in order for it to feel safe while you fulfil your intention or agreement. What does it want you to do?

If the answer you receive is not clear, ask your Advisor to clarify it for you. The answer should give you clear information about what the Rebel feels it needs.

Is this something you feel you can agree to and actually do? If it is not, discuss it with the Rebel and your Advisor, and try to reach an agreement on something you can agree to do that would help the Rebel to feel secure while you keep your promise.

It may not always be possible to reach an agreement, especially if the Rebel is finding what you have been asked to do really threatening. If the Rebel refuses to co-operate at first, see if you can find a compromise. Perhaps you could modify your agreement or intention so that you approach the new way of being or behaving more slowly, step by step. What do you need to do in order for the Rebel to allow you to proceed without hindrance?

When you have reached an agreement, clearly tell the Rebel and your Advisor exactly what it is that you are agreeing to do.

Now ask the Rebel to state clearly its agreement with you.

Do you need any suggestions or advice from the Rebel or your Advisor about what practical steps you need to take in order to fulfil this agreement? If so, ask for this now.

The Gift

When you have the information you need, I'd like you to imagine that you are holding your hands out in front of you. The Rebel will place a symbolic gift in your hands. This is the gift you will receive for keeping your agreement.

What does this gift feel like in your hands? Is it light or heavy? What is the texture like? What colours or sounds or scents do you associate with this gift? What is it?

Ask the Rebel what this gift symbolises. If you don't quite understand the answer, ask your Advisor to clarify it.

Is this gift something you want to accept? If you are not certain, discuss it with your Advisor and Rebel.

If you don't want the gift, give it back, and if you like, ask if there is another gift that you might feel more ready to accept.

If you do want it, give it back to the Rebel and ask it to place the gift in you or on you or around you, wherever it belongs.

What does the Rebel do with it? Do you notice any particular feeling when this happens?

Ask the Rebel and your Advisor if there is anything you need to know about using your gift. Is it for use in the inner world? The outer world? Or both worlds? How are you to use it in your everyday life?

Completion

When you have the information you need, thank the Rebel for being with you, and allow it to dissolve back into your inner world.

Then thank your Advisor for being with you and helping you, and say goodbye to your Advisor for now.

Go back to the place where you entered this inner world. As you go, notice if there have been any changes in your inner world. Is anything different or is it just the same?

When you reach the door or gateway through which you entered the inner world, come back through the cave or room to this world.

When you reach this world, take a couple of deep breaths.

And another.

Flex your feet and your fingers, and begin to pay attention to the sounds of the room around you.

When you are ready, open your eyes, and if you like, stretch, feeling rested, relaxed, and alert.

The logic of the imagery

You may have noticed that you went through the process of becoming acquainted with the Advisor, just as if you had not done it before. There are two main reasons for this.

First, the Advisor may take a different form at times. The unconscious has reasons and logic of its own, and may choose to present the Advisor in another guise.

Second, if the Advisor is the same as the one already encountered, the repetition helps the imager to become more confident and relaxed with the imagery. One of the ways that resistance may act is by making this particular journey challenging. Therefore, it is helpful if we make things as familiar and easy for the imager as possible before we get to the more difficult question and answer part of the imagery.

The same principle applies to having the Advisor, an already familiar and co-operative figure, there to help us, if we need it, in communication with the Rebel — or any other aspect of ourselves. We often experience resistance in the form of unclear answers to our questions. There is no real, objective reason why the Advisor should be able to clarify information for us when we don't understand the Rebel, but there is a kind of internal, emotional logic to it. The Advisor in an authority figure, and therefore, *of course* he or she can help us when we are stuck. The Advisor is wise and capable, and we have already established a relationship in which we listen to and, at least to some extent, trust the Advisor. We may even already have warm, co-operative feelings toward the Advisor. In addition to all of this, we are told in the imagery that, if we are having difficulty in understanding information or making a decision, the Advisor *will* help us — not 'might be able to' but simply will.

All of this means that the Advisor can give us powerful and authoritative assistance in clarifying confusion and in deciding what we really want to do.

The interpretation

To get the most out of this journey, write it out for your journal (as you did for *The Advisor*) and make an impressionistic painting of the Rebel. Use the visual and verbal techniques you have learned to gain as much understanding as you can of the part of you which rebels when you try to adventure into growth or unknown territory. The list of symbols following *The Advisor* (in Chapters 26 & 27) also applies to this imagery, of course.

The symbolic form of the Rebel itself shows the strength and character of your resistance to whatever issue you are discussing with it.

Possibilities for expansion

As suggested earlier, this particular journey can be used in many ways. In the example above, we have seen how we can ask our Advisor to help us to communicate and reach a better understanding with an aspect of ourselves. There are many other aspects of ourselves that it might be useful to meet. Any ectype — hero, huntress, trickster, mother — can be reached in this way, of course, but there are also many other possibilities. You can talk to the part of your psyche symbolised by your hands, your heart, your eyes, or the part of yourself that is in charge of your migraine headaches (or any other challenging issue) or is in charge of your relationship with your father (or anyone else). You can ask your liver what it needs, or you can speak to the artist or the musician within you.

If you are a student of the esoteric arts, you can speak with the aspect of yourself that is the psychic, the seer, the healer, the magician. If you are interested in astrology, you could speak to Jupiter or any other heavenly body, as it is in your horoscope and psyche. If you are interested in the tarot, you could speak to the Empress, the Charioteer, the Tower, as the energy of each one acts in your life at this moment. You can discuss things with your solar centre or any other chakra. The choices are limited only by our ability to think of them.

This inner communication can be used for problem solving, for improving health, or simply for getting in touch with ourselves and understanding our own needs better. Learning new tools for coping with the difficulties in our lives, and learning that we can solve more of our own problems will also improve self-confidence, self-esteem, and self-trust, all of which are important attributes of the well-balanced, creative person. We will be practising an example of an extended version of this imagery journey when we come to *The Healer* later on.

Please remember

The principle of resistance, which the Rebel personifies, applies not only to inner work, but to our outer lives as well. We can use this imagery journey to help us with difficulties, resulting from resistance, encountered in either realm.

You will probably need to come back to the Rebel again from time to time. Whenever our resistance is strong enough to keep us from doing what we want to do, the Rebel has taken up his weapons again. Each time this happens we can learn more about what holds us back — the fears, the insecurities, the old conditioning, the early traumas — and heal another hidden, hurt, fearful part of ourselves.

In doing this, our understanding becomes deeper and our compassion, both for ourselves and for others, becomes greater. We truly learn that the first step in healing anything is to love it, to recognise that it is a confused, perhaps badly hurt, part of ourselves, which is trying to do its very best to protect us from harm. If we genuinely recognise that, and if we treat that part of ourselves as we would a frightened or hurt child, change, healing, growth, and transformation become a way of life. If we make an adversary of our resistance and try to 'conquer' or 'destroy' it, we become locked into a battle in which, whatever happens, a part of ourselves will be hurt, perhaps grievously. I can't see the point in trying to grow in one direction by savaging ourselves in another.

There are many ways that resistance expresses itself. The imagery journey above is very useful for what we might call after-the-fact resistance, but often the resistance we experience is during or within the journey itself. There are a number of things we can do to help ourselves and others through that resistance and into growth.

Review

First, a reminder about posture — it really is important if you are to get the most from the journeys you take. If you find that you are working while slumped, or in a half-dozing state, perhaps you need to talk to the Rebel about this. Poor posture is an excellent way to sabotage yourself, while pretending you aren't.

Is your image directory up to date? Dream journal?

This might be a good time to review all the agreements you have made and the gifts you have received to see how you're doing with them. Do you need to go back and discuss any of the agreements with the aspect of yourself to whom you originally made them? With the Rebel?

Part VIII

Down the Wrong Path

The road, Hwel felt, had to go somewhere.
  *This geographical fiction has been the death of many people.
Roads don't necessarily have to go anywhere, they just have to
have somewhere to start.*
                    — *Terry Pratchett*
                    in Wyrd Sisters

30. Who Is In Charge Here?

If you are guiding an imagery journey for yourself or others, you might think that the guide is in charge. You'd be wrong. The imager (or the part of you that is the imager) is in charge. In a group practising individual imagery journeys, I heard the following exchange:

Guide: When you come through your door, where are you?
Imager: I'm in a prison yard, surrounded by high walls, and the door behind me is locked.
G: Find another door leading out of there.
I: There isn't one.
G: Yes, there is. Find it.
I: No, there isn't.
G: There *is* another door. Don't be stubborn.
I: There is NO DOOR. It's my mind and my prison, and if I say there is no way out then there isn't one.

The guide learned something from that, and later on she had a different exchange with another imager.

G: When you have finished petting your dog, please ask it to take you to your Advisor.
I: I don't want to see him. I want to roll down this grassy hill.
G: Fine. Go ahead and roll down the hill. (Pause, giving him time to start the action.) You'll find your dog and your teacher waiting for you at the bottom.

In the first example, the guide was missing the whole point. She would have done better to co-operate with the imager and explore the prison. If she had, she probably would have found that the information he needed to release himself from the prison was within the walls, but he needed to find it there, rather than being forced to pass through without investigating his true inner space. Having now made the statement that there was no way out (which was not at all the same thing as saying there was no door), the imager was thoroughly stuck, and the journey went no farther. The guide was stubbornly trying to impose her view of what the imager's inner reality 'should' be, instead of accepting that he felt imprisoned and working with that.

In the second example, the imager was obviously resisting going on with the imagery, and the guide used a very neat kind of 'psychic judo' to use his effort at distraction to get him where she wanted him to be.

So who is in control? The imager is — at all times. If we don't like what is happening, we can bring ourselves out of the imagery simply by deciding to do so. We must actively co-operate with our guide in order to get into it in the first place, and we must continue to co-operate in order to stay in it. All we have to do to get out is to stop co-operating. This is equally true whether we are guiding ourselves or being guided by someone else. We can choose whether we want to 'wake up' or to change the imagery and simply do it. This is taking place in our own minds and we are in charge at all times — however little it may seem so when we encounter our resistance.

31. Getting Through The Hard Places

We have *The Rebel* to help us work through our resistance, but there are some other things we need to think about as well. First of all, if at any time during the imagery the imager wants to quit, let her do so. Do not criticise or condemn her either verbally or *in your thoughts* for doing this. When she is ready to work on whatever problem she has, she will do it. Nothing will be gained by trying to push her into something for which she is not ready, and if you try to do so, you may actually delay the time when she will become ready to work on the issue.

Never try to bluntly force the imager. If we try to push people, it will sometimes work up to a point, but then they will rebel. And they may never really trust us again. We are supposed to be guides and facilitators, not adversaries or slave drivers. It is important that the imager feels that the guide is a helpful presence, which he can trust in aiding him to find his way. To get into a power struggle is completely counter-productive. If we have a need to be right, if we have a need to be in control, we will create difficulties for everyone when we try to facilitate guided imagery. Such ego needs will seriously interfere with our attempts to help others to explore and interact with their own inner world and with the aspects of themselves that they encounter there.

My theory of therapy

This is a simple theory:

Everyone knows, on some level, exactly what his problem is. And everyone knows, on some level, exactly what he needs to do about it.

All the guide/therapist/teacher/healer needs to do is to listen to the subject so carefully that the guide is able to hear clearly what he is saying. Then the guide needs to ask the questions that will enable the subject to hear his own answer — **when he is ready to hear it.**

In order for this to work, the imager cannot be pushed, but must be gently given the opportunity to find the needed insight. The guide needs to be patient and not to be overly directive in this. The type of question that begins with 'do you not think that' or 'isn't it true that' is *always* the wrong kind of question. If a question like that is asked before the imager has become ready to hear the answer, she probably will simply answer 'no' and turn that avenue of exploration into a dead end.

The other problem with being directive is that we, as guides, are not always right in what we think we hear. If we are right, and if we ask the right kind of questions, the imager will eventually come up with the answer we expect. I'd hate to have to count the number of times I thought I knew The Answer and the imager came up with something entirely different — and their answer was completely right for them at that time. If we are asking the right kind of questions, though, it won't matter too much that we have misunderstood — the imager will get the right answer anyway. We need to be careful not to put ourselves in the way of other people's processes.

This is a mistake that nearly all of us make, some of us more often than others. If you are working regularly with a group or with a partner as you go through this book, you might want to make an agreement with each other that you will each gently mention it when someone is being too controlling. However well we attempt to guide each other, it is all wasted if we start to push the imager, causing him either to feel hassled or to push back. People usually have enough resistance, without us evoking more in the guise of 'helping' them.

On the other hand, the imager may be just experiencing mild resistance and need a little encouragement to work through it. All of us spend much of our time caught between our resistance to the processes of growth and our need/desire to work with those same processes. This is especially true when we become involved in active

growth work of any kind, and our resistance feels a need to protect
our unconscious secrets and tender, hidden areas from the probing of
our conscious minds. The feeling seems to be that, if our conscious
mind knew what was really going on, knew the hidden fears and
motivations, it would decide to do something which is silly and/or
dangerous. Our resistance tries both to protect us from ourselves and
from dangerous change. Unfortunately, as we have mentioned, it
tends to view most, if not all, change as dangerous.

Nearly everyone will experience some form of resistance in doing
these journeys at some time. The unconscious fears that we will learn
things about ourselves that we don't really want to know or 'ought'
not to know. We are unconsciously afraid that, among other things,
we are going to ruin our 'coping mechanisms' — the habitual
responses and entrenched attitudes that we have developed over the
years to deal with some of the situations which confront us in our life.
Some of these responses and attitudes may create more problems than
they solve, but they are *our* attitudes and responses, we are accustomed to them and the way they work, we know what to expect, and
we know that they have worked for us at least once in the past. We are
firmly attached to them because we fear that, without them, we will
not be able to cope with life. 'Don't rock the boat, even if it is sinking'
sometimes seems to be the motto of the unconscious. This fear of
change in ourselves expresses itself as resistance which may be
experienced in any or all of several ways.

The ways we resist

Avoidance is probably the most common expression of resistance. Do
you find that you just never have the time to do inner work, either
guided or unguided? It sounds like such a good excuse, so important
and busy as we are, but is probably just common, garden-variety
resistance. Very nearly everyone can find the ten or fifteen minutes
needed to do some of this inner work. We can always find the time for
things we give priority to — and inner work often deserves a higher
priority than we give it.

If you find yourself saying that you really want to do the inner
work but you just don't have time, the chances are that you do have
the time, that you waste more time than that during the day, and that
you are letting your resistance get the upper hand. You are going to
have to be firm with yourself if you really want to do the journeys.
Schedule yourself a time for imagery and stick to it unless the house is

burning or falling down around your ears. And make certain that you haven't sneakily insured your failure by choosing a time that really isn't going to work. Get up that extra bit early in the morning or do whatever it takes to enable you to give that time to yourself. Then unplug the phone, lock the door, and get on with it.

Fatigue may be another manifestation of resistance. Perhaps you are one of the people who are so tired that they can't stay awake to do any of the journeys. There is a natural tendency for people to become so relaxed that they fall asleep. If you have this problem, try sitting on a straight, armless chair or in some other less-than-completely-comfortable position while you do the imagery. If you fall asleep there, you really do need some sleep and should be in your bed. Do your imagery when you have had some rest. If you are always tired, you should have a physical checkup and take a serious look at your lifestyle.

Succumbing to distraction is another common manifestation of resistance. We may find that, every time we sit down to do the inner work or even think that this might be a good time to do it, we remember something that we really must do first. Again, you have to be firm with yourself and give the inner work first priority.

Another form of distraction arises during the imagery itself. Actually, there are two forms — internal and external. You just can't concentrate because of the traffic, because the chair is uncomfortable, because someone else has the television on too loudly, because your toe/neck/ear/stomach hurts/itches/feels funny, because you're upset about your problems, because your mind keeps wandering, and half a hundred other 'becauses'. John Donne wrote, "I throw myself down in my chamber, and I call in, and invite God, and his Angels thither, and when they are there, I neglect God and his Angels, for the noise of a fly, for the rattling of a coach, for the whining of a door."[6]

Like Donne, we are perverse. Sheer persistence usually will overcome this resistance — eventually. If your resistance really is keeping you from doing the inner work you want to do, you might try talking with your Rebel again.

Not too surprisingly, interpretation is where we run into another level of resistance, when we have managed to get past acceptance. If we find ourselves immediately deciding that a particular image is impossible to interpret or that it doesn't make any sense, we are probably encountering our resistance again. We want to know — and we don't want to know. C. G. Jung wrote, "He argues vigorously against the existence of any components of great individual significance in this dream. It is true that the facade of the dream was not very transparent, and I could not know what was hidden behind it. My first deduction was that the dreamer had a strong resistance because he put so much energy into protesting that the dream was meaningless."[7]

The trick in dealing with this kind of resistance is, first of all, to recognise that it is resistance. We have looked at a number of ways of interpreting the unknown symbols and images that may come up for us, but we must actually use them. We need to persist in working with an image until it makes sense to us — even more, until we reach that indescribable feeling that we've really got it. There are no shortcuts around this.

Helping ourselves

When trying to deal with our own resistance, the main thing is always to remember that this work is done in our own minds and we are, ourselves, in charge of it. The mind is like a child — the less discipline it has had, the more unruly it will be. It can only be changed by well-disciplined practice. And the only way to do that is to do it.

You will find that the change can be made more quickly, of course, if your unconscious feels that you are behaving in a responsible, mature manner and taking good care of yourself as you try to make these changes. Use *Disarming the Rebel* and any other techniques you learn or invent to honestly face and work through your resistance.

And treat yourself with even more gentleness, patience, and consideration than you expect yourself to show to others. After all, they can get up and leave if they feel hassled, but you are stuck with yourself.

Helping others

Be patient with other people when you are guiding them through a journey, and they start expressing some form of resistance. Just be gently encouraging and see if you can help them past the resistance. However, if they want to quit, let them do so without saying or doing anything that will make them feel that you think that they should have gone on. In fact, you may even need to reassure them about this, explaining that it is unwise to push our resistance too vigorously. It may not be appropriate for them to deal with that problem at this time — and no one knows the right time better than they do.

When we are leading someone through an imagery journey and we find resistance, it is sometimes helpful to distract the person from it for a few moments by asking them some innocuous questions about the imagery environment or anything else that would be easy for them to answer. This may help in a couple of ways. First, it gives them a chance to calm down and become relaxed again. Second, there is something called a 'yes set' by psychologists. This means that, if you have established a good pattern of co-operation, the person is likely to continue to co-operate, even when it becomes more difficult or upsetting for them. Remember this whenever you sense that the imager is coming out of the relaxed state and becoming agitated. Rather than persisting with the disturbing image or concept, take a little time to ask some questions that give him a chance to relax, to re-establish the 'yes set' and get back into the flow of the imagery.

No matter what you are asking, keep your voice calm, soothing, and at the same pace as in the rest of the journey.

There is another trick to keeping the imager to the path of the imagery journey when you encounter resistance. The second example at the beginning of Chapter 30 is an exceptionally good demonstration of that, and it is worth repeating here.

Guide: When you have finished petting your dog, please ask it to take you to your guide.
Imager: I don't want to see him. I want to roll down this grassy hill.
Guide: Fine. Go ahead and roll down the hill. (Pause, giving him time to start the action.) You'll find your dog and your teacher waiting for you at the bottom.

This little bit of 'psychic judo' requires that we listen carefully, closely following what the imager is doing, that we correctly identify resistance when it appears, and that we think quickly. Then we appear to yield, as the judo expert yields to her attacker, and we somehow use the momentum of the imager to bring him closer to where we want him to go. Also, because he has what he asked for, he may well feel more willing (and perhaps more obligated) to co-operate.

And do try to keep the triumph out of your voice when it works.

If you encounter heavy, intractable resistance, go on to something else. The imager is not ready to investigate this and to try to push him into doing so will only make him less willing and less trusting when he works with you in future. Let it go gracefully after a gentle attempt to sidestep the resistance, and do something else. Remember! You are not in charge, the imager is.

The question is, then, when should we try to work through

resistance and when should we not? There are several possibilities.

1. When the imager is experiencing quite a bit of emotional distress, we should not go on without asking him if he wishes to continue. Let him make the choice — and let him know that he is making it. The questions should be asked within the context of the imagery so that it isn't an abrupt jolt out of the relaxed altered state of consciousness. For example, if the entry to the imagery world was through a cave and the imager was experiencing distress over seeing a particular image of a monster, we might ask, 'would you like to find out more about the monster just now, or would you rather come back out through the cave?'

2. If the imager is blocking on the images and repeatedly says things like 'I don't know' or 'I'm not getting anything' and efforts at re-establishing a 'yes set' have not succeeded, it might be best to bring her gently back out of the imagery and discuss the difficulty with her. It is possible that the initial relaxation and shift into the altered state needed more time or that the guide was not using tone and rhythm well. Some people, especially those who are inexperienced, need much longer to get into the imagery in the first place. If this is not the problem, resistance which manifests in this way is *unconscious* resistance and there may be little or nothing the imager can consciously choose to do about it. She may well be unaware of any feeling of resistance. Under these circumstances it is usually appropriate to wait and try again another time. Often this gives the unconscious a chance to become more comfortable with the idea of revealing some of what it has kept hidden.

3. If the imager is being difficult by wanting to go off on digressions or to change the direction and objective of journey, or if he seems irritable or angry with the guide or the process, the first step is to ask if he wishes to go on with the imagery. Sometimes the question, gently put in the context of the imagery, is enough to jolt him back into co-operation. However, if he wants to stop, gently bring him out of the imagery and discuss what is happening *without being judgmental*. It probably is appropriate to point out that you felt that he might be experiencing some resistance and ask for his comments. There may be a problem with the way the journey is being guided or there may be something that you, as the guide, could do to better facilitate the journey. In any event, it is important that the imager make a commitment to work in active co-operation with the process before trying it again.

32. When Not to Go — Cautionary Signs

The unconscious is an interesting and powerful part of ourselves, but it is only a part. When we temporarily surrender our ability to criticise in a relaxed altered state of consciousness, just floating along with whatever is happening, and when we are not exercising the controls of logic and reason as used by the conscious mind, we lose a safety factor. We become very suggestible. This is why guided imagery can be extremely helpful. It is also why it potentially can be harmful. Because of this, we want to be very careful of just what we do and of what is said to us in a guided inner journey. We want to be even more careful what we say to others when we are acting as guides.

The inner journeys given here are carefully planned to do whatever they are supposed to do without harmful or distressing side effects, assuming that the imager has normal mental health. In the earlier journeys, read them carefully before using them, and don't make much in the way of changes unless you are pretty certain that you know what you are doing. In later chapters, we will work on designing safe and useful journeys for ourselves and others.

Many guided inner journeys are simply research projects and your only objective is to gain information. Such journeys are generally quite safe to do, and it is rare for a reasonably normal person to have any sort of problem with them. However, guided imagery where you talk to your unconscious and endeavour to make changes in your attitudes or conditioning are often really a form of hypnosis, and hypnosis can be a very powerful tool for change. Just be certain that such changes are really what you want and that they do not have undesirable side effects. When in doubt, consult an expert.

You may find it helpful to have some sort of prayer or affirmation that you say before you begin using a guided inner journey yourself. Such a statement of purpose could be something like, 'I surround myself with the white light of the Christ Consciousness. I know that wisdom, growth, and good will come to me through this inner journey, and I accept them all. I also accept and am grateful for the wise help I receive as I search for my highest good'. You may desire to share such an affirmation or prayer with any person you are guiding through an inner journey.

The question then arises as to why you feel you need such protection. This brings us the major caution about doing imagery work. Never, never guide someone through an inner journey if you feel they are mentally or emotionally unstable to a serious degree — leave that for a professional. It is also advisable to avoid working with someone who is normally stable at a time when they are very upset or under a great deal of stress unless you are really qualified to do so. When in doubt, don't. Use common sense about it.

Some of the warning signs which tell us that people are inappropriate for us (unless we are highly trained and skilled) to work with are:

1. The subject is not able to explain coherently what the problem is. Her explanation involves a lot of innuendo, muttering, and evasion. This usually indicates either that she is lying or that she is living in a delusional world, which she expects you to understand and share. Her underlying assumptions about reality and human relationships may be radically out of touch with *consensus reality*, the reality that most of us share.

2. The subject contradicts himself often, giving you first one story and then another. Each story will be *almost* logically consistent. When questioned about the inconsistency, the story will change, sometimes radically. This is related to #1 above, but where #1 expects you to *understand* her version of reality, #2 expects you to simply *accept* his reality — and may be willing to appear to change it until you do.

3. The subject always has a reason why this, that, or the other won't work. Any suggestion for improvement is rejected, and if you offer ways around the objections, those too will be rejected. There is actually no desire here for change, but there is a great deal of self-pity. If you change tack completely and say something like, 'Oh, you poor thing! You really are being treated badly, aren't you?' the subject will be perfectly happy. Except, of course, that you will join the ranks of those who have 'failed' to solve her problem. What the subject wants is sympathy, not change, so trying to solve this kind of person's problems is pointless.

4. The subject is firm in blaming others for his difficulties rather than looking for solutions in himself or acknowledging his responsibility for himself. He probably wants some way to force others to change the way they behave, rather than changing his own behaviour or attitudes. It will be 'your fault' if he doesn't get what he wants. This is related to #3, but where #3 simply wants pity and sympathy, #4 wants actual change — but others are to be made to do the changing.

5. The subject believes that she is under some kind of (often non-specific or psychic) attack, sometimes by a specific person, but often by a mysterious 'they' who are causing her problems. The word is paranoia and the condition is not suitable for amateur treatment, nor is it amenable to calm and rational discussion. The gap between the reality of the subject and consensus reality is too great for ordinary communication to bridge.

6. The subject hears voices telling him what to do, which he believes he must unquestioningly obey. He may even believe that God is telling him what to do. He often fears these voices, and they may threaten him or those he loves. A manifestation of schizophrenia, this also requires expert treatment. People in severely delusional states do not operate by the same rules of logic and reason as the rest of us, and the guide without specialist skills may do more harm than good in these cases.

7. The subject is unable to look in your eyes and spends most of the time with her eyes shut or gazing elsewhere while you are talking together. When a symptom of severe emotional distress, this will be pronounced. This can also be simply a symptom of shyness or over-sensitivity, especially if she is just gazing at her fingers or the carpet, so look for other symptoms as well.

8. The subject does or says things that indicate to you that he does not live in consensus reality, but in a world of his own, in which reality can be expected to bend to his desires just because he wants it to. He is going, any day now, to write a best seller, to be recognised as a great master, to become rich, famous, and admired. He doesn't expect to have to study or work for what he wants. He needs expert therapy, but probably doesn't want it. He will be interested in imagery work as long as it supports his fantasies about himself, but not if it requires any actual work or change in himself.

9. Each time the subject does some inner work, it is amazing, astonishing, and completely changes her whole life — but she keeps coming back with the same problem. In many cases, this will not even be the real issue, but only a way of avoiding what is actually happening. The subject is out of touch with consensus reality, and she is indulging in a great deal of self-dramatisation. Working with such unreal issues is a waste of the guide's time, and it encourages the subject's belief in her fantasies.

10. Never coax someone who is reluctant to do an imagery journey.

This is a psychogame you can't win. If I manipulate you into coaxing me to do something, then it will be all your fault if it fails — and it probably will, since that is also part of the game.

On occasion the subject does not display any (or at least not many) of the above signs of extreme disturbance, but simply is going through a period of intense emotional stress. This may be caused by external events, such as a death or other major loss, or by severe internal conflicts resulting from choices that must be made. In either case, probing the wounds, if this is even advisable, should be left for experts. Imagery for relaxation and self-healing, however, could be helpful.

As you can see, there are several essentials if we wish to use imagery work for growth, healing, and self-transformation. First, we must recognise and accept that we, ourselves, are at least a part of the problem. Second, we must be willing and able to do the hard work of understanding and changing ourselves. Third, we need to be reasonably well in touch with the real world. Fourth, we need to be in a sufficiently healthy and balanced internal state to handle the additional stresses of doing this kind of work — because it *is* work and because any change in ourselves does involve a certain amount of stress — perhaps a little, perhaps a lot. Without these attributes, any inner work we do will probably just add to the confusion.

Now I may have upset some people by saying that inner work may add to our stress level. 'But I'm doing this to *relieve* stress,' they cry. Quite right. It will work, too. As we reduce the conflicts in ourselves, which is the whole point of this section of this book, we have less stress. Stress, like many of our other emotional problems, isn't really out there — it is within us. It's the result of one part of us trying to do something while another part is resisting. Stressful things may happen, but it's our response to them that is the real problem.

We all know people who handle most of the difficult situations they encounter with calmness and serenity, and we all know others who go into panic and high stress at the first hint of difficulty. We are trying to learn to become the first kind of people ourselves by finding ways of resolving that stress/conflict in ourselves. There are other ways to reduce stress and promote healing within ourselves as well.

Review

How are you doing with freeform imagery? Do you remember to use it in your daily life when you need answers to problems or insights into situations or relationships? The more you use it, the more valuable and informative it will become.

You also might want to consult your Advisor again, just to see what it would like to suggest to or ask of you at this time.

How long has it been since you last used the image association technique in Chapter 18? How long has it been since you *needed* to use it for something you didn't understand?

Part IX

Journey to Healing

"*I saved a man's life once,*" *said Granny.* "*Special medicine, twice a day. Boiled water with a bit of berry juice in it. Told him I'd bought it from the dwarves. That's the biggest part of doct'rin, really. Most people'll get over most things if they put their minds to it, you just have to give them an interest.*"
— *Terry Pratchett*
in Equal Rites

33. The Healing Place

Imagery affects us on many levels — body, mind, and spirit. Imagery for relaxation is an obvious thing we can do to help ourselves, but there is ample reason to believe that we can have much more profound affects upon our physical bodies than simple relaxation. We have all heard of spontaneous remissions and miracle cures, we may even know those who have experienced them, and a few of us will have experienced them ourselves. However, most of us are conditioned, by the belief system of the society in which we live, to believe that we *cannot* do these things ourselves.

In imagery anything is possible, and the conscious mind thinks of it only as a game, an imaginary nothing, not real. The censor of the conscious belief system is off guard and relaxed — this is, after all, just an image in your mind, not to be taken seriously. But the unconscious mind may take the ideas in the imagery very seriously, and it may even choose to act upon those images and concepts. Through imagery, we may enter into a space in which we can use the inner mechanism which enables such phenomena as spontaneous remissions and miracle cures to take place. A spontaneous remission and a miracle cure are exactly the same thing. We use these terms to describe what happens when someone gets well against the clearest and best medical expectation. 'Spontaneous remission' is a relatively new term, invented by those who feel uncomfortable with the word 'miracle' and who want to sound scientific.

If miracle cures are possible even *one single time* then they may be possible all of the time. I don't believe in a God of Dirty Tricks, who lays down hard and fast rules, natural law, that he sometimes, rather whimsically, chooses to break in some cases. However, I do believe that there are different sets of rules at different levels or states of consciousness. I know that there are many things we can do that our society doesn't officially believe in, but which stubbornly continue to happen — like healing.

Accessing the altered states in which these other sets of laws apply (and in which miracles occur) is what the training of a healer is largely about. These are the states and places in our minds that we need to learn to evoke and to stimulate in order to experience the self-healing process at its richest. Let's try an imagery journey to take us to one of those places.

Approximate travel time: 45 minutes.

JOURNEY TO THE WATERFALL

We are going to go on a journey to a waterfall for energy balancing and healing. As we do this journey, please remember that you are in charge, and if you wish to leave the imagery at any time you may do so simply by wishing it. To begin with, I'd like you to just take a couple of deep breaths.

As you inhale, imagine breathing in relaxation and peace, and as you exhale, just let go of any distractions around you. I'd like you to imagine that each breath you take brings in more relaxation, more peace, and especially that you begin to feel your forehead relaxing a little more with each breath. You may even actually feel the muscles in your forehead letting go, becoming softer, becoming easier, and as we count backwards from ten to one you may feel your forehead relaxing even more deeply.

Ten. Notice the incoming breath bringing in peace.

Nine. And feeling the tension leaving the forehead as you exhale.

Eight. You are breathing in ease, quietness.

Seven. And feeling the muscles of the forehead relax as you breathe out.

Six. Breathing in softness, so soft, so gentle.

Five. And feeling the muscles around your eyes letting go, letting go, letting go.

Four. You are breathing in peace and stillness.

Three. And letting go all around the eyes and all around the temples.

Two. Breathing in stillness.

One. Letting go. Letting go. Letting go.

And as your eyes become increasingly relaxed and quiet, your forehead soft and smooth, I'd like you to imagine that you are standing on a path. To your right there is a narrow strip of green, green grass, and in the grass there is a sprinkling of snowdrops in flower. Just beyond the grass, there is a silent, smoothly flowing stream. To your left there is a bank covered with brightly blooming daffodils. From the snowdrops and daffodils, you might suppose that it is very early in the spring, perhaps even as early as February, but as you walk along the path you notice that there are other flowers that usually bloom at other times of the year — roses of many colours, sweet-scented orange and apple trees bearing both blossoms and fruit, and hollies laden with bright red berries. As you look around, you see fruits and flowers from many climates and all seasons.

The sunlight has an unusual quality, almost as though it makes things glow as it falls softly upon them — the plants, the grass, and the trees seem to shine with their own inner radiance as the sunlight touches them. It has a particular luminous quality. You may even be able to feel a gentle tingling sensation where it touches your skin.

As you walk on, notice the path beneath your feet, the way the light falls upon it, the occasional stone that marks the edge of it. There are flashes of colour on the path, and as you look more closely you see that there are precious stones embedded in the earth.

And as you continue to walk along the path you come to a very large, beautiful tree. You place your hand upon it, and you are surprised to feel a living warmth of the tree, as if you were touching a soft, warm, living creature. Amazed, you look up into the branches and see that this is unlike any tree you have ever seen before. It has small, round fruits, and they are all the colours of the rainbow. And a delicious aroma is present in the air.

As you reach up to touch the closest of these fruits, it falls neatly into your hand and the enticing scent grows stronger. As you eat it, notice the taste. Can you describe its flavour?

If you like, you may pick some of the other fruits and eat them as well. Do the different colours have different flavours or are they all the same? Notice any sensations your body may feel as you eat these fruits.

As you walk around the tree, feeling the soft grass beneath your feet, you find that there is a plain wooden bench on the far side of the tree. It looks so comfortable in the sun that you sit down on the bench and rest against the tree itself. This tree is remarkably relaxing to lean against, and with its warmth on your back, the tingling warmth of the sun on the front of you, and within you the gentle sensation of the fruit you have eaten, you may feel almost drowsy. Your eyes close, in order to enjoy the sensation better, and your body gradually, gently, lets go.

When you look again at the scene before you, you notice that the flowers are moving in a very slow dance. Rooted in the earth, they sway slowly and gracefully. At first, you may think that a breeze is causing this, but you soon realise that there is no wind, just stillness, and the flowers are dancing to a song that only they can hear.

When you arise to look at them more closely, you notice a delightful feeling of lightness, of ease of movement, but you may be too intent upon the flowers and their dance to pay much attention to this at the moment. As you come closer to the many-coloured blossoms, you begin to feel, perhaps even to hear the faint, ethereal strands of the harmony, and your own body begins to move lightly in the rhythm of the flowers. And as you move in the dance, you happen to look back at the tree, and you see your own body, still sitting on the bench. It looks asleep, at peace, and like the plants and trees, it seems to glow from within.

And then you understand that your dancing body is your body of light, the network of power and energy that usually dwells within your physical body. For once, this body is free, free of the weight of the physical body, and you have a rare opportunity to enjoy that freedom. Your physical body looks so safe and so happy in the care of the tree that you are content to leave it there for awhile.

As you wander farther in your body of light, you find a stone pillar, about the height of your chest. And as you touch it, you notice that it, too, has a living warmth, warmth like that of the tree. On top of the pillar, there is a small globe of light. Although this light is very brilliant, scintillating and bright, the eyes of your body of light find it easy, even pleasurable to look at.

When you lift the globe in your two hands, you find that it, too, has a tingling warmth, and is almost weightless. As you hold the globe, you realise that the light within is healing power. You may even feel it in your hands. Inspired by this, you take the globe back to your physical body. On the way, you discover that you can make the sphere larger or smaller. It can be large enough to hold your entire body or small enough to hold only your littlest finger nail.

As you look at your sleeping body, considering it, think about where you would like the globe to be placed and how big you would like it to be.

While you are thinking about it, obedient to your desire, the luminous orb floats from your hands and moves to and then into your physical body. The globe and your body co-exist in the same space. As you watch, it becomes just the right shape and size to include all of the parts of your body that need and want healing. This may include areas you had not considered as well as the ones you were thinking of, but you can sense that the light has its own wisdom, and knows just what is needed.

As you watch for a few moments, seeing the light permeating the physical body and seeing the globe absorbing anything you don't want or need from that area, you understand that this is a natural process and will continue while you explore further.

Once again, you wander off, leaving your physical body in the care of the tree and the orb. You find that, wherever you go, you are always able to sense what is happening to your physical body, and you know that the tree holds it securely while you continue to explore.

As you walk on the soft springy grass, enjoying the airiness of your body of light, you come to a brook, gently flowing over a bed of pebbles. Among those pebbles, you see the same shining flashes of colour you saw in the path, and you realise that these precious stones must be every-where, even in the earth beneath your feet. Between the luminous sunlight and the many-hued stones beneath, the water sparkles like a multifaceted diamond. Intrigued by this, you wander upstream.

As you walk, moving lightly, you find a waterfall that is just a few feet higher than your head. In the waterfall, the sun creates a thousand, thousand tiny rainbows — one in each drop of water. The water looks irresistible, and you wade into the stream and stand under the fall. You might be a little surprised to find that your body of light is so subtle, so fine that the scintillating water can actually flow *through* it. As it flows, it washes away anything you don't want or need. If there are any shadows or dim places in your body of light, it fills them with rainbows, from your toes to your fingertips, to the top of your head.

Standing under the waterfall, you may feel an urge to stretch, to move, perhaps even to dance the slow dance of the flowers, and you find that the flowing rainbow water makes you even lighter and more supple, more supple that you can ever remember being before.

After a little while, when you are so full of light you almost feel as if you might float away, you move back onto the grass.

I'm going to give you a little time, about two minutes, to explore. As you walk, you may find other things you want to touch or taste. You are welcome to anything you wish here. Do whatever you want to do with this time. It is your time in your own place, and you may wander around to your heart's content.

Give the imager two minutes of silence.

What have you found as you explored? Have you enjoyed being free in your body of light?

As you walk through this space, so much bigger and more beautiful than you had realised, you notice a another bench by another tree ahead of you, and someone is sitting on it. As you draw closer, you realise that this person has been waiting here for you. You move slowly toward this person, and your new companion rises to meet you.

Is this being male or female? How tall is he or she? Taller or shorter than you? How old? When you reach this person, hold out your hand of light and let your companion take it.

Is your companion's hand large or small? Does it feel strong or delicate? What one word best describes the way you feel as you hold your companion's hand?

What are this person's eyes like? What colour are they? And what one word best describes the expression you see in those eyes?

How is your companion dressed? And what is this person's name? As you begin to walk together, what else do you notice about this person?

This is a good time for you to just enjoy some time together. You might want to talk and or you may want to just sit quietly together. You may have another couple of minutes to be with this person.

Give the imager another two minutes of silence.

I'd like you to say goodbye to your friend for now. When you come back to this place, you may meet again, or perhaps you may find other people at other times. Some of these people may surprise you by showing you things that you had not noticed before, or by helping you to see old things in new ways. And as you learn to know this place, the stream, the waterfall, the trees and flowers, you may find that being here begins to give you deeper peace each time you return.

I'd like you to go back to your physical body now. When you reach it, please lift the orb out of your body. You may find that it has become darker and heavier, perhaps even smaller, in your absence. Take the globe carefully back to its place on the pillar.

And when you replace the globe on the pillar, any darkness or heaviness in it drains out, down through the pillar into the earth. And the globe begins to renew itself, to fill with light from the magical healing energy of the sun, the moon, and the stars, and to gather up strength and warmth from the earth. As you watch the orb restore itself to its original beauty, you realise that you can come back here as often as you wish, and each time you come, you will find the globe fully charged with healing light, ready and waiting for you.

Once again you walk lightly back to your physical body. This time, when you reach it, you feel yourself being drawn into it. You may find that you want to simply turn and sit down, so that your essential body of light gently rests into your physical form. As you come to rest in the physical self, you may notice some change in the way you feel. You may be aware of the subtle sensation of the rainbow lights, or perhaps you may be aware of the gentle, warm feeling of the healing light of the globe, or perhaps both. It doesn't matter which, just be aware of the healing sensation of comfort and peace in your body.

You may even be able to hear the birds singing above you.

When you have left this place, you can come back whenever you wish just by thinking of the ancient tree in its centre, and imagining its fruit. As soon as you think of the tree, you will begin to sense the peace and stillness of this place, with your physical form resting against the security of the tree's strength, and your bright Self ready to rise and move lightly in the warm sunshine. This world is always within you, just as you are, in another sense, always within it.

Now I'd like you to become aware of your physical body, especially of your breath. And as we count from one to ten, you will return to normal consciousness, feeling rested, relaxed, restored.

One. Notice the incoming breath bringing in peace.

Two. Be aware of your physical body, sitting in its chair.

Three. Notice how your body feels, how peaceful it is.

Four. Take a deep breath. And let it go.

Five. Become aware of the room around you.

Six. And another deep breath. Now release it.

Seven. Flex your fingers and toes.

Eight. Open your eyes and slowly look around.

Nine. And one more deep breath. Now let it go.

Ten. You are now fully awake and aware. Notice how your body feels, and if you would like to do so, stretch and move around.

The logic of the imagery

In this structured imagery journey, the healing process begins with the discovery that this place does not conform to the ordinary, expected rules of the mundane world in which we think we live. We have entered a space in which those rules do not apply. This theme of the possibility of the impossible is expanded and developed by all of the unusual or 'impossible' things that happen later on.

Much of what happens or is logically implied in this journey is unstated. If we say you are feeling this or that, the conscious mind may argue. If, on the other hand, we can slip suggestions and experiences into the unconscious without conscious censorship, they may well be accepted. For example, the extraordinary profusion and variety of the flowers implies (without stating it for the conscious mind to argue with) that this is a place where we, ourselves, may experience nurturing and richness. They, and therefore *we*, do not follow the ordinary rules of the outer world in this place. These are statements to the deeper levels of the mind that we have entered a space in which our ordinary rules not only do not apply, but are superseded by extraordinary meta-rules, a higher law to which we can respond and within which we can act. In this higher reality, we can do what we could not so easily do (or perhaps not even do at all) in the mundane world.

The suggestion of healing itself is first touched upon in this journey by the unusual quality of the sunlight and the way it causes the skin to tingle. The unstated implication is that there is something almost magical in this — the plants even glow in response to it. Therefore, we, ourselves, must logically be similarly affected.

The fruit of the tree and the tree itself also imply the magical quality of this world. We all know from childhood fairy tales that, if we eat the special food of a magical land, strange things will happen to us, and so we are not really surprised by the almost immediate separation of our body of light from our physical body. We are even able to leave our physical body in the care of this nurturing and enchanting tree.

The globe of light is obviously a magical healing device. What is unstated here, but implicit in the action, is that the imager has the power to choose where and how this energy is applied and *by his own action* directs the healing process. This is an acknowledgement and affirmation to the self of the power of the Self. The body of light applies the healing instrument to the physical body — and then goes off to heal itself.

This particular imagery journey also gives us an opportunity to explore the possibilities of the body of light and its differences from the physical body. The light or energy body is that part of us most directly affected by laying on of hands, acupuncture, shiatzu, and other related healing techniques, as well as by visualisation. It is the framework, the matrix around which the physical body is built and to which the physical body conforms. The two bodies interact and inter-relate, but the 'decision-making' body is the body of light. This is why it is important to focus on healing it, as well as upon healing the physical body.

Lastly, we have a long cultural tradition of the association of rainbows and the renewal of life. They speak to us of the end of the storm and the return of the life-giving sun, the renewal of warmth and joy and hope for the future. Hope and joy are two of the most powerful agents of healing, and so we fill our body of light with them.

This imagery journey has nothing wasted. All of the symbolism, all of the experiences are pointed at accessing and utilising the healing power we all have latent within us.

Working with the imagery

Make an impressionistic painting of the feeling you had when standing under the rainbow waterfall. This may or may not be a painting of yourself. Paint the feeling as vividly as you can. You may also want to make a painting of yourself at some other point in the journey and/or of one or more symbolic images you encountered.

Use the tools and techniques you have for interpreting these paintings. What do they tell you about yourself? About your response to the healing imagery of the journey?

Was there anything in the journey that you felt uncomfortable with? If so, why? Paint it and see what you learn from the painting.

What did you enjoy most?

Was there any image you didn't understand? If so, use the image association technique (in Chapter 18), as well as painting the image and seeing what you can discover from the painting.

34. The Wounded Traveller

Journey to the Waterfall can be a powerful tool in the control of pain. Partly, this is achieved by simple relaxation — the more tense we are, the more we hurt — but there is more to it than this.

First, by moving the body of light away from the physical body, we give the mind space in which to detach itself from the pain, and we give the body space to mend itself in peace without the mind probing and nagging it. Both of these things allow healing to take place more rapidly.

Second, if the globe of light is used, especially if it is deliberately specified as removing pain, the suggestion is that pain and/or its source can be removed. If the imager is in a deep level of consciousness, this can function as a hypnotic suggestion to block awareness of pain. This may be a good thing or it may not.

Caution: Imagery pain control should not be used unless all needed medical and healing techniques are also in use.

Pain is like the temperature gauge in a car; it tells us that something is wrong. This is true of emotional pain as well as physical pain. When the gauge goes into the red, it would be pretty stupid to disconnect the gauge instead of fixing the problem — yet this is often our reaction when we have a pain. We try to disconnect it by taking a pill to block the pain, instead of asking ourselves what is causing it. The *source* of the pain, rather than the pain itself should be our first concern. Having said that, however, pain control through imagery can be very useful in helping to decrease (or sometimes even eliminate) the amount of anti-pain medication needed by the imager.

In order for imagery to work well in reducing or eliminating pain, the imager needs to be able to slip easily into a deep altered state of consciousness. Long inductions (the introductory, relaxation part) facilitate this. When we use a long induction, we need to remember to lengthen the time spent coming out of the imagery as well. As in any other activity, we improve our ability to relax with practice. Most people find that they go more deeply into the imagery as they do it again and again. If the imager understands this and if he knows that the more deeply we go, the more deeply we are affected by the imagery, it is an additional motivation to practise.

35. Consulting The Healer

When we first did *The Advisor* imagery, I mentioned that the original journey could be adapted to many purposes. We have used it to speak to the Rebel, and now we are going to use it to speak, with the aid of your Advisor, to your inner Healer. Your Healer is a very useful being (it might appear as a person or in some other guise) for you to know. First and foremost, it can advise you on your own self-healing process. Your Healer is the part of you that knows all that you know *consciously and unconsciously* about your body's needs. It knows the things that you have forgotten you know and the things you never even realised you were learning. It also knows how your body works *from the inside* — it may not know anatomical and physiological terms, but it does know what is working right and what is not — and quite often, it knows what you need to do to make it right.

Approximate travel time: 35 minutes.

THE HEALER

We are going on a journey to meet your Healer. Please be seated comfortably, and then I'd like you to take a deep breath. And now another. And take still another deep breath. As you exhale, be aware of your forehead and your eyelids. Allow them to relax, to become smooth and soft. Take another deep breath, and allow your fingers to relax, and then allow any tension in your arms, your shoulders, your neck to flow down and out through your fingertips. Take still another deep breath, and as you exhale, allow any tension in your body and your legs to flow down and out through your toes. Allow your whole body to become calm and still.

Breathe in peace, and as you exhale, breathe out anything in your mind that you don't need or want at this moment. And again, breathe in peace, and as you exhale, breathe out anything in your body that you don't want or need at this moment. You are in charge of this journey at all times. If for any reason you might wish to leave the inner world, all you need to do is to open your eyes, and you will immediately return to your ordinary consciousness in the outer world.

Now, I'd like you to imagine that you are standing in front of the entrance of a cave or a room. This entrance is big enough to walk into.

Please walk a few steps into the cave or room, and pause there.

What is under your feet? Is the floor hard or soft? Rough or smooth? What is the surface made of?

What does the air feel like? Is it warm or cool? Moving or still? Is it damp or is it dry? If it is damp, where is the moisture coming from?

If you were to reach out and touch the nearest wall, how would it feel to your fingers? What is it made of?

How big is this space? How high up is the ceiling and how far away is the farthest wall?

What colours or sounds or scents do you particularly notice in here?

Is there anything special or unusual about this space?

Where is the light coming from?

Now walk on into this space, until you come to a door or a passage to your left. You can go through this door or passage to your inner world. If it is a door and the door is locked, the key will be hanging on a hook to the right of the door. Go through the door or passage into the inner world. Your inner world may be an extension of the cave or room, or it may be some other kind of space altogether.

When you reach the inner world, stand still for a moment and notice what is under your feet here. Is the surface hard or soft? Rough or smooth? What is it made of?

Is the air warm or cool? Moving or still? Damp or dry? If it's damp, where is moisture coming from?

If you were to reach out and touch the thing nearest you, what would you touch, and how would it feel to your fingers?

And what do you see or sense in the distance?

What is above your head, and where is the light coming from? What time of the day or night is it? What time of the year?

What sounds or scents or colours do you especially notice? Is there anything else that stands out? As you begin to walk, notice your surroundings.

After you have been walking a short while, you meet a person, your wise Advisor. What is this person doing as you approach?

The Advisor

When you reach your Advisor, imagine yourself closing your eyes and reaching out with your hand, letting your Advisor take it. What does your Advisor's hand feel like? Does it feel strong or delicate? Hard or soft? Large or small?

What one word best describes the way you feel as your Advisor holds your hand?

What are your Advisor's eyes like — the first impression that comes to your mind? What color are they? What one word best describes the expression you see or sense in your Advisor's eyes?

What else do you notice about this person? Is it male or female? Large or small or in between?

What is your Advisor's name?

The Healer

Ask your Advisor to bring before you, in its symbolic form, the Healer within you, and the Healer will appear before you.

What form does it take? Is it a person, a creature, or some more abstract form? What colours or sounds or scents do you sense or associate with it? How big is it?

How do you feel as you look at your Healer? And how does it seem to feel as it looks at you?

At this moment, I'd like you to give your Advisor and your Healer permission to tell you the truth always, even if it happens to be something you don't want to hear.

Request

And now I'd like you to ask your Healer what it needs from you in order for the two of you to work together in your best interests. What does it want you to work on or pay attention to next?

If the answer you receive is not clear, ask your Advisor to clarify it for you. The answer will give you clear guidance about what is needed from you.

Is this something you feel you can agree to and actually do? If it is not, discuss it with your Healer and your Advisor until you reach an agreement on something you can agree to do that would help your Healer.

When you have reached an agreement, state clearly in your mind to your Healer and your Advisor exactly what it is that you are agreeing to do.

Do you need any suggestions or advice from your Healer or your Advisor about what practical steps you need to take in order to fulfil this agreement? If so, ask for this now.

Gift

When you have the information you need, I'd like you to imagine that you are holding your hands out in front of you. Your Healer will place a symbolic gift in your hands. This is the gift you will receive for keeping your promise.

What does this gift feel like in your hands? Is it light or heavy? What is the texture like? What colours or sounds or scents do you associate with this gift? What is it?

Ask your Healer what this gift symbolises. If you don't quite understand the answer, ask your Advisor to clarify it.

Is this gift something you want to accept? If you are not certain, discuss it with your Advisor and Healer.

If you don't want the gift, give it back, and if you like, ask if there is another gift that you might feel more ready to accept.

If you do want it, give it back to your Healer and ask it to place the gift in you or on you or around you, wherever it belongs.

If you have accepted a gift, what does your Healer do with it? Do you notice any particular feeling when this happens?

Ask your Healer and your Advisor if there is anything you need to know about using your gift. Is it for use in the inner world? The outer world? Or both worlds? How are you to use this gift in your everyday life?

Potential

Ask your Healer to transform itself to show you the symbolic form of what it has the potential to become. How does it change? What colours or sounds or scents do you particularly notice? How do you feel as you look at or sense this potential form? And how does it seem to feel about you?

Ask yourself if you are willing at this time to accept this kind of energy and power in yourself. If you like, discuss this with your Advisor.

If you wish to, hold out your hands, palms up, and ask the Healer-Potential to touch your hands. Allow yourself to feel its energy.

And if you wish to, ask this Healer-Potential to help you release any blocks or limitations to its power that you are ready to release at this time. If you do this, what does the Healer-Potential do? Do you notice any physical, energetic, mental, or emotional shifts or changes in yourself while this is happening?

Allow yourself to feel the energy throughout your entire being.

If you wish to, tell your Advisor and your Healer-Potential that you accept the fulfilment of this potential within yourself, and that you will try to use it wisely.

Completion

When this is completed, thank your Healer for being with you, and allow it to dissolve back into your inner world. And then thank your Advisor for being with you and helping you, and say goodbye to your Advisor for now.

Go back to the place where you entered this inner world. As you go, notice if there have been any changes in your inner world. Is anything different, or is it just the same?

When you reach the door or gateway through which you entered your inner world, come back through the cave or room to this world.

When you reach this world, take a couple of deep breaths. Flex your feet and your fingers, and begin to pay attention to the sounds of the room around you. When you are ready, open your eyes, and if you like, stretch.

The logic of the imagery

The use of the section on *Potential* (releasing blocks and limitations and fulfilling potential) is optional. Don't do it unless you really do want to make these changes, because what you are doing is to give your higher self, your spiritual assistance (the Advisor), and your innate healing energies (the Healer) permission to go ahead and start these changes in the way that they think best. This will take into consideration your tolerance for change and will not be faster or more drastic than you can handle, but it may shake things up a bit. This is a powerful tool — don't use it unless you really want this change.

If you are guiding someone else through the journey, discuss this with them before you begin and let them chose whether or not to do it.

Notice that it is the Healer-Potential who dissolves back into the inner world, not the original form of the Healer. This, too, is a tacit acceptance of the idea of integrating and fulfilling our potential for healing.

You may ask your Healer about any health issue you have — diet, exercise, courses of treatment for illnesses, et cetera. Such advice should be taken with due caution (see *Two Cautions* below).

In addition to guiding you towards better health, the Healer can also help you along the path of becoming a healer, or at least, of being a healing presence in the world, if you are interested in that.

Interpretation

The most important things to remember in this imagery journey are the promise or agreement you made, the gift you received, and the interaction with the potential healer.

Can you see a logical connection between the agreement made and the meaning of the symbolic gift?

It is also useful to look at the inner world to see what kind of an environment your inner Healer lives in. Would you say that part of you is a healthy or an unhealthy place? Does your Healer seem reasonably happy there? Did the Healer seem pleased to see you? Friendly? Hostile? Impatient? Satisfied?

Do an impressionistic painting of your Healer and the gift you were given. You may also want to paint the Healer's potential self and/or some other image from the journey. Using the interpretive techniques you have learned, what do these paintings tell you?

Two Cautions

As we have previously discussed, we cannot blindly follow the guidance we get from any part of ourselves, even the wisest parts. We may have emotional stuff that is interfering with reception, or we may have fixed conscious ideas that also interfere with accurately sensing what the Healer and the Advisor have to offer. But it is still always worth listening to the ideas.

It must be understood that healing and imagery work are not substitutes for medical treatment — nor is medical treatment a substitute for healing and imagery work.

Review

What were the symbolic gifts you received in the initial *Light Into Darkness* imagery journey? Do you understand them any better now than you did then?

This might also be a good time to go for another *Walk In The Forest* to see what changes have been taking place there. If an image has changed — and many probably will have done so — you need to consider carefully whether or not the meaning of it also has altered. If so, in what way and how much? Use both writing and painting techniques to learn as much as you can, especially about the more mystifying images.

If you have difficulty in carrying out your agreement with the Healer, remember to discuss it with the Rebel.

Part X

The Maps in Our Minds

It used to be thought that events that changed the world were things like big bombs, maniac politicians, huge earthquakes or vast population movements, but it has now been realised that this is a very old-fashioned view held by people totally out of touch with modern thought. The things that really change the world, according to Chaos theory, are the tiny things. A butterfly flaps its wings in the Amazonian jungle, and subsequently a storm ravages half of Europe.

Somewhere in Adam's sleeping head, a butterfly had emerged.

— *Terry Pratchett & Neil Gaiman*
in Good Omens

36. Travellers' Tales

In exploring our inner world, we find that we already have maps in our minds — maps that set out boundaries and limitations, maps that purport to tell us what is and what is not. These are marvellous examples of the cartographer's art, with the locations of dragons and other mythical beasts and much *terra incognita*. As art they may be wonderful, but as guides to reality, they often fall far short of objective accuracy.

Let us consider three travellers' tales about the use of mental maps. These stories will tell us something about images, affirmations, conditioning, programmes, and manifestation. These fables are all, by the way, both literally and allegorically true.

The last popsicles

The weather had been hot and dry in San Diego, with the wind blowing off the desert for several days, leaving almost everyone hot, frazzled, and irritable. Joe, who is a large, middle-aged friend of mine and a pretty good practical psychologist, went to the supermarket to replenish his popsicle (an 'iced lolly' to the British) supply — a necessity to him in such weather. As he was going toward the popsicles in the freezer, he noticed that the store had even run out of ice cubes. Then, just as he saw that there was only one carton of popsicles left, he realised that a woman was headed toward them. He moved a bit faster and picked up the carton just as she started to reach for them.

She looked at him accusingly and said, "You've taken the last popsicles!"

"They haven't any ice left," he explained.

"Oh, but they must have ice in the liquor store next door," she replied.

And Joe answered, "Yes, but they don't have any popsicles."

The woman looked at him, and her eyes glazed over. Joe said, "But I love you anyway."

"I love you, too," she replied, her eyes even glassier, and she turned and walked away with her shopping cart.

The monk and the mugger

For a meditation prayer, Fr. Joe uses the statement, "Father, into Thy hands I commend myself. Thy will be done." He repeats it whenever he is not occupied by other things, and it is very deeply imprinted in his consciousness.

In Pittsburgh one night to give a lecture, he was walking from his hotel to his destination, dressed, as he usually is, in ordinary street clothes. A man stepped out of a doorway in front of him, pointed a gun at him, and demanded his money.

Fr. Joe's mind went completely blank as he looked at the man and he said the first thing that came into his head, which was, "Father, into Thy hands I commend myself. Thy will be done." The gunman looked at him, confusion and bewilderment plain on his face, and Fr. Joe, a shrewd practising psychologist, said, "Bless you, my son," and, as casually as he could, walked on.

The black dog

There was a period of several years duration in my life when I was rather frequently exposed to physical dangers of various kinds. In order to calm (or at least reduce) what seemed to be becoming a permanent state of panic, I started mentally saying, 'I am safe in Thy hands' over and over in stress situations, until the excessive fear had been replaced by relative calmness and even confidence, perhaps to the point of foolhardiness.

Very late one night, feeling extremely confined by the apartment in which I was temporarily staying in Glasgow (another large city where wise people usually do not walk alone late at night), I went for a walk. As I walked along a deserted street by the park with a high, dense hedge to one side and the closed, dark university to the other, a dirty, dark-coloured delivery van pulled up beside me.

The driver asked if I wanted a lift, and I said, "No, thank you," and kept walking. The driver started to get out of the van, and I thought, "Well, Jesa — what now?" He was quite a bit larger than I. Just then an enormous, black dog burst out of the hedge beside me and viciously snarled at the man. The man sensibly stopped right where he was. The dog was very large, very black, and appeared to have rather more than the usual number of teeth. He clearly had hostile intentions toward that man.

The man asked me, "Is that your dog, missus?" I just nodded

because the dog was getting louder as it began to move toward him, fur bristling. The man backed slowly to his van, jumped quickly in, and drove away with a desperate grinding of gears.

I looked at the dog and said inanely, "Good doggie." It waved its tail and panted good-naturedly at me, obviously a perfectly harmless teddy-bear of a dog, and then it disappeared back into the hedge.

37. Understanding These Tales

The fables in the preceding chapter illustrate the following principles of mental activity:

First Principle: When emotion overwhelms the rational mind, humans react to the situation in which they find themselves in accordance with the programmes (habit patterns or conditioned response or images or belief systems) they have developed as a result of their conditioning (verbal or experiential repeated and/or traumatic experiences). We often use these unconscious programmes for dealing with emotion-laden situations, whether they are appropriate or not, helpful or not.

Second Principle: When emotion overwhelms the rational mind and a programme takes over, it only works as long as everyone and everything responds 'appropriately' — that is, in one of the ways that the programme expects and for which it is prepared.

Third Principle: When the rational mind is not functioning (because emotion has caused a programme to take over) and someone or something behaves in a way for which the programme is not prepared, the programme ceases to function — in computer talk it 'crashes', leaving a void. We cannot think, and we do not know what to do. We are confused and bewildered.

Fourth Principle: When we are bewildered because emotion has shut off our rational mind and something has caused our programme to crash so that we are unable to function for the moment, we become very susceptible to programmes put forth by others (especially those for which we have a programmed response) or to suggestions made by others.

Fifth Principle: We programme ourselves through life experience, we allow ourselves to accept programming by others, and we can reprogramme ourselves through experience or in various other ways such as the use of hypnosis, imagery, affirmations, et cetera.

Sixth Principle: We unconsciously put out physical and energetic messages about who and what we are and about how we expect to be treated, and other beings respond appropriately (either in accordance with their own programmes or through considered, conscious action).

Seventh Principle: The universe knows our programmes and it treats us accordingly. We create our own reality.

What has all this got to do with imagery and affirmations and manifestation?

Everything.

Conditioning is something we have all experienced, and as a result of that conditioning we have developed programming, which takes the form of unconscious belief systems. These belief systems manifest in our minds as images, mental maps, that limit and confine us. They manifest in our behaviour as unconscious choices — habits or patterns or programmes of behaviour. Some of our programmes help us and are useful, but sometimes they are self-destructive, self-defeating, or they give us pain or unhappiness in some way. We don't believe we have a choice, because we automatically make the same choice each time. We are sleep-walking.

Once we have learned of an old programme, a false entry in our mental map, through imagery journeys or other means, affirmations, which are consciously-created self-programming devices, are tools we can use to break old patterns of behaviour while simultaneously replacing them with new.

38. The Mental Map

Whatever we are programmed or conditioned to expect tends to be what we get. Unconsciously, we even look for beings and situations who will be or will provide what we expect, who will fit neatly into our mental map, so that our programmes can function without crashing. Often we even fail to really see or hear what is actually happening because it doesn't fit our programme and we are unwilling or unable to do the thinking necessary when we are confronted by a situation for which we have no programme.

The Zen Buddhists say that an enlightened person never reacts with a conditioned response in any situation. Instead, he always consciously chooses his actions and responses. He acts thoughtfully and purposefully, with full awareness of the reasons for his actions. He considers before he acts. Most of us are not so aware of ourselves and our actions/reactions. We have developed various response patterns to certain types of situations, and we react with that programming (which is a result of conditioning), especially when we are too tired, distracted, uncaring, or emotional to think.

All our programmes came into being because they were useful. They worked better than anything else we could find, and they got us, more or less safely, through certain situations or types of situations. We respond to things in our life dozens of times each day with conditioned responses. I meet you on the street. "Hi, how are you?" "Fine, and you?" "Great. How's the family?" Conditioned responses. You hold out your hand, I shake it. The anthropologists have a name for this — they call it *phatic communion*. It is a social noise acknowledging a general friendliness toward another person without actually communicating anything beyond that.

Many of our conditioned responses are useful. They probably are necessary in order to survive in heavy or fast traffic. Such *physical* responses take care of all the things that we haven't time to think about — we must just do, and do them quickly. However, our *mental* response programmes lock us into patterns of behaviour, and they are by no means always benign and helpful. Let us look at the story of Jack and Jane, two mythical but entirely plausible people. Jack yells at Jane. Jane bursts into tears. Jack apologises. Conditioned responses — but why?

Jane's father was prone to fits of rage. Children consciously and unconsciously search for and find ways to protect themselves from those who have power over them. As a very small child, Jane, frightened by one of her father's rages, ran away, was caught, and was spanked. The next time, she screamed back at him and was again spanked. The next time, still frightened and utterly helpless, she cried and he stopped shouting. Thus, Jane learned at an early age that tears got the desired response.

Later on, when she went to school, the same thing worked — usually. This never was a conscious tactic. At first it was the only thing she could do and then it became a conditioned response. However, as she grew older, this response didn't always work — in fact, sometimes it made matters worse instead of better. Some people actually get satisfaction or pleasure from seeing someone else cry, and such people were quick to exploit Jane's weakness. Sometimes,

especially after such an occasion, Jane thought about what she might
have said or done to change the situation if only she could have kept
from crying. She didn't like the helpless feeling that went with the
tears, and sometimes was angry with herself for responding as she did.

Jack was raised by a mother, who was what we might call a 'weepy
manipulator'. Her technique for manipulating others into doing what
she wanted was to invoke their sympathy or to make them feel guilty,
using a variety of specific techniques — tears being one of the most
effective. (We won't go into how or why she programmed herself to
handle things this way — we could wind up going back for genera-
tions.) Jane's tears were a defence, but Jack's mother's tears were a
weapon. Being a decent sort of child, Jack didn't want to make his
mother suffer and cry, so he learned to respond to tears with apologies
and promises to do better in the future. This worked, and as he got
older he learned to go his own way and still please his mother with
promises and apologies without always actually doing things he really
didn't want to do. He learned to do what he wanted and apologise
afterward, and he learned to make promises he had no real intention of
keeping.

How high would you estimate the chance of Jane and Jack for a
happy marriage?

The funny thing is, it may be better than you expect. We are
unconsciously attracted to the people who seem to fit our mental
images of how people can be expected to behave, *and* we are, at the
same time, unconsciously attracted to people and to situations which
will challenge our weaknesses and give us the opportunity to learn
new and more satisfactory means of coping with everyday life. Quite
often we manage to find both attributes in the same person.

Think of the implications of that.

Jane could be attracted to Jack because her behaviour would get
unsatisfactory results, as well as because it seemed to get favourable
results. Her higher self, her unconscious spiritual attunement, her
inner Advisor, would recognise this as a learning opportunity and
draw her toward it at the same time that her blocked and limited self
would be attracted to a familiar response to its programme. If she tried
new ways of responding to Jack, she would at least not meet with
violence, because his programme is to evade rather than to confront.

Jack could be attracted to Jane both because she is a weepy woman
and he 'knows' how to cope with them and because she is not
manipulative in the same way that his mother was, but is instead
someone in genuine pain, with an honest desire to be a good person.

Since she is that kind of person, Jack's behaviour is inappropriate and may lead to feeling of guilt and genuine regret on his part. He might even go so far as to change his behaviour.

In this situation both Jack and Jane have the opportunity and motivation to find new and more positive ways of functioning in the world. Should they fail to take advantage of this opportunity, they will simply reinforce their old programmes and make it that much harder to achieve this growth when a loving universe offers them another chance to do so.

But the universe is patient — it gives us chance after chance until we finally do learn.

In fact, it doesn't stop giving us opportunities to see the underlying motivations of our actions and to change our behaviour until we *do* learn. And the slower we are to get it, the sharper and more pointed the lessons seem to become.

We have been talking a lot about 'programming' and 'conditioning' — it all sounds very mechanical. There is a school of thought that believes that people are purely mechanical beings, that we can only respond as we are conditioned to do, and that we really have no choice in the matter. This is not the kind of book that appeals to people like that. We are assuming here that we do have a choice, that we can examine our actions and thoughts, our programmes, habits, and conditioned responses, and that we can consciously choose to let go of them, and through greater self-awareness, give ourselves choice of action rather than simple reaction. We are only mechanical beings when we choose to react out of old habits or programming, sleep-walking through life, rather than choosing to think and to consciously make choices.

Of course, the ability to make such change presupposes certain knowledge and character traits in the person who intends to change her conditioning, whether by the use of affirmations or by any other means. First, we are assuming that she recognises that she herself is the one with the problem. With this kind of situation, it is often disastrously easy to believe that other people or circumstances are responsible for our unhappiness and that we would be happy if only they would co-operate. We must recognise that it is our response to a situation that gives us pain, not the situation itself.

Second, we are assuming that we have accurately identified the problem.

Third, we are assuming that we have the perseverance needed to make these kinds of changes in ourselves. The more deeply ingrained the programme is, the more difficult it is to change and the longer the time required to effect that change.

Thoughts are things. They are, like everything else in the universe, made up of energy. We shape them with our own energy and they are with us and of us even after we send them out into the universe. They are, again like everything else in the universe, subject to change. We create our thought patterns, and they do much to create our lives. We have the power to change our thoughts — especially our habitual, programmed thoughts — and, in so doing, to change our lives. There are several ways of doing this and one of the most effective do-it-yourself methods is through the use of affirmations.

39. Correcting The Map

The following are basic principles for creating and using an affirmation:

a) be specific;

b) use a positive approach;

c) accept it now;

d) accept responsibility for yourself;

e) keep it simple;

f) make it irresistible;

g) make a mental image of it

h) use body language

g) check it for other meanings;

h) use it;

i) give it time; and

j) reinforce it.

Being specific

If we really want to accomplish anything with our affirmations, we must be specific. We need to pinpoint our problems as accurately as we can and create specific affirmations for specific problems. Generalisations used as affirmations do not accomplish much — they often require too big a change in attitude or belief on the part of the unconscious. We need to figure out exactly what we want to change and create our affirmations with that and only that in mind. Trying to create an affirmation that will take care of all of our problems usually results in an affirmation that does not give the unconscious anything specific to go on, and therefore it (the unconscious) does nothing. 'Every day in every way I am getting better and better' may just possibly help us to feel better about our self-images, but it is unlikely to do much else. Be specific, be concrete, and be practical.

Using a positive approach

The unconscious is largely nonverbal. It is especially sensitive to emotions and is readily aware of visual symbols. It is not as adept with words as the conscious mind, and it tends only to understand the ones that catch its attention because of their emotional impact. If the affirmation used is 'I am not afraid' the unconscious picks up the concept of self-identity and the emotion associated with the word 'afraid' — which is, of course, fear. The connection of these two concepts is not desirable, and is, indeed, exactly what one is trying to eliminate.

The unconscious in not good at picking up subtle (or not so subtle) verbal distinctions, such as the difference between is and is not, do and don't, can and cannot. It needs to be told in positive terms just what we desire. Don't use negatives like 'no' and 'not' and avoid words with negative connotations, such as 'guilty' or 'afraid' or 'sad', which will actually reinforce the negative attitude that you are trying to change. Always use positive terms.

Sometimes it is quite tricky trying to work out a positive way to put something. I think this is because we are so focused on the negative that we cannot even conceive of the positive. However, there always *is* a positive way to put it. For example, if the issue is about a characteristic, such as fearfulness, we need to think of its opposite, bravery or courage, and affirm that.

Accepting it now

Avoid affirmations like 'I will meditate' — that says that I am not meditating now, but I will do so *sometime in the indefinite future*. Avoid words like 'will' and 'shall' and 'going to' and use words like 'am' and 'do.' For example, it would be better to say, 'I meditate every day'.

Taking responsibility for ourselves

We need to exercise the power that we have over our lives — and not to hand it to someone or something else. Don't use an affirmation that gives others or circumstances power over you by making your feeling of self-worth and your well-being dependent upon their approval or love. For instance, if we feel unlikable or unlovable, the real problem is our attitude, our ability to accept love, not that of other people who may or may not be offering love to us. It is our attitudes toward ourselves that need to be changed. Therefore, an affirmation like 'I am worthy of love' or 'I am lovable' might be useful.

It would NOT be useful to say something like 'people love me'. After all, no matter how lovable you may be there will inevitably be some people with poor taste or warped personalities who don't love you. Every time you encountered such a person, your efforts to reprogramme yourself would receive a nasty setback, and you would probably fall back into your old response of 'nobody loves me — I'm awful'. If you are affirming 'I am worthy of being loved and I love me', you can then accept love as your due when it is offered and recognise that the fault does not necessarily lie with you when someone rejects you. Focus on self-respect and a sense of self-worth in your affirmations and not on the approval of others.

Keep it simple

A good affirmation is simple. Remember, the unconscious is really not verbally oriented, so keep it simple and don't give it a lot of complex verbal instructions. Don't try to do too many things at once with an affirmation like 'I am serene and peaceful and I have confidence in my ability to make good decisions'. Focus on one thing at a time, no matter how eager you may be to reform yourself completely overnight. It probably took you years to get yourself in this mess, so allow yourself plenty of time to make the changes you desire.

Make it irresistible

Can you make your affirmation rhyme? Can you put it to music? Can you make it so that, once you start saying it, is it difficult to stop? When we do any of these things, it makes the affirmation much more effective, partly because we will use it more, and partly because the rhythm or rhyme will make it more appealing to the unconscious. Instead of 'I release my old ideas and I allow myself to grow' try something like 'I let go and let grow'. The advertising industry uses this concept very effectively. Ask yourself, will it sell me on this?

Make an image of it

The unconscious isn't verbal, but it is visual. Can you make a simple, positive, mental image that you can easily call to mind as you say the affirmation? It should follow the same rules as the affirmation itself.

Use body language

The unconscious freely uses body language to communicate, and you can consciously use your body language to communicate a message to the unconscious. What body language (posture and movement) says *this affirmation is true — I really feel this way?* What posture would say it was untrue? Notice your posture and movements when you repeat the affirmation, and make certain that you are conveying the same message with your body language, your image, and your words. If you are not, your unconscious self-programming mechanism will probably believe the body language rather than the words.

Check it for other meanings

When you think you have your affirmation worked out, write it down and show it to some of your more intelligent friends. Ask them what the affirmation means to them. You may get some surprises — not all of them good. It is safer to assume that your unconscious will respond to *all* of the possible meanings, unless they are contradictory. If they are contradictory, it will choose the meaning that most nearly agrees with the beliefs and programmes it already has — and that will probably be the meaning you want least.

Even very bright people frequently make absurd mistakes. Partly, this is because the unconscious resists reprogramming — it knows that the old programmes work, some of the time anyway. It resists changing them for the untried, and it attempts to help you to create an affirmation that will not disturb the status quo, even though your conscious mind may intend differently. This is why it pays to get several opinions on what possible meanings are inherent in your affirmation before you start using it. Remember! We create our own reality. The universe responds to the messages we transmit. Be certain the reality you are creating is one you really will enjoy.

Use it

You cannot use an affirmation too often — unless it's a bad affirmation, producing results you don't want. The more often you use any affirmation, the sooner the unconscious will become conditioned to react in accordance with it. Pick something that you do several times a day and use it to remind yourself to say your affirmation. For example, if you drive a lot, tell yourself to remember to repeat your affirmation every time you stop for a traffic light. Repeat your affirmation while you are changing your clothes, dressing in the morning, putting on makeup or shaving, sitting on the toilet, washing dishes, sharpening pencils, or during any activity which you perform frequently and which really doesn't require concentration.

Giving It Time

Consider this equation: *Time x Intensity = Results*. Any process takes time and energy. The more energy involved, the less time needed; the less energy, the more time. Sometimes we acquire conditioning very rapidly — for example, in a really traumatic situation we may programme ourselves to respond to certain stimuli with specific behaviour patterns in a matter of seconds or minutes. Because of the emotional intensity (energy) of the moment a new programme can be established rapidly. Other conditioning may be acquired because of a low intensity stimulus repeated over and over until it is accepted by the unconscious. Either way, it took time and energy to get us into these messes. It will take an equivalent amount of time and energy to get ourselves out of them. Keep saying it until it becomes true — not just true once in a while, but true all of the time.

Reinforce it

Reinforce your affirmation by saying it when confronted with whatever situation it is designed to cope with. If your affirmation is, 'I am self-confident at board meetings', say it a lot (silently to yourself would probably be best!) at board meetings. And as much as you possibly can, *act* — in both the sense of taking action and of pretending — as if you were self-confident. This reinforcing of the affirmation, regardless of how you may feel at the moment, will speed up the process of change greatly. The stronger your feelings are when you say the affirmation, the more effect it will have — just as an emotionally traumatic experience has more effect upon us than an experience about which we have little feeling.

Most of all, say it and say it and say it until every part of you believes it.

Let the universe do its work

Tell the universe what you want, not how to give it to you. If you want financial security, ask for exactly that, instead of asking for a particular job that pays $500,000 a year. They are not the same thing. If you want a healthy, loving, growing relationship with someone, don't ask for a specific relationship with a specific person. You might well get what you ask for, although it will not necessarily be what you thought it would be when you asked. Be certain that you are asking for what you really want.

For example, you may get that $500,000 a year job — but with a company which goes bankrupt within a year. Not much security there. Or you may get that relationship with that special person — and later find out that she is a secret but confirmed alcoholic and not at all the person you had expected. This is not conducive to happiness.

Of course, when you ask with an undivided heart for what you really want, rather than a specific thing which you believe would be the manifestation of what you want, you have to be open and receptive to what the universe does offer you. What you are asking for may come in a totally unexpected form, and you need to be open enough, alert and attuned enough, and daring enough to take the opportunity offered you.

The use of affirmations is the use of power — the use of the creative life force that shapes the universe. It is real magic.

CREATING AFFIRMATIONS

1. Make a list of things you want to change about yourself.
2. Mark the things on the list that you feel your old attitudes prevent you from changing. Don't be too surprised if nearly everything on the list turns out to be something like that.
3. Choose one of these things for working on with an affirmation. Pick the

one that looks like it might be the least complicated, and if possible, the one with which you are the most anxious to work.

4. You will need to know:
   a) what the attitude is that you are trying to change, and
   b) what kind of situations you have problems with because of that attitude.

5. Create at least one affirmation, using the information given here as a guide.

6. If you are working with a group, help each other check the affirmations. If you are working on your own, get an articulate friend to tell you what she thinks it means.

7. Use it over and over and over.

Sometimes it is quite useful to discuss our affirmations with our Advisors, and you might want to try that. Later on we will use an affirmation within an imagery journey, but for the moment, I'd like you to see how much it can do alone.

Part XI

Travel Broadens the Mind

"I've walked through walls," he said, slowly and deliberately.

"Of course you have, of course you have," mumbled Cutwell.

"Only before I did it I didn't know that I could, and when I was doing it I didn't know I was, and now I've done it I can't remember how it was done. And I want to do it again."

"Why?"

"Because," said Mort, "if I could walk through walls I could do anything."

"Very deep," agreed Cutwell. "Philosophical. And the name of the young lady on the other side of this wall?"

"She's —" Mort swallowed. "I don't know her name. Even if there is a girl," he added haughtily, "and I'm not saying there is."

— Terry Pratchett
in Mort

40. The Far Reaches of Space-Time

The important thing, of course, is to be able to walk, at will, through the walls in our minds and to explore the far reaches of our inner worlds, instead of being confined to our little circles of light at the top of the mountain. The following imagery journey is an exercise in the dissolving of walls.

In the last chapter we said we would try a guided imagery exercise that uses affirmations in conjunction with an altered state of consciousness to reprogramme the deeper levels of mind. Here it is.

Approximate travel time: 50 minutes.

POOL OF WATER

This is the imagery journey to the Pool of Water, an exploration into expanded consciousness. Twice during this journey you will be given an opportunity to make some kind of a choice, an affirmation about yourself. You may plan this ahead or just allow it to arise from your greater Self at the appropriate moment.

Let us begin the journey.

Please be seated comfortably, upright, and with your feet on the floor. Allow yourself to relax into this position, your body balanced in an effortlessly relaxed yet erect posture.

First, just close your eyes and take a couple of deep breaths. As you inhale, breathe in relaxation and peace. As you exhale, breathe out all of the tensions and distractions of the day.

Be aware of your breath. As you breathe you may notice that some of your breaths are longer, some shorter, some more shallow, some more deep. The natural breath changes from moment to moment, and the movement of air becomes easier as you relax, as you become more still. Be aware of the natural breath and its flow within you, and you may choose to allow yourself to let go of any need to control, to *do*, and just allow yourself to *be* with your breath for a moment.

As you sit there, being aware of your breath, breathing in, breathing out, I'd like you to imagine to yourself that you are inhaling through your navel, and as you inhale through your navel, your breath rises, rising up to your throat, and then as you exhale, your breath flows back down to your abdomen, and out through your navel. Imagine each breath, inhaling through your navel, the breath rising up to your throat, and descending again, exhaling through your navel, like a wave, washing in and up the shore and back out to sea.

Don't try to do anything special with your breath, don't try to control it in any way. Just allow your breath to be free and natural, each breath in its own time. And imagine with each breath that the breath comes in through the navel, up to the throat, and back down to the navel. All through this imagery you may allow your breath to continue coming in peaceful waves, waves washing in and up, and down and out.

As you continue to breathe gently and naturally, your breath washing in and washing out like the waves of the sea, I'd like you to imagine that you are standing in a small clearing within a wood and the wood is surrounded by gentle, rolling hills. In the center of the clearing there is a small pool, surrounded by soft, green moss. The pool is very deep — very deep and very still. And although the water of the pool is the clearest water you have ever seen, it is so deep that it seems to have no bottom at all, and so still that it looks as if it had never moved, not in all of time.

As you stand there on the soft, green moss, observing the quietness of the pool, you may be aware of the very gentle movement of air around you — not enough to call it a breeze, just a gentle movement, touching you lightly. The myriad leaves of the trees move lightly in the air, but the pool remains perfectly still, still and deep.

As you sense the stillness of the pool and the gentle movement of the air, you may be aware of certain sensations in your body, sensations of tension or perhaps discomfort. These sensations belong to you, they are something that you have, something that you own, but they are not you. They are not you — they are just something you may hold or let go of whenever you wish.

If you would like to at this time, you may allow any of these sensations that may be in your head to fall down to the earth. There on the earth, on the soft moss, that sensation you might have had takes on some kind of symbolic form, some kind of a shape, and it moves across to the pool, and it goes into it. As this symbolic form enters the water, you feel it radiating a sense of bliss, of joy, and you notice that it is blissfully dissolving in the pool, which remains perfectly still, still and deep. And the pool becomes just a little larger.

As it dissolves, any similar sensations that might be in your neck are already falling down to the soft moss, where they also take on a symbolic form. In this form they move across the moss and slide gently into the still water. As they dissolve in the water, you sense their joy and relief. And they become one with the water, which is still and deep.

As they dissolve, any similar sensation you might have in your shoulders is also falling down to the soft moss, where it too takes on a symbolic form. In this form it moves across the moss and slides gently into the still water. As it dissolves in the water, you sense its joy and relief. And it becomes one with the water, which is still and deep. And the pool becomes just a little larger.

As it dissolves, any similar sensation you might have in your arms and hands is also falling down to the soft moss, where it too takes on a symbolic form. In this form it moves across the moss and slides gently into the still water. As it dissolves in the water, you sense its joy and relief. And it becomes one with the water, which is still and deep.

As it dissolves, any similar sensation you might have in your chest is also falling down to the soft moss, where it too takes on a symbolic form. In this form it moves across the moss and slides gently into the still water. As it dissolves in the water, you sense its joy and relief. And it becomes one with the water, which is still and deep.

As it dissolves, any similar sensation you might have in your abdomen is also falling down to the soft moss, where it too takes on a symbolic form. In this form it moves across the moss and slides gently into the still water. As it dissolves in the water, you sense its joy and relief. And it becomes one with the water, which is still and deep.

As it dissolves, any similar sensation you might have in your pelvis is also falling down to the soft moss, where it too takes on a symbolic form. In this form it moves across the moss and slides gently into the still water. As it dissolves in the water, you sense its joy and relief. And it becomes one with the water, which is still and deep.

As it dissolves, any similar sensation in your back is also falling down to the soft moss, where it too takes on a symbolic form. In this form it moves across the moss and slides gently into the still water. As it dissolves in the water, you sense its joy and relief, as it becomes one with the water, which is still and deep.

As it dissolves, any such sensation you might have in your legs and feet is also falling down to the soft moss, where it too takes on a symbolic form. In this form it moves across the moss and slides gently into the still water. As it dissolves in the water, you sense its joy and relief. And it becomes one with the water, which is still and deep.

Any other similar sensations you might have still remaining in your body may also choose to fall to the soft, green moss at this moment. There they take on their symbolic forms, cross to the still water, and dissolve, dissolving in bliss. You may sense the ecstasy of release as each one lets go, letting go into the deep stillness of the water, becoming one with the silence of the pool, deep and still, still and deep. And the pool becomes just a little larger.

While all of those sensations were blissfully dissolving in the pool, you may have been aware of some thoughts in your mind. These thoughts are yours; they belong to you, they are your tools, they are something you own, but these thoughts are not you — they are just something you may hold or let go of at your own pleasure.

You may allow these thoughts to drop down to the soft, green moss. There they too take on their symbolic forms, cross to the still, deep water, slide into the pool and dissolve. You are easily able feel the relief and joy of each one as it lets go into the stillness of the deep water, serene and silent.

All of your thoughts may enter the pool, and whenever you find yourself thinking about anything during this exercise, you may also choose to allow that thought to fall onto the soft green moss, to enter the still, deep water, and to dissolve in joy. And you may sense the release and the bliss with which they dissolve.

You may have noticed, without really thinking about it, that the pool of water has become a little larger as each form entered it. As you watch the last of your thoughts joyously entering the pool, you may sense that it is noticeably larger now, and yet it is even more still, even more deep than it was in the beginning. And the water of the pool is becoming luminous, a gentle glow as the pool expands.

As you stand there, observing the pool, noticing its stillness and deepness and the soft light glowing within it, you may find that your memories also begin to drop down to the soft moss. These memories are yours, they belong to you, they are something you own, but these memories are not you — they are something you may hold or let go of at your own pleasure.

First, all of your conscious memories, all of the memories of which you are aware, sink down to the soft moss. They take on their symbolic forms and they move across to the deep, still water, where they dissolve. And as they dissolve, you may feel their sense of release and bliss. One by one, they enter the stillness, the deepness of the flowing water, and they are gone, with a sigh of joy, and you sense them dissolve in the glowing water, still and deep, deep and still.

As the last of your conscious memories dissolves joyously in the deep, still water, your deeper, unconscious memories begin to follow them. They also fall to the earth, to the soft moss, where they take on their symbolic forms, and move across to the deep, still water. There they dissolve, dissolving in joy and relief, letting go into the water. These are things that belong to you, but they are not you, and you sense them dissolve in the luminous water, still and deep, deep and still. And the pool expands and grows lighter.

As the last of your memories dissolves into the deep stillness of the luminous water, your emotions may also begin to fall away to the soft moss. These emotions are yours, they belong to you, they are your tools, and they are something you own, but these emotions are not you — they are something you may hold or let go of at your own pleasure.

First, all of your conscious emotions, the ones of which you are aware, drop down to the soft moss. Your joys and your fears, your loves and your hates, your sorrows and your griefs, your enthusiasms and your pleasures all take on their symbolic forms, and they move across to the deep, still, luminous water, where they dissolve, and as they dissolve you feel their sense of relief and bliss. One by one, they enter the stillness and light of the deep water, and they are gone, with a sigh of joy and release.

As the last of your conscious emotions dissolves joyously in the deep, still water, your unconscious emotions, the ones you didn't even know you had, may begin to follow them. They also fall to the earth, to the soft moss, where they take on their symbolic forms, and move across to the deep, still water. There they dissolve, dissolving in joy and relief, letting go into the water. These are things that belong to you, but they are not you, and you sense them dissolve in the deep, luminous water, still and deep, deep and still. And the pool expands still further.

As the last of your emotions dissolves into the deep stillness of the water, any physical sensations you may still be feeling in your body may also begin to sink down to the soft moss. These sensations are yours, they belong to you, they are your tools, and they are something you own, but these sensations are not you — they are something you may hold or let go of at your own pleasure.

All of your physical sensations, all of the feelings in your body, drop down to the soft moss. They take on their symbolic forms, and they move across to the deep, still, glowing water, where they dissolve, and as they dissolve you feel their sense of release and bliss. Each sensation, one by one, enters the stillness, the deepness of the water, and they are gone, with a sigh of joy. And you sense them letting go, becoming one with the water, deep and still and luminous, filled with silence and serenity.

As the last of your physical sensations dissolves into the deep stillness of the water, you may notice that the pool has expanded very greatly. Much of the soft moss around the edge has dissolved, and you may notice with pleasure that the deep, still water is touching your feet.

Your feet themselves begin to dissolve and you may distantly sense their pleasure as they become one with the pool, so deep, so still. As your legs and body, your hands and arms, your neck and head dissolve, you realise that this body is yours, it belongs to you, it is your tool, and it is something you own, but it is not you — it is something you may hold or let go of at your own pleasure — and you sense its relief and joy as it becomes one with the water, deep and still and filled with light, serene and silent.

You are easily able to sense your body as it dissolves into the pool, and the pool becomes even larger, slowly and gently expanding to encompass the entire clearing, the trees and even the surrounding hills. And they melt joyously into the water. This space is your space, it is something that belongs to you and you alone, but it is not you — it is something you may create or dissolve at your own pleasure. And as the trees and the hills dissolve, you may sense their pleasure, the release of joy as they become one with the water, deep and still and luminous, filled with serenity and silence. And the pool expands still further.

As you sense the hills dissolve joyously in the expanding pool, you also may notice that the land around them is sinking gently and lovingly into the water, the towns, the roads, the animals and people each dissolving joyously into the pool. And they become one with the water, deep and still, filled with light, filled with silence.

And the entire country, the whole continent dissolves in the expanding pool, gently received into the stillness of the water, releasing a feeling of serenity and joy, as you sense them becoming one with the water. And the water is deep and still and luminous, serene and peaceful.

And the whole of the earth dissolves into the stillness of the expanding pool, gently dissolving into the deep water. You may feel her joy as you sense her becoming one with the glowing water, deep and still, filled with light, filled with silence.

And as the earth dissolves, the moon follows her into the expanding pool, gently dissolving into the deep water. You feel her joy of release as you sense her becoming one with the water, deep and still, still and deep.

And as the moon dissolves into the expanding pool, the pool expands yet further, and the sun and the planets, the entire solar system — the asteroids, the comets, and even the dust of space — begins to dissolve into the expanding pool. You may feel the joy of release as you sense it becoming one with the water, deep and still, serene and filled with peace.

As the pool expands yet further, the space between our solar system and the nearest stars, light years of space, is gently absorbed into the water with a sense of relief and joy, water more deep, more still than space itself, filled with silence, filled with serenity.

And as the luminous pool continues to expand, it gently dissolves our entire scintillating galaxy. You may feel the vast pleasurable release as uncounted stars and planets, moons and comets, pulsars and quasars, black holes, and even the dust between the stars all dissolve, dissolving gently and joyously into the expanding pool, and the water becomes lighter and brighter, yet more deep and more still, serene and filled with peace.

And as our galaxy fully dissolves into the expanding pool, all of the other galaxies, blazing brightnesses scattered the length and the breadth of the wide universe, begin to gently dissolve in the infinite pool. As they dissolve they release a sense of joy so vast, so deep that it resonates deeply within you. And the entire universe dissolves into the living water, infinitely deep and utterly still, glowing with life.

And as the farthest reaches of the universe dissolve into the infinite, luminous silence of the pool, you may sense the pool expanding in yet another way, expanding in time, and you sense the past, the long, long history of the entire universe as it dissolves blissfully into the pool, the pool which is more deep and more still than eternity itself.

And as the past dissolves and the infinite, luminous pool expands within eternity, the future also begins to gently dissolve — not only that which is to be, but also all that might or could be — the unknown, the unmanifest and the potential of the universe dissolving blissfully into the infinite and eternal pool, infinitely deep and eternally still.

And as the last of space and time dissolves into the infinite and eternal pool, you may realise that this pool is at last big enough to hold you, your Self, and you allow your Self to dissolve within it. You may allow yourself to rest within the eternal light and power, the infinite stillness and serenity of the living water.

Within that infinite and eternal living water rests all that is, that was, that might have been, or that yet might be. And within the pool, everything is still and yet it is filled with life, with the potential to be. And the pool itself is infinity and eternity. It holds all love, all compassion, all wisdom, all power, and the infinite possibilities of time and space.

Within that vast reach of infinity and eternity you become aware of your own greater Self, encompassed within that love and wisdom, compassion and power, and yet as large as all time, all space, all possibility. You are the pool, and it is you, wisdom and grace, tenderness and love.

As you experience that greater Self, you can make a choice, an affirmation of what you choose to own for yourself.

Be aware as you make your choices. Be aware of what is really you and what is just something that belongs to you as you make the choices in your life. You may make a choice about yourself at this moment if you wish. Allow this choice, this affirmation of yourself, to come from your infinite and eternal self. Let it arise within you like a bubble from the depths of the pool. As this choice arises, repeat it to yourself three times.

Allow time for the affirmation to arise and for three slow repetitions.

And then within this living water of yourSelf you may become aware of the universe, a vast wheel turning from the past to the future through space and time, deep within the living water, deep within yourSelf.

And within the living water of yourSelf you may become aware of our galaxy, filled with a multitude of dancing stars, filled with life and energy, with love and power, held within the embrace of the living water.

And within the living water of yourSelf you may become aware of our solar system, sun and planets and moons, living and growing, held within the embrace of the infinite and eternal pool.

And you become aware of the earth, our mother, alive and dancing through space with her moon, joyous in her Self, held within the embrace of the infinite and eternal pool.

And you become aware of the hills and the wood, and the small, still, deep pool where you began, held within the embrace of infinite and eternal living water of yourSelf.

And you become aware of your own body beside the small, still, deep pool where you began. This body is not you, but it is something that belongs to you in all of its complexity and glory. Its thoughts and feelings, sensations and emotions, its memories and personality are all tools that belong to you and you may use them as you will, within the embrace of all that is, of your own greater Self.

Be aware of your body, of its place on the earth, of its place in space.

Be aware of yourself as you are at this moment, at this point in time.

Be aware of yourself within the embrace of all that is, that was, and that yet might be.

This belongs to you, and this moment in time, this point in space is your place of power. In this place of power, allow your affirmation to arise again in your mind, and repeat it three times.

Allow time for three slow repetitions.

Now take a deep breath.

And another.

And another.

Become aware of your whole body, of the sense of relaxation, of peace, of energy in your body. Allow yourself to be aware of just how relaxed and energised you really are.

You have now completed the journey.

Become aware of your feet upon the floor or earth.

Flex your toes. Flex your fingers.

Another deep breath.

Become aware of the environment around you — the sounds, the scents.

Open your eyes and look gently around you.

When you feel ready, stretch and move around.

Enjoy.

The logic of the imagery

The accepted point of view of many religions (and all mystics) is that our 'real selves' are neither our bodies nor our minds. We are instead that mysterious thing sometimes called a soul. This structured imagery journey explores that concept of our souls as an integrated, undifferentiated wholeness with all that is now, has been, or might be. It also evokes the emotions we might have about releasing the things that normally limit and define us.

After consciously letting go of our limitations and definitions in this imagery, we accept a new definition of ourselves into our being, an affirmation. This can be a very powerful way of impressing a new programme upon the unconscious because of the internal state we may have reached in the journey. Pay careful attention to the principles discussed in Part X regarding affirmations when choosing your statement for use with this imagery.

An important part of the journey is its length, which gives imagers time to become very profoundly relaxed. Immersed in that tranquility, physical bodies have an opportunity to restore themselves at a very deep level and to experience an unparalleled sense of well-being. Attaining this depth is not something that everyone does easily. The ability to let go, to surrender into relaxation, while maintaining a focus of awareness, is a skill that can be acquired. To those who have not yet learned to do that fairly well, this journey may seem difficult or boring. Feelings of frustration or discomfort are counter-productive to the journey. For those less experienced, practice should be gained with shorter journeys until they are ready to handle the length and depth of concentration needed to work with the unusual concepts embodied in this imagery.

Possibility for expansion

Instead of using an affirmation in the *Pool of Water* journey, we can ask for the solution to a problem or an insight into an issue. To do this, the issue needs to be as clear in your mind as you can make it. Then there are three things to bear particularly in mind.

First, you need to be able to put your issue into a simple question or request for enlightenment — not some incredible compound question with clauses and sub-clauses and sub-sub-clauses and conditions.

Second, avoid prejudicing or confusing the response by making assumptions about the issue.

Third, leave the unconscious room to work by making your request as open-ended as possible.

A request like 'please give me the insight I most need just now into my relationship with X' is far superior to a question like 'what am I doing wrong that causes X to get so angry with me whenever we are trying to enjoy time together?' The latter question has all three faults: it is too long and too complex, it assumes that the imager is 'wrong', and it tries to address a single aspect of the relationship, which may not be the most important thing, rather than considering the issue as a whole.

This use of the imagery journey can occasionally produce some startling insights. The insights, startling or subtle, may come during the journey itself, or they may occur within a few hours or days after the journey. This is related to the technique of going to sleep after asking for a dream to explain something you need to know or understand — but you don't have to be able to remember your dreams for this imagery to work.

41. The Heart of the Matter

These journeys take us further into ourselves, and in so doing, offer us the opportunity for transformation. Fantasy and imagination are important in our lives from childhood on into extreme old age. In regard to the long-term effects of fantasy and the consequences of fantasy deprivation, Muz Murray wrote:

> Over the years, in my capacity as psychotherapist and spiritual counsellor, I have noticed that a great number of people of the unimaginative and 'dry-brained' type, with an inability to be enthralled by the mystery of existence, are very often those who

have never had bedtime stories read to them as children. Adults whose childhood imaginations have never been stimulated by flights of fancy and wondrous tales which stir the soul, usually have no inner resources to fall back on later in life when overcome by world-weariness.

. . . one of the best ways of soul-shaping is by offering children mind-stretching stories which can awaken and elevate their inner selves. Although the tales may not be remembered in later life, the magical *feeling* of them remains to colour the consciousness with wonder. Such seeds which are sown in early years tend to germinate later in more creative and visionary adults, full of ideas and positive possibilities for life. [8]

I believe fantasies are important on two levels, inner and outer. The fantasies that are read to us as children, and which we read for ourselves in later life, stimulate our imagination and expand our boundaries. The fantasies that we consciously make up or which arise from the unconscious mind are even more important. These two levels are closely connected in that the outer fantasies may inspire us and liberate our inner fantasies. Children who didn't have fairy tales and imaginative stories read to them often had parents who disapproved of the inner imaginative life, and actively encouraged the child to suppress her inner life — or at least to feel guilty about it.

One of the reasons such suppression creates long-term problems is that fantasy is the entry point for new ideas and hopes, as they move from the unconscious well of creativity into the light of the conscious mind. Virtually all new plans and hopes start as fantasies in our minds, except for those suggested by outside sources — which are immediately turned into the kind of fantasy that begins 'wouldn't it be lovely if . . .' or 'what if . . .' If that gateway is closed, life is very dry and grey, and our possibilities are extremely limited.

Fantasy is the way we try out new ideas in our minds. Long before an idea can be properly called a 'plan' it is a fantasy, turning around, taking different shapes and colours in our minds. We try it on to see if it fits us. It gives us a chance to experience, at least in part, new ways of being. Some of our fantasies will eventually become hopes, then plans, and then manifest results, but others will be discarded. Does this mean that the discarded ones were useless? A waste of time? No, because fantasies have other uses to us.

First, our fantasies can be pressure-relief valves. We can tell the boss just what we think of him. We can have an affair with anyone we fancy. We can rebel against the strictures placed upon us by society and convention and by our own choices *without incurring consequences.*

In addition to the relief of internal desire pressures, we can explore unknown ways of being. We can be rich and powerful. We can be humble and saintly. We can live in far-away lands, and experience the amazing. We can be heroes, villains, saints, and sinners — without hurting ourselves or anyone else. Many of these fantasies we would not want to come true. They would disrupt our lives in ways we might find quite distressing. In the privacy of our minds we can enjoy lifestyles that we either can't or wouldn't want to have in the 'real' world. Through fantasy we can have both — all of our heart's desires.

And another thing — the whole question of fantasy or reality can now be seen to be irrelevant, in a way. There is another way of defining reality, which is simply: *if it affects you, it's real.*

42. Would You Rather Have Chocolate?

The problem with fantasies as a tool for change and self-transformation is that some people become confused between what they only want to dream about and what they really want. I remember a man coming to me once because he was so bored with his marriage, bored with his wife, bored with his job, tempted by this wonderful, exciting woman he knew and by the possibility of running off to Hawaii with her. However, you must understand that he had been married to his wife for over twenty years and had never been unfaithful to her. He had been working at his job almost as long and had never seriously looked for another. These two facts tell us that it is probable that something more than a mere sense of inertia is holding him there.

After some imagery work and a great deal of discussion, he finally realised that he loved his wife and would be devastated if *she* left *him*. He also understood that he got a great deal of satisfaction from his job and lifestyle. What to do, then, with his wonderful, vivid fantasies of other lives? He started to write, and last I knew he was doing reasonably well as a novelist, with several books published. He is not yet on the best-seller list, but that's a fantasy that may still come true.

I have a fantasy of my own. I (or at least a part of me) would like to own nothing but two changes of clothes (one for wearing and one for washing — see how practical my fantasies are?), a towel, a tooth-brush, and a bag to carry them in. With only this to burden me (and I might even learn to do without it as well), I could travel lightly through the world, a healing, learning, sharing, meditating, serene, and merry presence, gently touching those I passed.

Of course, I wouldn't miss my warm fireplace, shelter in the rain and snow, contact with old friends, being able to pick up the phone and speak to my children, my daft cats, my garden, books, even my friendly computer — would I? You can just bet I would. But when I pass through a particularly lovely bit of countryside, when I look at the pictures in someone else's travel books, when I read about Nepal and Greece and Afghanistan, and when I think of the road to Damascus and the ancient ridgeway of England and the road to the Scottish isles — well, I can just go there in my mind. In my inner world the sun is not *too* hot, the wind not *too* cold, the people kind, the adventures just as dangerous and exciting, just as fulfilling as I could possibly wish. And I come back here, refreshed and renewed, ready to deal with another stack of paper or the laundry or whatever. And sometimes I sneak off for walks closer to home — I have to sneak because otherwise I'll have two Abyssinian cats trailing behind me, protesting that we have gone beyond our home territory and should return right now and play in our own trees.

The wonderful thing about fantasy is that you can do or be anything. If we don't like the world as it is, we can explore other possibilities. The first step in personal growth is to realise that things could be better, that we could be different. The second step is to ask ourselves, 'If I don't like it, what are my alternatives?' Then we look at all our fantasies, however strange and unlikely, because sometimes, just sometimes, a totally weird idea may contain the seed of something practical, possible, and wonderful. My daughter says that all her best ideas and intuitions start out as jokes.

In self-transformation and personal growth, as in much else, fantasy is essential. Until we have thoroughly explored something in our minds, we don't know, can't know, whether it is practical or impractical, something we desire in the real world, or just something wonderful to think about, but not wanted in our daily lives.

Life is the only game I know where you are supplied with your pieces and told to start playing — and you must figure out the rules as you play. Oh, yes, there are sets of rules available — volumes and volumes of rules. The problem is that there are so *many* of them, and some contradict others in very important ways. This induces even more muddle, as if there were not enough already.

When I was a small child, I was absolutely convinced that *I* could fly. I was certain that there was something anyone could do, a special way to hold your mind or your body or both that would enable anyone to fly. I used to dream about it, and would awaken confident that I had it right — or could at least get it right on the way down. So I jumped out of trees and off the roof. To give myself more time to get it right on the way down, I made parachutes out of my mother's best sheets, which was not exactly well received. The parachutes didn't work either.

At about the age of eight, I gave it up — not because I had become convinced that flight was impossible (I *knew* I could do it), but because I was becoming old enough to object to the bruises. I decided to wait until I really understood what was needed before I tried it again, and I rarely jump off high places now — and I make certain there is something soft, like water, underneath before I do. Have I given up? Not really, not quite, not in my heart of hearts. Others before me have settled for inventing parachutes and airplanes and hang-gliders, but I'm holding out for the real thing.

We are like this about many things in life. We are certain that, if we just find the key, the magic word, the precise right action, everything will be all right. Whatever we want will happen. People spend years married to alcoholics in the belief that, if they just get it absolutely right, the alcoholic will stop, *must* stop drinking. 'Impossible' is not a word that humans really, truly, honestly believe in, no matter how logical and rational we try to be. We believe this about life in general, as well as about specific things: there is a 'right' way, and if we find that right way, nothing will ever hurt us and the universe-god-fate will give us what we want because we've got it right, and we'll live happily ever after.

So, why do you want to change?

Is it to transform yourself or to transform the outer world?

Is it because you can't stand yourself the way you are?

Is it because you believe that what you are, in yourself, is somehow wrong?

Is it a way of punishing yourself for being who you are?

Is it because you're addicted to the excitement and drama of change — especially change that doesn't really mean that you have to actually *be* different?

Is it because you want others to love you? To approve of you?

Or perhaps it's a kind of pseudo-magical bargain you are making with the universe: I will change and be a better person, and then You will give me what I want.

Be Warned! These motivations can hold us back.

We need to come to terms with the real world, a world in which things go the way they go, people do what they do, and our choices don't always get us everything we think we want — even when we get it as 'right' as is humanly possible.

Some religions deal with this problem of bad things happening to good people by deciding that the only answer is to be without desire or attachment — because then we would never experience the pain of disappointment or loss. This doesn't feel quite right to me, but maybe I am not 'evolved' enough. It seems to me that compassion requires a certain involvement in humanity. Being unattached to outcomes or to goals is one thing, and very useful, too, but being unattached to everything seems to me to be going too far. Yes, things sometimes hurt, but this isn't necessarily the worst thing that can happen to us. Loss and grief can be powerful tools for growth.

I rather feel that, on the whole, the best that most of us can hope for is that, by learning and growing and transforming some of the weeds and thorn bushes in our inner world into fruit-bearing vines, we can make a contribution to healing the outer world, so that the whole place becomes just that little bit better for everyone. We could each become less of the earth's problem and more of its solution. This kind of growth is the purpose of these imagery journeys. They are not escapes from being human, but ways of creatively, constructively, compassionately discovering and expressing our humanity. I think we are missing the point if we try to bypass our human nature rather than fulfilling and then transcending it.

And fantasy can also take us beyond the bounds of the mundane world's understanding of 'possible' into the farthest reaches of the mind and the unknown universe, expanding our conception of what is possible.

On the other hand, if we just want to feel better, rather than going to all the trouble and thought involved in self-transformation, I recommend chocolate. It contains substances similar to those we manufacture internally when we genuinely feel good, and although both fattening and mildly habit-forming, chocolate *is* legal.

Review

By now, I would hope that the use of freeform imagery would have become a daily habit. All you need to do when you have a question about anything or anyone is to ask yourself what symbolic image represents them. And then interpret it.

Are your image directory and journal (including dreams) up to date?

What do you know about yourself that you didn't know when you began this book?

Review your past imagery journeys for agreements made and gifts received. How do you stand with keeping your agreements? Is there anything you need to discuss with your Rebel? Are there any agreements you need to discuss with the aspect of yourself with whom you originally made them?

Part XII

The Meeting Place

Little particles of inspiration sleet through the universe all the time travelling through the densest matter in the same way that a neutrino passes through a candyfloss haystack, and most of them miss.

Even worse, most of the ones that hit the exact cerebral target hit the wrong one.

For example, the weird dream about a lead doughnut on a mile-high gantry, which in the right mind would have been the catalyst for the invention of repressed-gravitational electricity generation . . . was in fact had by a small and bewildered duck.

. . . Why the gods allow this sort of thing to continue is a mystery.

— *Terry Pratchett*
in Sourcery

43. Two Travellers

As we travel through our inner worlds, everything is seen by the twins in our minds, the two basic modes we have for processing information. The *analytical* twin uses a kind of *linear thinking* that deals with one thing at a time. She perceives things as separated from one another. She is interested in *detail* and *fact*. She is largely *verbal*, not visual, and she doesn't *think* that she understands something unless she can *describe* it in a *logical, sequential, rational* way. She believes in *cause and effect*. She also likes to make *judgments* about right and wrong, better and worse. She is interested in *classifying* things, *labelling* and *defining* them. When she looks at a forest, she *counts* different kinds of trees. When she looks at a mountain, she counts vertical feet and labels types of rock. She likes word games and puzzles and the rules of logic. She accepts *logic* as proof.

The analytic twin values things for *usefulness, realism, and conformity* to an accepted norm. She accepts *authority* and is comfortable with *hierarchy*, which gives her a structure for her *judgments*. She likes to be in *control* and to have well defined *boundaries*. She may be frightened by things she can't name, categorise, and control. She has *ideologies*. She can't establish priorities effectively (although she thinks it can) because she gives most importance to whatever is immediately in front of her. She is very conscious of time and the sequential tic-toc of the clock, but because of her difficulties with priorities and with seeing relationships, she is often late.

This twin does not understand or see the point in art or music unless she can analyse them mathematically or logically — or judge them by the *sets of rules* developed by analytic mode thinking. She does not understand that a good painting or piece of music should grab you just under the heart — and that, if it doesn't do that, it isn't good art, no matter how clever or inventive or technically 'correct' it may be. She might describe a wine as 'witty' or 'presumptuous' or some other *non-sensory* word, usually pertaining to verbal processes. This twin is essential to function effectively in a *technological* society. She is not creative. Some authorities say this mode is the natural function of the left hemisphere of brain — and others disagree.

The other twin could be described as *associative* because he connects things to other things. He uses words to make *metaphors, similes, and puns*, finding *similarities* and *connections* between unlike things. He sees the *whole* of things — and perhaps the holiness as well. He sees *patterns* and thinks *globally*. He largely works with *images, sensations,* and *emotions,* and he communicates through *body language* and *gestures.* He doesn't *feel* he can understand something unless he can *see the whole* of it. He needs a *sense of meaning or purpose* to fit facts and details into. He is aware of *spatial relationships*. For this twin, facts and details are like the pieces of a jigsaw — without meaning in themselves until enough of them have come together to give a *sense* of the *whole*. He either likes something or he doesn't, based on a *gut-level, emotional* response — or on associations with previous experience. He accepts *experience* as proof.

The associative twin values things for the *feelings* they evoke. He recognises and values *sensual perceptions*. Because he responds to feeling and cannot always verbally articulate why he is doing something, he says he 'just has a feeling' that guides him, annoying the analytic twin, who wants a logical, factual reason. He is more . interested in *relationships* between people than in things or facts. When he looks at a forest or a mountain, he responds by saying something like 'Wow!' and feeling a *sense of awe and beauty*. He can't count and may be confused by numbers. Because he can't understand linear mode judgments of right and wrong, good and bad, and because he often *cannot articulate* his sense of *appropriateness*, he cannot defend his own feeling-based judgment, and often fears he is wrong. Because he doesn't use words well, he may often be over-persuaded by the articulate analytic twin.

The associative twin likes *fantasy* and believes in fairies, Mother Nature, and/or God (or gods and goddesses). He is fascinated by colour and form and movement. He has no concept of priorities and does not know what to do first or next. This mode is essential to appreciate a painting or a piece of music or to grasp the essential meaning of the theory of relativity. He is not creative. Some authorities say this mode is the natural function of the right hemisphere of the brain — and others disagree.

The twins see time differently. The analytic mode views time as a rigid, sequential flow, divided into pieces which follow one another with great rapidity, an endless succession of *now*, dividing the past from the future. The associative twin sees time as variable — moments may seem like hours and hours may seem like moments — or he may experience a sense of timelessness.

The associative twin does reason, but unlike the reasoning of the analytic mode, he does not do so linearly. He finds connections and sees relationships and interactions. In working a 1000 piece jigsaw puzzle, the analytic twin divides the pieces into separate groups, sorting them by colour. She picks out all of the edge pieces, and she probably starts with the corners. However, it is the associative twin that holds the overall pattern in his grasp. Together they see that *this* shape fits into the pattern *here*.

Both modes *think*, both modes *reason*, but they do so in very different ways. In speaking of the associative mode, Jean Houston writes of "a patterning of ideas and images gathered up in a simultaneous constellation." She adds, "And the brain can process millions of images in microseconds, and images seem to have their own subjective time not related to serial clock time, a great deal can be experienced in imagistic thinking in shorter times and in ways that evidently cannot occur in verbal thinking." [9] The associative twin thinks globally. He is like someone who is capable of being everywhere and anywhere, simply by focusing his attention *here* or *there* — so different from the analytic mode, which must go from *here* to *there* one precise step at a time. This quality of instantaneousness is why the associative twin perceives time differently.

By now, you may be bouncing up and down in your chair, saying, "She's got it backwards! Obviously the analytic twin is male and the associative twin female." The is the stereotypical view in our culture, but it isn't true. Modes of thinking are not genetically gender specific. All of us have and can use both modes, but in most of us one or the other dominates.

In our technological society, the analytic mode is more highly valued, especially in the education of men. Women have had to fight for the right to that kind of an education because of cultural prejudices. It is more acceptable to be a scientist than an artist — and usually better paid as well. Houston writes, "The strong emphasis on verbal-linear processes appears to have grown out of the medieval scholastic system of educating clerics in such a way as to weed out the high-sensory types from the more austere students given to conceptual, verbal thought (who would be less trouble in the monastery). This was fine in medieval Catholicism, but its long arm is still felt in modern education to the detriment of the many natural nonverbal thinkers."[10]

This exaggerated valuing of one mode of thinking over the other has had rather dire consequences for us — both as individuals and as a community. Our educational system works to develop the analytic mode *at the expense of* the associative mode. Reading, writing, and arithmetic are taught analytically, not associatively. Predominately associative mode activities such as music or art often are only acceptable to contemporary education if they are taught within a framework of analytic rules and judgments — even though the analytic mode cannot actually understand the real value of the arts at all. This means that predominately associative thinkers are taught to think in the mode in which they are less competent — like the teaching of left-handed people to write with their right hands. This is something which we now know to be quite damaging to left-handers. Left-handed people are often naturally associative thinkers, who are being handicapped and frustrated on both the physical and the mental levels.

I was listening to the radio the other day and heard an excellent example of a strongly analytic man's response to a culture in which associative mode thinking is much more commonly used and more highly valued than in ours. He had just returned from Russia and was asked for his impressions of the Russian people. He started off by saying they were very open, very friendly, but went on to say that they made him feel acutely uncomfortable. "They read one's face," he said. "They watch one closely while one converses with them, as if they can see one's emotions written upon one's face. One feels that they know more about what one is feeling than one knows oneself." Then he added, with real horror in his voice, "And they *touch* one another and even oneself."

Typically, an analytic mode thinker, especially one who has learned to suppress associative mode, finds expression through body language and communication through touch unacceptable, even frightening. But, on the other hand, the strongly associative mode thinker may find communication through words difficult and confusing. Working with a couple I heard the following exchange:

"I tell her and tell her I love her, but she never says it to me."

"Well, I show him all the time how much I love him. I sit close to him and cuddle him, but he just backs off because he doesn't really love me."

"But I keep telling you and telling you I *do* love you and you never tell me!"

"That's only words. If you really loved me you'd cuddle me and *show* me you do."

Guess who is strongly analytic mode and who is strongly associative? It took a very long discussion before they really understood that they simply had a communication problem caused by their differing modes of thinking — and that, if they really wanted to communicate, they each had to do so in a way that seemed real to the other. He had to hug her when he said 'I love you' in order for her to *really feel* it, and she had to say 'I love you' when she hugged him in order for him to *really hear* it. And they had to learn to watch and to listen *consciously* for communications in the other's preferred mode.

He came back later and said, "I've learned something I wouldn't have believed. Two people can have completely different ideas about something and *both be right*." That was his suppressed associative mode speaking at last.

If one person is expressing himself in analytic mode and the other in associative mode, communication often fails to take place. In an ideal world, every child would be taught the mode that he could best understand — and would be gently led to understand and use the other mode as he developed. If we did this, more and more people would develop the capacity to think holistically, thus gradually changing the value system of our culture into one where practicality, aesthetics, and spirituality would balance in a more harmonious whole.

There are so many things that neither twin can do alone. They can't establish priorities, think intuitively, have real insight, or apprehend any concept in its entirety. They cannot create. When these two modes combine, we invoke the *holistic* mode. Then we see inter-relationships, and we understand meaning. Facts and feelings combine and recombine into new ways of being. Used together, they are creative, and in this creativity we find meaning and purpose to life. We feel whole, integrated, and we become able to access our own inner power, and we grow to be at peace with ourselves.

Associative-analytic balance is essential if we are to discover and expand our creativity and fulfil our potential. Working, as we have been, with a combination of painting and writing helps to integrate and enhance these two functions of our brains. Only through such integration can we perform the magic that makes us into who we were meant to be.

There are a variety of ways to enhance the integrative process. A person with a dominant analytic mode needs to learn to allow the associative twin to draw and paint like a child. She needs to learn to pay more attention to the associative mode's understanding of the physical senses and their input, to dance and move, and to play. On the other hand, once a person with a dominant associative mode has properly learned to use his strongest mode, he needs to learn to listen to the analytic mode, to apply the rules of logic, and to use sequential

thinking as a *supplement to* associative thinking — not *instead of* it, as our present established educational system would have us do.
And of course, imagery work can also help.

44. Travelling Together

The following imagery journey is designed to help to integrate left brain-right brain, forebrain-hindbrain, and analytic-associative modes.

When doing the imagery journey below for the first time, there are three things you need to know:

1. Ignore the markings >>>*return*> and <<<*return*<.
2. Leave out anything you see printed within (parentheses).
3. Treat the words in *italics* like any other words.

These things are explained in *Possibilities for expansion*, following the imagery, but the first time you do the imagery, just follow the above instructions — otherwise chaos will result.

The pace of this imagery is unlike that of most other journeys. Do the relaxation in the beginning slowly, allowing time for the sensations to be experienced and the relaxation to take place. Begin the imagery at that pace, but very gradually increase the speed. The imager should have to work to keep up by the time you reach the end of the main body of the imagery, where it is marked <<<*return*<. Slow down to do the ending, giving everyone enough time to come back into normal consciousness.

Caution: If you have epilepsy or another disorder of the brain or nervous system, the following exercise may not be for you. There are various possibilities. You can skip this imagery altogether. You can do the imagery, but leave out the parts to do with light/energy. Or you can proceed with caution. You will have to be the best judge, but my advice would be when in doubt, don't.

Approximate travel time: 30 minutes (one round) plus 15 minutes for the first additional round.

ROUND THE WORLD IN 15 MINUTES

First, be seated comfortably in an upright position, with your spine and neck erect and relaxed. Take a couple of deep breaths. We are about to begin an imagery exercise on integrating some of the different functions of the brain.

Now, focus your awareness on your feet — the toes, the soles, the arches, all the bones and muscles and tendons. Just allow them to relax, to be soft, resting on the floor. Let any tension or strain in your feet drain down and out through the soles and into the earth, while you take another deep breath, inhaling — and exhaling.

Lift your awareness up into your ankles and lower legs, and allow any tension or strain in your lower legs and ankles to drain down through your feet and into the earth, as you take another deep breath, inhaling — and exhaling.

Let your awareness rise up into your thighs. Notice how they feel, and then let go of any tension or strain in your thighs. Allow it to flow down through your legs and feet, and into the earth, as you take another deep breath, inhaling — and exhaling.

Next, your awareness rises up to your hips and pelvis, your lower back. Observe the feelings there, and allow any feelings you don't need or want to flow down, down through your legs and feet, down into the earth, as you take another deep breath, inhaling — and exhaling.

And your awareness rises up into your abdomen and the small of your back. What are you feeling there? You may allow any feelings you don't need or want to flow down, down through your hips and pelvis, down through your legs and feet, down into the earth, as you take another deep breath, inhaling — and exhaling.

Your awareness continues rising, rising up into your chest. Feel the motion of your chest as you breathe. You may even be able to feel your heart beat. Notice the feeling in your chest and shoulders and arms. If there are any feelings you don't need or want, you can simply allow them to flow down, down through your abdomen, down through your pelvis, down through your legs and feet, down into the earth, as you take another deep breath, inhaling — and exhaling.

Your awareness rises further, up into your head. Notice the way your head balances on your neck. Allow it to be erect and well-balanced, so that your neck is comfortable. If there are any feelings in your head, your scalp, your face, or your neck that you don't need or want, allow these feelings to drain away, flowing down through your neck, down through your chest and abdomen, down through your pelvis, down through your legs and feet, down into the earth, as you take another deep breath, inhaling — and slowly exhaling.

Allow your awareness to rest in the center of your head.

I'd like you to imagine that you are looking at the inside of your eyelids.

Be aware of your left eye.

And now be aware of your right eye.

Become aware of the optic nerve that goes from your right eye to the back of your brain on the left side. Move your awareness along that nerve from the back of the eye to the back of the brain. Be aware of that part of your brain, in the back of your head, at the level of your eyes.

Now bring your awareness to your left eye. And slowly move your awareness to the optic nerve that goes from the left eye to the back of your brain on the right side. Become aware of that part of your brain.

Let yourself become aware of both optic nerves. They run from the back of the eyes, and crossing one another, they carry visual impulses into the opposite sides of the back of the brain. Notice the point where the nerve cables cross. Let your awareness rest for a moment at that point.

Allow your awareness to shift to the left side of your brain. How does it feel? Do any spontaneous words or images or feelings come to you as you focus on your left brain?

Now let your awareness move to the right side of your brain. How does it feel? Do any spontaneous images or feelings or words come to you as you rest your awareness in your right brain?

Let your awareness move to your forebrain, just behind your forehead. How does it feel? Do any spontaneous images or feelings or words come to you as you rest your awareness in your forebrain?

And now move into the midbrain. What do you find here? How does it feel? What comes to you as you rest your awareness in your midbrain?

And now move into the oldest part of the brain, the hindbrain, the brain stem where it arises from the atlas vertebra, which holds and supports the world of the head. How does it feel here? What comes to you as you rest your awareness in the hindbrain?

Allow your awareness to move back to the center, and rest there a moment. We are going to begin exploring some images, which will appear alternately in the left and the right chambers of your brain. As I speak, you can simply allow the image to arise in your mind. If an image fails to come, just go on to the next, and keep up with me. Just allow the images to arise naturally, without effort.

In the chamber of your right brain, I'd like you to imagine a frog. In the chamber of your left brain, I'd like you to imagine a male voice singing.

>>>restart>

In your right brain, a silver harp with five strings. In the left, a golden crown with five rubies.

In the right, a clear blue sky. In the left, the taste of honey.

In the right, the feeling of running, in the left the number three with little legs, dancing.

In the right, an enormous formal flower garden with a topiary bush, shaped like a pig. The bush needs trimming. In the left, an orchestra playing the 1812 Overture. One trumpet is off key.

In the right, three bears, discussing politics and eating porridge. In the left, an open door, leading to the land of unicorns and smelling of honeysuckle.

In the right a wedding in a cathedral, with sun shining through the stained glass, all of the statues singing Hallelujah, and the bride's mother crying. In the left, a football game, with the spectators howling with rage while the referee runs away with the ball.

In the right, all the stars of the galaxy, singing. In the left, a caterpillar eating a rose, crunching.

In your right brain begin saying the alphabet. When you reach the letter C, begin counting in your left brain. Count and say the alphabet simultaneously in whatever way seems best to you.

Let go of that image. In the right, a white candle with a multicoloured flame. In the left, a vast, silent waterfall.

In the right, the taste of a lemon. In the left, the sensation of playing a piano.

In the right, *a vast plain with a single hill in the distance* (a mountain valley surrounded by sharp, icy peaks). In the left, *the hill itself, with a single tree on top* (in the valley, a farm with four fields). In the right, *a branch on the tree* (the house in the center of the four fields). In the left, *a nest on the branch* (a window, with a windowbox full of flowers). In the right, *a bird in the nest* (a tiny blue flower with a golden center). In the left, *the eye of the bird* (a dewdrop on the petal of the flower). In both sides, *your own eyes reflected in the bird's eye* (your own eyes reflected in the dewdrop).

In the center of your brain, a shining white statue two inches high. The statue begins to contract, shrinking smaller and smaller, until it becomes a pinpoint of brilliant, coruscating white light in the very center of your brain. The light begins to pulse slowly, expanding and then contracting back down to the pinpoint of light. With each pulse, the light expands further, until it fills your entire head, contracting back down to the point between each expansion. When it fills your entire head, feel the sensation on the inside of your skull.

Let the light contract again, fading, winking out.

In your right brain, your own face at the age of three. In the left, the place you now live.

In the right, a tiny, gnarled, ancient tree on a windswept rocky ledge. In the left, a lush field, full of ripe corn.

In the right, a peaceful pastoral scene, horses grazing in a field, with the hedgerows in bloom. The sky is blue and the sun is warm. In the left, smell the scent of the sun-warmed hay. Allow that scent to expand into the right, filling the scene with the scent of the hay.

In the right, the same scene, warm and bright, the horses moving lazily in the sun. In the left, a gentle breeze. Allow the breeze to move into the scene on the right, gently moving the grass and the manes and tails of the horses.

In the right, the same scene, warm and bright, horses, grass and flowers gently moving in the soft breeze. In the left, a single daisy with a bright golden center. Allow the golden pollen from the center of the daisy to drift across the scene in the right brain, filling it with golden light.

In the right, the same scene, expanding to the left. Both sides, filled with the golden light, the scent of the sun-warmed hay, the movement of the gentle breeze. The horses shimmer in the light. A stallion gallops to the center, tosses back his head, rears, and neighs at the sun.

The scene disappears, and in the center of the darkness, you hear the distant sound of a wolf singing to the moon.

In the right, the feel of the wolf's fur against your fingers. In the left, the sensation of your own body, dancing slowly.

In the right, *the ocean, seen from outer space* (the vast sweep of the sky, electric blue with strong white clouds). In the left, *the ocean, with gentle waves* (between the clouds, a tiny dark speck). In the right, *a sailboat on the ocean* (an eagle flying between the clouds). In the left, *a strong man, with shining golden hair, at the helm of the boat* (a soaring eagle, with feathers shining in the light of the sun). In the right, *the bright face of the man* (the gleaming, feathered head of the bird). In the left, *the man's blue eyes* (the golden eye of the eagle). In both sides, *his eyes, with both of your eyes reflected in his* (the eye, with both of your eyes reflected in it).

With both eyes, in the center of your head, see a faint, tiny blue light. As you watch, the blue light grows brighter, and rises to the inside of the crown of your head. When it reaches the crown, it begins to sparkle in all colours. Moving slowly, the light follows the inside of the skull, first to your forehead, where it pauses, and then arching up and back and down to the base of the skull, the brain stem, the top of the spinal cord. The light sparkles and fizzes as it moves all the way down your spinal cord to the sacrum and the coccyx, the base of the spine. Let it rest a moment at the base of the spine.

Then the many-coloured light rises again, growing brighter and brighter as it comes up the spine, becoming brilliant as it reaches the base of the skull. Radiant as a sun rising, it fills the skull and the brain with multi-hued light. Notice the feeling of the light on the inside of your skull.

The light fades, and there is darkness and silence in both sides of the brain.

In the right, a single atom comes into being, radiating a faint silver light. In the left, a single atom, radiating a faint golden light. Both atoms move to the center of your brain and join, forming a faint light that has the qualities of both gold and silver. When you look more closely at the tiny atom, you see that it is a spiral galaxy, rotating, seen from a vast distance. As the galaxy expands, you can see that it is on a horizontal plane, level with your eyes. The galaxy continues to expand, growing brighter as it does, rotating slowly until it almost touches the inside of your skull.

There is a great, scintillating mass of suns at the center of the galaxy and uncountable billions of suns, planets, moons, comets rotating in the spiral arms, all rotating within your head on a horizontal plane. As the stars grow even brighter, the galaxy spins faster and faster, its outermost stars just brushing the inside of your skull.

As you sense the power and the immensity of the galaxy, it begins to tilt, the left side rising and the right falling, until it is spinning vertically in your head. The same tilt continues on around, spinning and spinning, until the galaxy once again rests in the position in which it began.

And now the galaxy begins to tilt in the opposite direction, the left falling and the right rising. Again, it becomes vertical, and then continues on around until it returns to its starting position, brighter than ever.

The galaxy continues to expand, extending farther and farther, filling the solar system, continuing to expand to the farthest reaches of time and space. Spinning majestically through all time, all space, the galaxy moves with grandeur and precision.

Now once again, see the tiny galaxy in the center of your mind, small and bright and distant, becoming smaller and smaller in the distance, until you cannot see it at all.

<<<return<

As it disappears, you hear a single plangent sound, as of a perfect silver bell being struck, at the center of your mind. You may be able to feel the vibrations of that ringing note in the bones of your skull.

Be aware of your breath. Let your breath fill your head, and as you exhale be aware of the feeling in your head.

Be aware of your breath in your chest. In your abdomen. Be aware of your pelvis, sitting. Be aware of your legs, your ankles, your feet.

How do you feel in your body? In your mind? In your energy?

Flex your toes. Flex your fingers.

Take a couple of deep breaths.

Open your eyes.
When you are ready, stand up and stretch.

The logic of the imagery

The imagery incorporates the senses of sight, touch, scent, taste, and hearing. It evokes the kinesthetic sense of movement and of the body's position in space. It touches into memory and imagination. In doing this it activates the parts of the brain concerned with these functions. In switching from side to side and occasionally using both simultaneously, we are focusing attention on the integrated use of the two sides of the brain. We are also energising the brain by working with light which is a metaphor for energy.

Working with the imagery

Make an impressionistic painting of the *sensation* you had inside your head when you completed the imagery. If you like, make a second painting of the sensation you had at another point during the journey — you choose which. Use the tools you have learned for interpreting these paintings. What do they tell you about the effect of the imagery upon you? Do they tell you anything about yourself that you didn't already know?

You want this imagery to 'stretch' you. Ideally, at the end of it, you want to feel as if you really have been doing something — perhaps a sensation not altogether unlike exercising a muscle that is unaccustomed to hard work.

When you first do this imagery, just go through it once, and then stop and think about it. If you found it difficult for any reason, continue to practise it once through each time, until it becomes easier. Some people, particularly those who are strongly one-sided, may find a substantial difference between the response of the left and right sides. Most people will experience odd sensations (which we will discuss in Chapter 49) at one time or another. This is all quite normal. It merely tells you that something is actually happening, just as it is supposed to do.

If you feel really tired at the end instead of energised, it may be an indication that you are trying too hard and need to remember to simply *allow* the images to arise, not to force them. If that doesn't work, I would suggest shortening the journey by deleting the section on the hill, tree, and bird and the one on the statue, which follows the bird.

What differences, if any, did you notice between the feelings and experiences of the two sides of your brain? Was either side easier to work with than the other? How did you feel in your body, in your head, in your energy when you finished the imagery?

Possibilities for expansion

When you find that the imagery is (or has become) fairly easy, and that you do not feel 'stretched' by it, you can lengthen it, until you feel as if you had been really working at something — which you have. The easiest way to lengthen the travel time is to repeat part of the imagery. It is not necessary, or even advisable to go all the way to the end and then begin at the beginning again. To make this a little easier, I have marked the imagery for you. When you come to the place marked <<<return<, go back to the place marked >>>restart> and continue from there. You can go through the imagery as many times as needed, cycling back through the main body of the imagery each time.

When doing repeats, you may want to do the first round slowly, speeding up with each succeeding round. The fastest round should be read through at a normal speaking rate.

I have also suggested alternate images, which you may want to use the second time through, to give yourself a little variety. These are in parentheses, and they are meant to replace the images in italics. You can also invent other image sequences that work the same way to make it even more interesting for the imagers (and you). As you probably realised in the imagery journey, these sequences take the imager from a very long view to a very short one, switching from one side to another, and then to a unified close view.

You may also make substitutions where there is a sequence of unconnected images like those just after >>>restart>. Use similar images for those in the script — that is, a scent for a scent, movement for movement, sound for sound, et cetera.

Do not change the sections that involve the use of light/energy.

45. The Alchemist's Tower

Running through this book there is the theme of the Seeker, the Magician, who quests within his inner world and discovers the magical being there. His quest takes place in a landscape, the world of Sun–over–Mountain. In writing something as long as a book, I found it helpful to use an old alchemical imagery memory technique to keep track of what I was saying and to see/remember how one part related to another. Hopefully, my having used this technique here and there in the book will be helpful to you, as well, in working with these concepts. With luck, it will aid you in using the information as stepping stones to further insight and understanding.

Many people use this particular technique in various ways, but not all of them are conscious of its purpose and full possibilities. Nor are they aware that it is a part of the alchemical tradition. A room, a building, a garden or any other place can by used, but it helps to have a well-defined and memorable layout and design.

The first step of the alchemical memory game is to create a mental setting. Either an imaginary place or a familiar, real one can be used. After the setting has been established, the concepts or data we wish to remember are attached to things in the scene. This is then refined further, in as much detail as is needed. In this memory game, images are used to remind us of the relevant concept or datum, as a key unlocks a door. This technique can be used to store any kind of knowledge.

For example, we could create a mental laboratory to store chemistry formulas — the Bunsen burner reminds us of one formula, the old-fashioned balance scale reminds us of another, the rack of test tubes holds one in each tube, a chart on the wall by the door holds another, and so on. The greater the association between the thing to be remembered and the 'storage place' the easier it is to remember, but such an association is not essential in this process. It may also be helpful, if the information stored has a built-in sequential nature, to place it around the memory space in order, so that you come to each thing in its proper turn as you travel around the space. This exercise obviously aids our memory and helps us to develop even greater memory skills — but it also can do much more.

It is believed that the analytic mode operates the short-term memory, while long-term memory is the province of the associative mode. Placing the concepts or things to be remembered in the mind by using associative techniques logically would make it easier for the associative mode to remember them. This is why symbols are often more vividly remembered than abstract concepts.

When a person has used the memory game for a while and has become proficient with it, interesting things begin to happen. Things may shift about while we are not looking. The Bunsen burner might move itself to sit beside the test tubes. This is an action of the unconscious, the meta-rational mind, operating associatively. It is trying to bring to our awareness a connection (which we may not previously have seen) between two or more things. This is a process of discovery, of making better and more extensive use of the knowledge we have.

Symbols may also appear in such a scene spontaneously, representing things that we have forgotten, or even information that has always been below the surface of conscious awareness. These symbols may carry their own meaning just as clearly as the symbols we have consciously placed in that area. Because they really are our own inner knowledge, we can recognise and understand them, and they, too, can form surprising connections.

If a great deal of our knowledge is stored in this way, in one continuing and interconnected space, quite important realisations and juxtapositions may occur. Under the double impetus of intently focused concentration and the experience of a mental breakthrough, we may even make the big breakthrough out of 'mental' space into creativity and even to spiritual realisation.

In writing both this book and *Moon over Water*, the use of this technique helped me to see things from different angles, finding new insights and making new realisations as my symbols took on lives of their own and formed unexpected relationships. I hope it will help the readers to do the same, perhaps seeing things that I didn't see and finding their own insights.

And apart from all that, using this technique is fun. But it takes practice to keep it all straight.

The alchemical memory game makes use of two modes of thinking — analytical and associative, combined holistically — and from the combination of the two, creativity is evoked.

46. Speaking the Language: Puns

The unconscious has a sense of humour, which it presents in both dreams and imagery work. It seems particularly fond of visual puns, and sometimes even verbal ones.

One imager, talking to his Rebel, was asked to dress in yellow. He couldn't make sense of this, and even though the Rebel was insistent, he kept refusing. Finally, he agreed to wear yellow socks. In discussing the journey later, he realised that yellow symbolised caution — as in a yellow or orange traffic light. We say that someone is 'yellow' when we feel that they are overcautious or cowardly. The Rebel was simply trying to surround an impulsive person with caution, but it was willing to settle for just the feet, for going more slowly and not rushing into things. Since the imager was notoriously impetuous and quick, this seemed a reasonable request.

Someone else, on a *Walk In The Forest*, found his container by the roadside to be a box with a sheep in it. When questioned more closely, he said it was a 'ewe'. Another member of the group asked, "Do you feel that 'you' are in a box then?" Which, of course, turned out to be the explanation.

An Advisor called himself 'The All' and the imager objected to this on the grounds that it sounded pretentious. The Advisor responded, "Then call me Max." It was only when the group was discussing their imagery that the imager realised that 'max' is slang for the maximum — or The All.

Watching for puns is an art. People who like making puns themselves or like to play with words are more likely to spot them. All I can suggest is that you keep your eyes and ears open for significant weirdnesses, and remember that the associative twin likes its little jokes — which may have much meaning.

We have been talking about the division between the associative and the analytical parts of our minds, but there is another division as well — the rational and the archetypal — and creativity demands a balance between these aspects as well.

Review

Are you using imagery for healing whenever you need it? Are you well enough in tune with your inner Healer that you anticipate your needs before they become critical?

How are you getting on with your affirmations? And with the *Pool of Water* imagery? Can you see changes in yourself that may stem from the use of affirmations and/or that imagery?

Make an impressionistic painting of who and what you were when you began this book and one of yourself now. Don't think about this before you do the paintings — let them be as spontaneous as possible. What do they tell you?

Part XIII

In the Company of the Gods

Wizards don't believe in gods in the same way that most people don't find it necessary to believe in, say, tables. They know they're there, they know they're there for a purpose, they'd probably agree that they have a place in a well-organised universe, but they wouldn't see the point in believing, *of going around saying, "O great table, without whom we are as naught". Anyway, either the gods are there whether you believe or not, or exist only as a function of the belief, so either way you might as well ignore the whole business and, as it were, eat off your knees.*

- *Terry Pratchett*
in **Reaper Man**

47. The Home of the Gods

The gods live on the far slopes of our mountains and in the deep valleys. Below them there is only the one sea, from which we all come. These gods are the archetypal energies and ectypal images who dwell within us in the deep unconscious. We have already briefly discussed archetypes and ectypes back in Part III, but let's take a deeper look at them and consider their role in the processes of creation and transformation.

As mentioned before, the dictionary definition of *archetype* is 'the original pattern from which copies are made' — a prototype. The original definition of *ectype* is 'an impression of a seal or medal' but it also has come to mean 'of the nature of a copy' as well.

In Platonic philosophy, *archetypal* is applied to the idea or form as present in the divine mind before the creation of the *ectypal* object. We are able, Plato believed, to comprehend intellectually such archetypes, partly by considering the *ectypal* object, the material thing-in-the-world. Thus, there would be an ideal, archetypal Tree in the divine mind, and all of the trees in the world are ectypes of that Tree, variations on a theme of Treeness.

This is contrasted by the view of C. G. Jung, who saw humans minds as a series of layers or levels of consciousness. Three of these levels are ordinary consciousness, the personal unconscious, and the collective unconscious. (There are others as well, but we'll leave them out of this discussion.) The collective unconscious, he felt, is the deepest of the three, and it is common to all people. It is hidden below the personal unconscious, which contains our individual pasts, the experiences, feelings, and ideas that we have forgotten or repressed.

Jung believed that the collective unconscious is the storage place for the past of the entire human species and that individuals are influenced by both the personal unconscious, and the collective unconscious, the heritage of humanity. Much of this heritage, he said, takes the form of archetypes, myth-figures like the Wise Old Man, the Great Mother, the Trickster, the Hero, and others, and these archetypes are universal among humans.

Jung did not agree with the Freudian view that the unconscious was simply a place where we hid unpleasant experiences and parts of ourselves that we did not approve of. He believed that it was the foundation of our being — the source of our truest hopes and aspirations. In fact, he thought that many of our emotional problems and mental suffering stem from the fact that we, for the most part, have lost touch with this deep collective unconscious.

As we learn and grow, we overlay the myth-making substratum of the collective unconscious with the personal unconscious material, the individual's experience of life. This also means that, as we grow older, we increasingly tend to lose touch with the collective unconscious, as it becomes buried under the layers of the personal unconscious. As children we have a sense of magic and mystery, of purpose and meaning. As we have already discussed, how much of it we lose depends on how great or little a part fantasy and imagination play in our lives.

In Jung's view, the collective unconscious is the level of the psyche that has the task of making sense of our experiences and giving meaning to our existence. A great deal of his work with clients focused on working with archetypes and the archetypal images, ectypes. He felt these were most easily accessed through painting and imagery work, both dreams and waking imagery, which he called *active imagination*.

However, the modern emphasis, for many Jungian analysts, is on analysis — words and rational mental processing (analytic mode) of the 'irrational' matter of the unconscious. I don't think Jung meant it to be like that. He, himself, seemed to regard dreams and paintings as the important matter — the analytical words were their servants, not their masters. Jung placed a great emphasis on the use of associative mode interpretative techniques. Perhaps the mistake was in calling the process 'analysis' instead of something like 'integration' or 'reconciliation' or 'unification' or 'attunement' or something else that acknowledges the essentially balancing and integrative function of the process. Whatever the cause, some Jungian analysts now seem to regard the intuitive (associative mode) as an 'inferior' function, and there seems to be almost an underlying suspicion of the activities of the unconscious. This creates a problem, an imbalance, where we are only using half of our minds to understand ourselves.

Archetypal psychology goes the other way. The archetypal level of consciousness is considered to be of primary importance, and analysis (the analytic mode of thinking) is viewed with suspicion. There seems to be a role-reversal taking place, where the 'superior' analytic mode becomes the 'inferior' and the 'inferior' intuitive mode becomes the 'superior', the preferred way of processing inner world activities. This seems to be the old problem, imbalance, in the opposing direction.

So here we see three views of archetypes: Plato's view that they were prototypes in the divine mind, Jung's view that they are an integral and powerful part of the collective unconscious of all humans, and statements like Alan Bleakley's that, "Archetypal psychology stresses that an archetype is not a thing, but a move one makes; and an image is not a thing, but a way of seeing, of re-visioning."[11]

Psychology is an old art and a young science — if it is a science at all. For a while, when psychologists first began thinking of themselves as real scientists, they tried to abolish the concept of consciousness and to replace it with a kind of mechanical process. Feelings were said to be *caused by* certain glandular processes in reaction to pressures from the outer world. 'Soul' and 'spirit' did not exist; there was no such thing as 'mind' or 'consciousness' — only brains, nervous systems, and glands. This point of view is still prominent. James Hillman writes about Freud and Jung, "For their ideas, as *idees-forces*, are still a scandal today, academically unacceptable, a *bouleversement* of the vested interests of mulish minds, who refuse the reality of the psyche as the primary human fact."[12]

We basically have two branches of psychology — the machine model and the consciousness model. When I first went to college to study psychology, the predominant model was the machine — rats in mazes, behaviourism, physiology, neurology, hormones, glandular secretions, and Pavlovian dogs. The information gained by this kind of scientific experimentation is valid — but what is not valid is the assumption that the machine is all there is. In fact, we might almost say that the machine-model is only valid when we are unconscious, when we are sleepwalking through life, and even then it may be tripped up by other levels of consciousness.

Since then, psychology has grown up a bit with the recognition of something that is not entirely explicable by our present physiological knowledge — consciousness. However, the acceptance of consciousness opens up a whole can of worms. If you have consciousness, then presumably you can have unconsciousness and perhaps even super-consciousness. How do you decide what is and what is not? Can an object (or is it a process?) — mind — possibly investigate itself accurately and objectively? We can see that the philosophical basis of the study of consciousness is fraught with difficulty and confusion.

On a more practical level there is a problem that psychology may be incapable of facing. Psychology is, by its nature, reductionist — that is, it takes things apart to look at them, usually using analytical mode thinking. When it has an associative mode insight, it cannot accept the insight until it has taken it apart and reduced it to logic. When we do this with anything, taking a wholeness into pieces and then reassembling it, the thing we leave out is the magic and life and significance of the original whole. If you dissect a live kitten and then reassemble the bits, you will have a dead kitten. The same is true of ideas and feelings and experiences. The more we analyse them, the more we are in danger of talking the life out of them.

Additionally, there are things in us that need the darkness. They are like the delicate new shoots of plants, hidden in the sheltering darkness of the earth. New ideas, the earliest stages of the creative process, the beginnings of love — these are things that should not be brought prematurely into the bright light of consciousness, lest we think them to death.

We have been looking at a lot of interpretation techniques for taking things apart so that we can 'understand' them, but it's important to realise that this is only an *intermediate* step to something else. We are using all these techniques to retrain our automatic, unconscious process of thinking, to get ourselves out of the either/or of analytic/associative modes into our own wholeness. We are learning to think holistically.

I occasionally teach a short experiential seminar, sometimes called *The God and Goddess Within*, which looks at the way we give form to and nurture the archetypal energy of the creative life force in ourselves. We do this through imagery journeys and other interactions with a selected group of our personal ectypes. During this seminar, someone always asks, 'But do you mean that the god and goddess are *in* you, or are they something *outside* you?' My answer to this is simply 'yes' — and the usual response to this, because they have already begun to find the meaning of the experience in themselves, is something like, 'I was afraid you were going to say that.' Then I know that they are on their way to getting it. The 'it' I want them — and you — and me — to get is the sense of meaning and purpose that exists in each of us — and indeed, in everything there is. And we can't find it by taking things apart.

So why are we learning all these techniques for taking things apart? When we learn to drive, we begin by learning techniques, logical steps. The process is taken apart for us so that we can deal with one bit at a time. Dealing with all those bits is very complex, especially when we are hurling down a fast road, surrounded by others doing unpredictable things.

However, at some point in this learning process, we make a

quantum leap. Suddenly, we are able to pull off the road and stop without chanting to ourselves: check rear view mirror, turn indicator on, begin braking, clutch down, shift to lower gear, clutch up, pull over, clutch down, out of gear, clutch up, hand brake on, brake pedal up, turn indicator off, ignition switch off, resume breathing. We learn the process so well that it becomes automatic and unconscious — we just do it. We can even do it and breathe at the same time.

The same thing will happen with the imagery interpretation techniques, both associative and analytic, when they are practised enough. They will become automatic and unconscious, a richer way of processing information without consciously and laboriously thinking about it. Given enough practice in this kind of thinking on the conscious level, the quantum leap will take place and we will attain the ability to think holistically — meaning and purpose will present themselves to consciousness without all those slow, arduous steps. We will be able to ask for a symbolic image and just *know* what it means; we will better understand the meaning of our dreams; our lives will be filled with a sense of meaningful purpose — and from that, creativity will flow freely. And when we get stuck, we have our step-by-step techniques to fall back on.

Mystics have known all along that life has meaning and purpose — even if we cannot always analyse and verbalise or even intellectually grasp that meaning or define the purpose. Physicists and psychologists, after having heaped scorn on the mystics for a very long time, are finally coming around to the same understanding. They seem to be finding growth a very painful process (as we all do, from time to time), and there is much resistance. And of course, one manifestation of that resistance has been the insistence that soul (meaning) and spirit (purpose) don't exist. Consequently, schools and universities all over the world continue to teach us to take things apart, killing them in the process, and without teaching us to redeem them by learning to see them in their wholeness. Thus, we learn, from childhood to adulthood, not to see the magic and power, the divine spark, in the wholeness of ourselves.

What we are trying to do here is to reclaim that divine spark and restore it to its rightful place in our lives. It is the well-spring of meaning and creativity. Archetypal energies and ectypal images are an expression of that divine spark, and by attending to them, we return to the roots of our creativity.

As we work with imagery, we will inevitably encounter our ectypes frequently. They are easy to recognise — they are the figures in our minds with power, the ones that make a lasting impression on us. When they enter our dreams, as they often may, they are more vivid than other things, we remember them more clearly, and they stay in our memory longer. They have a numinous quality, a kind of larger-than-lifeness. Mythology is full of ectypes — not only the gods and goddesses, but also people who may once have been historical figures, but who have assumed the focus and power of an ectype. The film stars and pop stars of our times are also given some of this archetypical quality by their fans, who see them as something better or worse, but definitely different from and bigger than the ordinary human.

When we meet an ectypal figure in our own images, we know that we have met something out of the ordinary — and the closer they are to the pure energy of the archetype, the more powerful they seem — and the more intense their impression is upon us. By connecting with these energies in ourselves, we begin to recover some of the sense of wonder — the magic that we lost by being too closely bound by one mode of thinking, while suppressing another, and encouraging the rational while denying the archetypal.

It seems that creativity, then, is something that flows from the integrated whole self, rather than from any one part. And the more that integration takes place, the more creative we become.

48. Exploring the Unknown

There are several ways of becoming better acquainted with our deep archetypal energies. We can, as Plato suggests, deduce information about them from their ectypal manifestations — but this analytic process hardly seems a way to *know* them. There is, however, a way in which we can invoke and experience them, a way in which we can expand our consciousness to include more of their energy. The following imagery journey explores the experience and expansion of a particular archetypal energy of consciousness. This energy is defined by your sense of the figure you chose to work with.

The first step is to decide which energy is the one we want or need to enhance at this time. The imagery journey below focuses on the heart centre, whose primary attributes are love, compassion, mercy, generosity, gentleness, empathy, joy, and charity. It also recognises the qualities of detachment, serenity, tolerance, wisdom, and grace.

Having chosen the appropriate attributes, we then can choose a suitable focal figure.

One way of doing this is to think about which of the gods, goddesses, or potent beings symbolise a kind of energy we want to invoke in ourselves. For example, if you see the Buddha as detached and serene, the qualities experienced and amplified are those. The goddess might represent the qualities of mercy and compassion, like Kuan Yin, who gives us what we ask for, whether we deserve it or not, as long as so doing will cause us no harm — or she might be the nurturing mother principle, the Earth Mother. We have worked with the Wise Elder, the Healer, and the Advisor, and each of these are possibilities.

You might wish to choose the figure of Christ or of a saint, although the more complex the figure is in your mind and the greater the variety of characteristics you see in it, the less focused the energy is into a simple quality, which is what you need for this imagery journey. For this reason, it may be better to choose a figure about whom you know little. For the same reason, it is usually better to avoid using the image of a real person, either someone you have known personally or have admired from afar. Such a figure usually lacks that numinous quality, the power of an archetype. Having said that, I must acknowledge that sometimes real people have assumed archetypal qualities in our minds, and they appear in our images as the god or goddess of whatever. I still wouldn't use them — they are too near the human and have too much complexity in our minds.

We can also invoke our own ectypal figures, as we did with the Wise Old Wo/Man. If you do this, you need to make the figure real in your mind. Get the Advisor to introduce you, as you were introduced to the Healer. Ask to speak to the god or goddess *within you* who represents whatever quality you wish to work with. Notice what kind of an environment it has within your inner world. Find out what it wants of you, and begin to work with it. Then paint it, and look at the painting with all the tools we have used. Ask to meet it in your dreams. Get to know it well.

Choose your primary image with great care to enhance and balance your personal qualities. For example, if you are a compassionate and generous person, you might feel drawn to the Kuan Yin archetype, but you might *need* the experience of serene detachment that is associated more with the Buddha.

Remember, these archetypal energies already exist within you, and this is an exercise in evoking and experiencing their qualities. Some

believe that this is where the gods and goddesses come from —
energies and impulses in the deep unconscious, the human spirit,
filtered and shaped by personal experience, an interface between the
depths of our own beings and our conscious minds. I'm don't think
this is the entire explanation myself, but some do.

When you first begin the journey, hold the concept of the archetype
you have chosen clearly in your mind. Once your concentration is
fully focused on that concept, just let go of it and follow the imagery.
Don't try to keep thinking about the 'significance of it all' during the
journey — just be. The important thing in this is to stay focused on
the image of the chosen figure.

Because the impact of this imagery is especially enhanced by a deep
altered state of consciousness, the relaxation induction at the beginning is longer than usual. As you go through it, pause between each of
the paragraphs of the relaxation instructions long enough to allow the
imager to take several breaths before you go on to the next paragraph.

Approximate travel time: 20–25 minutes.

META-MIND

Please take a couple of deep breaths, letting yourself relax in a centered,
earthed position. This is an imagery journey for the purpose of expanding
consciousness. To begin with, I'd like you to become aware of your
breath, the natural breath. Just observe your breath as it moves through
your nostrils.

And observe the movements of your chest and abdomen as you
breathe. This is just your natural breath — some breaths will be longer,
some shorter, some deeper, and some more shaliow. Simply observe your
natural breath, feeling it move in you and through you, and back out
again.

Now I'd like you to begin focusing on a particular thought as you
breathe. As you inhale, think of breathing in truth. And as you exhale,
think of breathing out not-truth. This is just the natural breath, breathing in
truth, breathing out not-truth.

With each breath, you continue to breathe in truth, and breathe out
not-truth. You don't have to know what truth is; you don't have to know
what not-truth is — your higher self knows and will take care of it for you.

As you continue to breathe in truth and breathe out not-truth, your
breathing may become quieter, more regular — or it may not. It really
doesn't matter which, as you continue breathing in truth, breathing out
not-truth.

As you breathe in truth and breathe out not-truth, you may notice a different quality in the incoming and the outgoing breaths — or you may not. It really doesn't matter which, as you continue breathing in truth, breathing out not-truth.

As you continue to breathe in truth and breathe out not-truth, you may notice that your breath becomes easier — so easy that it's hardly like breathing at all. If this hasn't happened to you yet, it probably will as you continue through the journey, automatically breathing in truth, breathing out not-truth.

About an arm's length in front of your heart, there is a tiny shining figure, seated in the air. It is about the size of your thumbnail. Allow your focus of awareness rest upon this figure. This figure has a luminous quality, a bright aura around it, as if it were glowing from within.

Who is this figure?

What energies or qualities does this figure have?

Now, I'd like you to forget all about those qualities and just focus on the image itself, there in front of you. Small and glowing, it sits before you.

I'd like you to imagine that the figure is moving toward you, until it pauses just in front of your heart. It slowly turns in the air, until it is facing the same direction as you are. And then, very slowly, it enters your body, coming to rest in the center of your heart.

Just let yourself be aware of this luminous figure in the center of your heart. As you observe it, it begins to expand. It expands, growing larger, until the top of its head touches the top of your heart and the soles of its feet touch the floor of your heart. Be aware of your breath moving around that radiant figure, as you breath in truth, breathe out not-truth.

The glowing figure continues to expand, growing larger, filling your chest. The top of its head reaches the base of your throat, and the soles of its feet rest on your diaphragm. Notice your breath moving through and around that bright figure, as you breathe in truth, breathe out not-truth.

And the shining figure continues to expand, growing larger, until the top of its head reaches the top of your head, and the soles of its feet occupy the same space as the soles of your feet.

And the luminous figure continues to expand, growing larger, until the top of its head reaches the height of a tall building, and the soles of its feet rest on the earth.

And still the bright figure continues to expand, growing larger, until the top of its head reaches the sky, and the soles of its feet rest at the center of the earth.

And the figure of light grows larger, larger yet, until it is as big as the whole of the earth.

And the radiant figure continues to grow, larger yet, until it is as big as the entire solar system, the sun and the earth, and all of the moons and planets revolving within it.

And the shining figure continues to grow, growing larger yet, until it is as big as our entire galaxy, uncounted billions of stars dancing their spiral path within it.

And the luminous figure continues to grow, growing still larger, until it is as big as our entire universe, the whole of space, with galaxies uncountable circling within it.

And the bright figure continues to grow, growing larger still, until it contains the whole of the universe and the whole of time, the past, the present, and the future — all that is, was, and shall be.

And the figure of light continues to grow, growing larger still, until it contains the whole of the universe and the whole of time, manifest and unmanifest. It contains that which was and which might have been, that which is and is not, that which shall be and that which might be — all the possibilities of time and space.

And then the bright figure begins to become smaller, becoming smaller still, until it only contains the universe and time, the past, the present, and the future — all that is, was, and shall be.

And the luminous figure continues to become smaller, smaller still, until it is as small as our universe, the whole of space, with galaxies uncountable circling within it.

And the shining figure continues to become smaller, becoming smaller yet, until it is as small as our galaxy, uncounted billions of stars scintillating in their spiral dance within it.

And the radiant figure continues to become smaller, smaller yet, until it is as small as the entire solar system, the sun and the earth, and all of the moons and the planets revolving within it.

And the figure of light becomes smaller, smaller yet, until it is as small as the earth.

And still the bright figure continues to become smaller, smaller yet, until the top of its head just touches the sky, and the soles of its feet rest at the center of the earth.

And the luminous figure continues to become smaller, smaller yet, until the top of its head just reaches the height of a tall house, and the soles of its feet rest on the earth.

And the shining figure continues to become smaller, smaller yet, until the top of its head just reaches the top of your head, and the soles of its feet occupy the same space as the soles of your feet.

And the glowing figure continues to become smaller, smaller yet, until the top of its head just reaches the base of your throat, and the soles of its feet rest on your diaphragm. Notice your breath moving through and around that bright figure, as you breathe in truth, breathe out not-truth.

And the radiant figure continues to become smaller, smaller yet, until its head is touching the top of your heart and the soles of its feet rest on the floor of your heart. Be aware of your breath moving around that luminous figure, breathing in truth, breathing out not-truth.

And the bright figure continues to become smaller, smaller yet, until it is just as high as your thumbnail, in the center of your heart.

And the figure moves forward, pausing in front of your chest, slowly revolving until it is facing you. Then very quietly, it moves out to a point about an arm's length in front of you. Be aware of the resonance between yourself and this figure, the bond of shared energy and love.

As you sense the figure in front of you, it begins to grow transparent, until it fades from sight, still there, but unseen.

Your journey to the outermost reaches of space and time and beyond is complete. You may be feeling rested, relaxed, and refreshed as you return from your journey. How does your body feel? Your emotions? Your mind? Your energy?

Once again, be aware of your breath, breathing in truth, breathing out not-truth. Be aware of the feeling of the breath in your nostrils, in your throat, in your chest and abdomen as you breathe in truth and breathe out not-truth.

Take a few deep breaths, and become fully present in your body.

And another deep breath or two as you become conscious of your environment.

Flex your fingers and toes. And when you are ready, take a couple of deep breaths, and gently open your eyes. Has your perception of your environment changed in any way?

When you are ready, take another deep breath and stretch.

The logic of the imagery

Note that at no time does the imagery actually suggest that you, the seeker, have actually become one with the archetype — and yet this is an assumption that we automatically make — at least the associative mode makes it while the analytical mode is otherwise occupied, thinking about relative sizes. This is an example of the use of indirect suggestion, which we will consider further in Chapter 54.

You may have noticed the similarity between *Meta-Mind* and the

Pool of Water, but where the *Pool of Water* was about *letting go of*, *changing* or *understanding* something, this journey is about *being*, about evoking qualities and energies in ourselves that already exist and emphasising them in our consciousness.

Working with the imagery

First, make an impressionistic painting of the way you felt at the end of the journey. If you can, make another of the way you felt when extended beyond time and space. These are paintings of feelings, emotions and sensations, and they may or may not include your physical self. Use all the tools and techniques you have for interpreting these paintings.

How did the sensations and emotions during the imagery compare with the way you normally feel?

Remember! These are not perceptions and feelings from outside of you — they are evocations of something that already exists within you. We have these attributes, and if we wish them to become stronger, there are two things we must do. First, we must constantly monitor ourselves, and when we find ourselves losing touch with those qualities, we must re-evoke them. Practising the imagery helps us to become more proficient at this. Second, we must do our best to act upon these feelings. In order to do this, we may have to invent new responses to old situations and create new patterns of behaviour in our daily lives.

People sometimes have a feeling of discomfort, or even vertigo, when they get into the furthest reaches of space-time, while others take to those concepts like a duck to water. The former is usually a simple lack of experience, and will disappear with practice. The relaxation induction to this journey was meant to facilitate reaching a deep altered state of consciousness, and this also may produce odd symptoms occasionally. This is discussed in the following chapter.

Possibilities for expansion

There are other centers we could work from as well as the heart. In a way the heart is the safest to work with because of the qualities it represents. The *hara*, for example, has to do with balances of power, both within ourselves and between us and external powers. It has to do with will, courage, physical well-being, and both physical and moral strength. The *hara* is located about two inches in front of the spine and two inches below the level of the navel.

The brow center, located at the level of the eyes, in the center of the brain, has to do with serenity, intelligence, insight, intuition, wisdom, discernment, and grace.

49. Trans-Dimensional Travel

There are many other dimensions in our minds, not accessible to ordinary consciousness. The magic words *altered states of consciousness* (ASC for short) fascinate — and sometimes alarm — many of us. Most imagery work is done in a light to deep altered state, so it will be useful to consider just what that means and how we can recognise such a state. It is also useful to know that some of the more unusual sensations, perceptions, or emotions we may have are actually quite normal, both in deliberately induced ASCs, such as meditation and imagery work, and in 'accidental' ASCs, such as daydreams, concentrated mental or physical effort, or highly charged emotional states. ASCs are much more common than many people realise.

First, let us consider what we mean when we speak of 'normal' or 'usual' consciousness before we look at variations from it. 'Normal consciousness' might be best described as a state of general attentiveness to the things that are going on in our environment and in ourselves. It is usually a rather diffuse state where part of our attention is on what we are doing or thinking, and another part is scanning the environment. We might be attending to paperwork, aware that it is nearly lunch time and we are hungry, and simultaneously listening to the conversation between two co-workers at the next desk. We might be making a mental shopping list, washing the dishes, and also aware of the children playing outside. In either case, a particular sequence of words by our co-workers or sounds of distress in the children immediately will move our main focus of awareness to them, even though, if asked, we would have said we were doing the paperwork or the dishes. We would give different answers to the two questions 'what are you doing?' and 'what are you thinking about?' at the same time, and we might not even be consciously aware that we were actually listening to something as well.

This state of diffuse consciousness enables us to notice and attend to changes in and around us at the same time that we accomplish a not very demanding task. We probably are not doing any of these things at maximum efficiency, but we are getting them done adequately. We are so used to switching our attention back and forth between two or more internal and/or external processes that we hardly even notice that we are doing it. It is part of the way we survive in a world that frequently produces sudden changes without warning.

We tend to change from this diffused state to a more focused kind of awareness when we become so intently involved with one thing that we cease to notice other things. We might become so involved with balancing a recalcitrant bank account that we don't even hear the telephone ringing, or so lost in a daydream that we don't notice our name being called. Some people would consider these states of conscious also to be 'normal' — but if we consider the amount of time most of us spend in such deeply focused concentration, they certainly cannot be considered usual.

My son's employer once told me with amusement that ordinary people don't understand computer programmers. He had just picked up one of his programmers, who was doing some on-site programming for a construction company. When he arrived to pick up his man, the receptionist asked him in nervous and lowered tones if the programmer was 'all right' or if there were something wrong with him. It seems that the programmer had wandered out of the room where he was working, had come to her desk, completely ignored her, and removed, one by one, the wrappers from the peppermints in the dish on the corner of her desk. He didn't eat them. He carefully aligned all the unwrapped peppermints along the edge of the desk, equally spaced, and then smoothed out all the paper wrappers, neatly stacking them in a pile in the precise centre of her desk. As a final touch he put the dish on top of the papers. Then he sauntered back into his room, all without ever seeming to notice her presence.

The boss assured the receptionist that such behaviour was perfectly normal in programmers and not to worry. He said to me, "What I didn't say was that, if I had asked him why he had done that with the peppermints, he would probably have said 'what peppermints?' I thought that might have worried her."

My son, I must mention, was not the programmer involved, but he easily could have been.

The thing that is relevant here is that the programmer was obviously in an ASC. Doing something as difficult as a complex computer programme, where the programmer must hold the whole shape and sense of the programme (associative mode) in his mind while simultaneously working out each detailed part of it (analytic mode), requires full attention. It is quite likely that the whole business with the peppermints was, in fact, a symbolic acting-out of something that he was trying to do in the programme, the equivalent of certain kinds of doodling or perhaps related to sleep-walking. To many of us, such deep and lengthy absorption in a mental process may seem abnormal, yet we may do such things ourselves on a smaller scale quite often. How often have you found something in an unlikely place, and then not been able to remember having put it there, probably while thinking about something else?

Perhaps, then, we can say that one borderline between 'normal' and 'altered' states of consciousness is the place where we lose that diffuse awareness of self and surroundings and become focused on one thing — which brings us to the first sign that we have entered an ASC.

Signs of altered states

Unusual power of concentration.   In an ASC we often find that we have a remarkable ability to concentrate — in fact, this ability to concentrate so intensely indicates that we must be in an ASC. This concentration may focus on an idea or train of thought, an image or series of images, a physical sense and the sequence of information received through that sense, a feeling of energy or of the movement of energy in the body, or an object or person and its activities. We may simply become acutely aware of things that go on all the time, but that we are usually distracted from by the many calls upon our attention. This exceptional ability to concentrate upon one thing to the exclusion of all else may be the explanation for many of the other changes in awareness during an ASC.

Changes in vision.   Things may appear flat or unusually far away. Glowing lights may be seen at the edges of things or lights may be seen independently of any explanation for them. Colours may seem brighter or more intense or may appear to shimmer. More rarely, things may be seen spontaneously that are not physically present, as in visions.

Physiological changes.   The breath and heart rate may speed up or slow down. Quite often, they first speed up as we go through an unstable transition stage, and then slow down as we become securely in a stable ASC, such as meditation, concentration, or sleep.

Control of muscles may be improved or decreased. At one extreme, we have the small, not very strong person lifting a car off of a child, while at the other, there can be the dream-like feeling of being unable to move or act. We may also twitch or jerk, as we often do when going to sleep, as the body releases muscular tension.

Another change that may occur is in the quality of our voices. Many people's voices naturally drop in pitch, becoming quieter and smoother, as they relax. There may be other changes as well — perhaps in accent or vocabulary. Our voices may become quite unlike our usual voice.

Unusual feelings about one's body. Our bodies may seem to be changing shape or size or position. There may be a feeling of energy and/or of the movement of energy in the body. Feelings of floating or lightness or of being particularly heavy are quite common. When I first began meditating, I could recognise a certain level of consciousness by the feeling that, while remaining in the same position, I was floating upside down. As is usual with such feelings, it disappeared when I became more familiar with that depth of concentrated relaxation.

If we are moving about during an ASC, we may move differently, or at least feel that we are. This is often experienced in the mild ASC in which people do exercises like yoga or t'ai chi. As they become more relaxed and focused in on the exercise, their movements often become smoother and their bodies more supple.

Unusually strong sensory response, or at the other extreme, very little sensory awareness. We may feel more involved with or more detached from our environment. Sensitivity to colours, sounds, scents, textures may be exceptionally vivid. One sense — such as smell or hearing — may become unusually acute, perhaps even to the point of temporarily becoming the dominant sense. Alternatively awareness of the body and the physical senses may be lessened as the focus of attention moves to mental or emotional realms. This is part of the explanation of the ability of hypnosis to decrease and, sometimes, even to eliminate pain.

Changes in emotional response. We may overreact, under react, not react, react in an entirely different way than our usual emotional response to almost anything. Extreme intensity of emotions or, alternatively, a lack of emotional response may also be experienced. We might find that we can think calmly and objectively in an ASC about something we have been quite upset about — or the reverse may happen. For example, a woman might begin to cry about her mother's death, even though the death had happened many years ago and she had not felt strong emotional reactions to it for a long time. We often allow ourselves only incomplete emotional release, suppressing some or even most of our feelings. In an ASC we may relax some of the walls that keep these unexpressed and unreleased feelings from conscious awareness, and they come welling up, unbidden. We will come back to this subject later on in Chapter 61.

Unusual mental response to one's environment. Special or remarkable significance or meaning may be seen in the ordinary things in the environment or in the actions or words of others. We may hear and see things in quite a new way.

Our communications with others may change in some way. Many of us have had the experience of talking to a very sleepy person who believed that he was making sense, but who, in fact, was quite incomprehensible. The words he uses may be clear as individual words, but they don't make sense collectively. In a deep ASC, we may perfectly understand what we wish to say, but have difficulty putting it into words or find that people don't seem to understand what we are saying. I suspect that the associative mode may be in charge, using words in a very different way.

Alterations in memory. In an ASC, we may experience memories so vividly and completely that we can even remember details we didn't notice at the time of the original event. Hypnosis is sometimes used to retrieve such memories, as in the cases of hypnotised witnesses being able to remember the licence number of a hit-and-run car. This kind of information has to be taken with great care, because we can also 'remember' things, in the same vivid way, that didn't really happen, especially if they are suggested by the hypnotist.

On the other hand, in an ASC we may have gaps in our memories. We usually assume that these gaps were times when we were asleep. This may be true, but often they mark times when we were in such a deep ASC that we didn't bring the memory of it back into our usual awareness.

There is a phenomenon called 'state specific memory' — which simply means that we tend to remember some things more easily when we are in the same state of consciousness that we were in when we first experienced it. One example of this is the continuing dreams that some people have — an unbroken sequence may be dreamed over several nights or even several months, each dream continuing where the last one on the same subject left off. There may even be other dreams in between the episodes of the continuing dream. Another example of state specific memory is the boring drunk who always wants to tell you about the singularly fatuous things that happened when he was last drunk. Probably the most common example of all is the way a dream slides out of our conscious minds unless we go back over it, either writing it down or telling it to someone immediately after awakening. This is why it is so important to keep a journal and to jot things down immediately after completing the imagery journey. We may think we will remember, but we probably won't.

Fluctuations in the sense of the passage of time. We have all had experiences of times that seemed to rush by, and other times that seemed to drag on forever, and we usually recognise that this is largely because of our own state of mind. When we are enjoying ourselves or working frantically to meet a deadline, time often seems to go very quickly, but if we are bored or unhappy, an afternoon can go on and on and on. In the first situation, when we are working intently or are pleasurably involved with something, we are usually in a mild ASC of focused attention. When we are bored or unhappy, we tend to be very easily distracted and our attention even more diffuse than usual.

Anyone who meditates knows that a meditation *feels* good when they have remained intently concentrated on the meditation focus. It then either seems to go very fast or to be atemporal, somehow outside of time. On the other hand, the times when we fidget and cannot seem to hold our focus clearly seem to glue the hands to the face of the clock.

Another type of unusual perception of time we may experience in an ASC is the feeling that the past and/or future is mixed up with or happening at the same time as the present.

In doing imagery work, we may often experience this dilation or contraction of apparent time. We may also have an unusual sense of here-and-nowness — or the opposite extreme of feeling outside of time, as if the normal flow of time were somehow irrelevant. We may pack seeming hours of vivid experience into a few minutes of clock time. You can see why a guide finds it so tricky to get the timing right in an imagery journey.

Changes in mental processing. Along with our changed perception of time we may be thinking more quickly or more slowly than usual. We may also find that our thoughts seem sharper or more clear than usual — or alternatively, that they have dream-like jumps and irrationality. The whole question of logic in ASCs is fraught with confusion. I remember once working out a wonderful Five Year Plan when I had a fever. It seemed to cover all my needs and be the solution to all my problems — it all seemed so simple and obvious that I couldn't imagine why I had not thought of it before. Unfortunately, my fever-induced sense of logic doesn't seem to work by the same rules as ordinary reality, and in a non-feverish state, the wonderful plan clearly wouldn't work.

"If you can touch a clock and never start it, then you can start a clock and never touch it," said the Golux. "At least, that's logic as I know and use it."[13] This is the point — logic as we know and use it seems to change with our state of consciousness. Dream logic is different from waking logic. In an ASC, our logic may become much more rational and clear than usual, or we might go the other way and become like the Golux, using our own brand of logic — which makes perfect sense to us within the context of the inner world we are experiencing. (Incidentally, the Golux was right, and the princess did start the clocks without touching them.)

What I am trying to say here is that the logic of ASC imagery may well be different from our ordinary rules of logic — but those different rules may work well within that inner world. We considered this idea briefly in regard to *The Waterfall* back in Chapter 33. Amazing things can happen. We can fly, animals can talk, mythical animals and beings can exist in these inner realities, we can remove bits of ourselves and replace them with new parts, and we can do far more magical things than these. The only problem comes when we try to apply ASC logic to the ordinary world — or ordinary world logic to the inner worlds.

Alterations in the sense of identity.   One of the most useful things about guided imagery is the ability it gives us to see ourselves and aspects of ourselves from new and unexpected angles, giving greater breadth and depth and a different perspective to our sense of ourselves. A person can never feel the same about their fear of heights once they have seen it symbolised as a garden gnome or as a turnip in an imagery journey — and both of those images have actually turned up for people in that situation. Nor can we feel the same about ourselves when we have seen our Inner Healer as a radiant being of light or a towering, vibrant tree. We are grander, more powerful, more ridiculous, more vulnerable, more delightful, and more creative than we may realise.

It is not only in guided imagery journeys that we may contact these altered views of ourselves. In dreams and daydreams and in other ASCs we may have the sense of an unusual identity or role, or we may encounter alienation or detachment from or a new perspective on our usual sense of ourselves. We may dismiss any of these experiences as being 'just imaginary' — but they change, subtly or radically, both our sense of who we are and our sense of who we have the potential to become.

I have spent as much time on the phenomena of ASCs[14] as I have because it is important that we understand that the 'weird' sensations we occasionally experience in ASCs are simply versions of things that commonly happen in our daily activities, in deep relaxation, and in sleep. The important thing about imagery work is the degree of insight and self-transformation that it facilitates — not whether or not we have weird feelings, which are only markers that indicate that we are deeply relaxed and in touch with a part of ourselves that is usually obscured by our mental and physical activities. The biggest problem is not in achieving an ASC (which we do spontaneously and frequently in our daily lives anyway), but in staying awake throughout the journey rather than entering the ASC of sleep!

One of the things that people occasionally worry about with hypnosis and guided imagery is 'what if I can't wake up again?' Don't worry about it — you always can. The worst thing that might happen is that you would drift from the journey into a dream state, probably to continue to work on the problem you are dealing with, and from that move on into a normal sleep. You will waken from such a sleep in the usual way, either when you are sufficiently rested or when something disturbs you.

If you are worried about this, you have probably been watching too much television or movies or reading too many horror stories written by people who don't really know all that much about ASCs.

Using altered states

In guided imagery, we allow ourselves to move into an ASC in which we may access information and/or do things that are difficult, if not impossible, in our ordinary waking state. The first part of a guided imagery journey is usually designed to facilitate entering the desired type of ASC, hopefully producing a state that is deeply relaxed both physically and mentally, in touch with the deeper aspects of ourselves and our creativity, and with our minds open to new possibilities and ideas.

In the imagery journeys, we have used several different ways of helping to make that transition. Most of these techniques can be adapted for use as the induction to many other guided imagery journeys.

All of the imagery journeys we use are designed to facilitate two-way communication between the conscious and the unconscious minds in one form or another. By allowing ourselves to relax and respond freely and spontaneously to the imagery, we enable the unconscious to project ideas and feelings into consciousness. This trans-dimensional (or should it be trance-dimensional?) travel is a major factor in developing and enhancing creativity.

Review

How would you assess your own analytical-associative balance? What effect does *Round the World in 30 Minutes* have on you now? Do you need to lengthen it? I recommend practising it regularly — once a week or so — until even 45 minutes of it is easy.

How are you doing with integrating the use of imagery and associative thinking into your daily problem solving and decision making?

How are you getting along with your Elder Self and Rebel? Make an impressionistic painting of the Rebel as it was when you first met it and another as it is today. Have there been any changes? How do you feel about the Rebel now?

Do you communicate well with your Advisor? Are you taking full advantage of what your Advisor has to offer in your daily life?

Part XIV

Creating New Paths

It is now known to science that there are many more dimensions than the classical four. Scientists say that these don't normally impinge on the world because the extra dimensions are very small and curve in on themselves, and that since reality is fractal most of it is tucked inside itself. This means either that the universe is more full of wonders that we can hope to understand or, more probably, that scientists make things up as they go along.

— Terry Pratchett
in Pyramids

50. Choosing a Destination

The first question is, what are we attempting to accomplish with the imagery? It seems an obvious question, but these obvious things often get forgotten.

Are we looking for information and/or guidance, or are we interested in some form of self-transformation?

If we are looking for information, exactly what are we seeking to learn? Which part of ourselves, which aspect of our beings might have the needed information? In what kind of an inner world might we find such information? When guiding someone I don't know well, I like to let them provide the landscape and the inner guide as much as possible, as we did in *The Advisor* and in other interactive journeys.

If we are working toward transformation, what are we transforming from? And what are we transforming to? Which aspect of our being is undergoing transformation? Which aspect of ourselves might be resisting transformation?

When designing an imagery journey, we need to be clear about our purpose. Once we have that, the rest is relatively simple. Some sample objectives are:

to relax deeply and release the stress we are carrying
to facilitate our own healing process
to discover more about a particular relationship with someone
to let go of an old behaviour, perhaps replacing it with something
 new
to find the resolution to a personal dilemma
to access our inner wisdom for guidance in making a choice
to see a personal issue from a different point of view
to explore our creative potential.

Define the specific issue for the particular journey carefully:

Who is involved besides yourself, if anyone?
Which aspect(s) of yourself do you need to communicate with? One of your ectypes or some other part of you?
If you are trying to learn something, precisely what is the question?
If you are trying to do something, exactly what is the intention?
Which type of imagery journey is most suited to your purpose: freeform, interactive, or structured?

Next, let's consider the symbols you might want to use.

51. Landmarks

Choosing the representative symbols, the landmarks on the journey, may seem like the hardest part of creating an imagery journey, but it really isn't all that difficult. The important thing is to remember that the symbols we use are a metaphor, an analogy, for the intended idea or object. This is the province of the associative twin, which is probably why we have so much trouble with the *idea* of doing it — it is associative logic rather than linear logic. This gives us the clue we need — there must be an *association* in the mind of the imager between the symbol we choose and the thing it represents.

We've been going the other direction in our interpretations of imagery, from the symbol to the meaning. We only need to reverse that process to go from the meaning to the symbol. If you have been keeping up your image dictionary, you will have, by now, an extensive list of symbols and their meanings to you. These are your personal vocabulary of meanings, but some of them will probably be shared by many people.

In the list of a few possible general interpretations in Chapter 27, some examples of this kind of (possibly) shared symbolism were also given.

Remember, too, that a symbol can be an action as well as a thing. For example: going up can symbolise moving into the mental and spiritual realms; going down can indicate connecting with the repressed, suppressed, or unconscious self; going in can indicate exploring within ourselves or a part of ourselves; we can go back (or down) into the past and forward (or up) into the future.

The following are a few examples, from imagery we have used, which illustrate how some of the symbols have been chosen.

In *Light into Darkness*, the Sun God symbolised consciousness and the analytic mode of the mind, while the Earth Goddess represented the associative mode and the unconscious. In *Pool of Water* we needed a perfectly calm place (the deep, still pool) in which to let go of (dissolve) the sensations, emotions, perceptions, thoughts, memories, and so on of the small self to connect with a greater self. In *The Advisor* we went into a cave in order to go into our minds, and then beyond that to another world, our inner world of sensation, emotion, and belief to gain information and a point of view unknown or forgotten by the conscious mind. The Rebel and the Healer symbolise other aspects of ourselves.

In the *Walk in the Forest* we went into the obscuring woods to find feelings hidden in ourselves. There we explored eight things we found in the forest that symbolised aspects of ourselves. We could easily have extended that, except that trying to do too much in a journey makes it very hard to keep straight in the imager's mind. Some of the other things we could have looked at are:

1. Rubbish heap — this reminds us of the attitudes and feelings we hold that are of no real constructive use to us. These may be things left over from childhood or from the more recent past. Often we find these images particularly difficult to interpret because no part of our psyche really wants to be thrown out, and it may resist being brought to conscious notice.

2. Something in the air above us — this can symbolise unconscious goals and ambitions. These either tend to be really easy to interpret or very difficult, depending on how well our unconscious desires harmonise with our conscious ones. If, for example, our conscious goals require much hard work and striving and the object seen or sensed is a balloon floating gently in the breeze, it may be quite hard for us to allow ourselves to see the meaning of the balloon, which perhaps symbolises drifting gently, being carried by the current, being relaxed, even passive, rather than striving. The opposite way around would probably be even more difficult to interpret.

3. Any ectype — a jester, hero, healer, magician, hermit, fortune teller, king (father/authority image), queen (mother/authority image), wise man or woman, or any of the gods and goddesses of particular arts or sciences, like poetry, music, dance, painting, sculpting, mathematics, et cetera. We could ask any of these a question or we could just give them an opportunity to give us a bit of advice or information — or even to give us a symbolic object, with a special meaning for us.

In *Journey to the Waterfall*, both the waterfall and the orb of light symbolise specific sources of healing, but the entirety of the space is a magical, healing place. The sun, the earth, and the special tree all have unusual qualities which are symbolic of energy and nurturing. Although it is a structured journey, there is even time for the imager to find her own symbols of healing and to have spontaneous healing interactions with others and with the environment. In using this imagery with others, I have often noticed that the important things, the things that give the most insight and healing, seem to happen most often within the silences. *People know what they need, and given the right opportunity, they will find it for themselves.*

As you can see, thinking back over the journeys we have done, many of the symbols have been created by the imager, himself. The actual structure of the imagery, as set by the guide, is often minimal. In freeform imagery, all of it comes from the imager. There is only a simple outline for most of the interactive journeys, where much of the imagery is elicited by the guide's questions. Only in the structured imagery does the guide have to provide all or nearly all of the symbolic images. When creating structured imagery journeys, it is important to use symbols that will 'speak' to the imager. This can be tricky.

Consider, for example, the symbolic sun and the variety of sun gods in human history. In the hotter latitudes, we find that the sun gods often develop vengeful, unforgiving, harsh characters, and they are sometimes even death to look upon directly. In more temperate, hospitable latitudes we find Apollo, a spectacularly beautiful figure who is also the god of music and poetry, the gentle arts. In the far north we find poor Baldur, lovely and gentle — and murdered.

When we think of it, it seems obvious that the sun has an entirely different set of meanings for a person living in a harsh, hot desert than it has to someone who lives near the Arctic circle, where the sun is weak, easily overwhelmed by storms and even 'dies' at midwinter.

Even within a single culture, a simple concept like 'father' varies widely from person to person, depending greatly on their own experience of their personal father and their experience of other father/authority figures. The archetypical Father may be benign or malign, loving or cruel, absent or present, active or passive, depending on the individual's own experience.

We must realise how differently others' minds work if we are to do imagery work really effectively. We have to let go of the analytical twin's desire to judge rightness or wrongness, and just accept images the way they are, both in ourselves and others. Nothing is to be gained by denying the validity of an image and a great deal is to be lost.

Because of these individual differences, it is helpful to learn the meaning of another's symbols if we wish their imagery journeys to be as rewarding and useful as possible. If, for example, we wanted to use the sun as a symbol of courage for someone in an imagery journey, we might want to ask several questions first. If the sun were a god, what would it look like? Is it male or female? Old or young? Is it like a human, an animal, or some kind of magical creature? What are its emotional qualities? Personality? We might then decide that the sun was not a suitable symbol for courage for that person, after all. Easiest and probably best, we could ask the imager what his personal symbols of courage are. In the end, we will find it most effective to use the symbols of the imager whenever possible.

52. Signposts

Visual puns can work in two ways. We have already considered how the associative mode/unconscious may use puns when speaking to us, but we can also use images whose names have a double meaning to slip an idea past the analytical–critical part of the mind to the associative mode and into the unconscious. Words can point two or even more ways.

For example, if you want to promote the idea of change, an altar (either in a church or some other type of holy place) might indicate a need for alteration or that something is altering. To place an offering on the altar might represent letting go of an old programme or attitude.

To suggest taking 'the right path' also has multiple meanings — when we think about it, which the associative mode does virtually instantaneously and the analytic mode hasn't time to do. There is right as in right hand, right as in correct, rite, wright, and write. Take your choice.

In *Round the World*, the 'neigh' of the horse to the sun resulted in sudden darkness. In *Meta-Mind* the 'soles' of the image touch your 'soles' and you are soul-to-soul. Then your/its 'soles' connect with the heart of the earth, our mother.

English has many words with double meanings as well as words that sound nearly alike but have completely different meanings. The associative mode always considers all of the meanings — and *it may well accept more than one*. It is not hampered by the one-thing-at-a-time logic of the analytical twin. Don't struggle to introduce ideas like this artificially, but do use them if you happen to think of them. In fact, you may sometimes discover that you have used them *without* thinking about them — that is just your associative twin trying to be helpful.

53. Caravans

We can help others and ourselves along these journeys by making caravans, connecting images and ideas together. There are several aspects of this. First, there is the need for the imagery structure to have its own internal logic. If miraculous or magical things are to happen, they need to be foreshadowed by something that has gone before. For example, in the *Journey to the Waterfall* we had various clues of light and environment to tells us that we were in a magical place, outside of the boundaries of the commonplace rules, before the conspicuous magic began. We also ate something, in the best of fairy tale traditions, which transformed us enough so that we, too, could do the impossible.

If one thing, no matter how unusual, seems to lead us naturally to the next in the journey it is easier for us to stay on track. I suggest you read fantasy, especially old fairy tales and myths, if you do not already have a sense of what I mean by internal logic. These are our common heritage, and the associative twin easily relates to them.

Another technique for connecting ideas is to use extra connecting words in the imagery. Words like 'and' and phrases like 'as you continue to do this, you also . . .' at the beginning of sentences can connect unlike ideas and actions. As we have learned, the associative mode uses and accepts a different logic than that of the analytical mode. It may be poor grammar, but it makes good imagery.

We can also repeat words and phrases, even whole sentences or sequences. The familiarity is reassuring, and lulls the imager into a deeper ASC and even greater cooperation. Such connections are especially useful in the relaxation process at the beginning of the imagery, and throughout structured imagery journeys, such as relaxation, stress-reduction, and healing imagery, where a deep ASC is desired. They are less needed in the main body of interactive imagery, unless the imager needs to be calmed, soothed, and relaxed again for some reason.

Another way we can fruitfully use connections is to sneak in an action or idea likely to be difficult among some easier ones. Connecting a new and possibly more difficult action with an action already accomplished implies that they are equally easy.

Consider the following sequence:

I'd like you to begin walking along the path, noticing the feeling of the path under your feet and the breeze on your face. And as you walk, notice the flowers around you — their colours, their scents, the feeling of vibrant life they seem to have. As you breathe in deeply to catch the scent better, you notice that one of the flowers is moving in a way that cannot be accounted for by the breeze, and it seems to be cheerfully nodding at you.

In that short example a great deal happens. We start with the simple, familiar physical action of walking, so the phrase 'as you walk' in the next sentence obviously connects back to it, but 'breathe in deeply' returns less obviously to noticing the scent of the flowers. And if you can 'notice' the scent, you must be able to smell it, even though the idea of actually smelling it may seem a slightly more difficult thing to do, especially to the analytic mode, than merely noticing it. One thing has lead imperceptibly to another, slightly deeper experience.

When we ask the imager to notice the colour and scent of the flowers, the associative mode takes over — and it does not have any problem with the idea of them also having a particular vibrancy. The analytic mode would doubt, but we have hooked the concept into the ordinary functions of the associative mode. Thus, this first small step out of the ordinary world is accepted, preparing us for a slightly bigger one to come.

In a deeply relaxed state, which we need to be in to work well with imagery, people tend to be more suggestible. When we suggest that they breathe in deeply in the imagery, people usually do this with their physical bodies as well as in their imagination. In paying attention to this, which is more complex than simply 'noticing' something, they are distracted from the 'weird' sight of a flower nodding to them. Also, attending to deliberately breathing deeply is another function of the associative twin, who is quite inclined to accept and enjoy a friendly, cheerful flower. The analytic twin, who is more likely to say, 'wait a minute — flowers can't *do* that' is relaxed and less attentive to what is going on. This is another step further from the ordinary world and deeper into imagery, where anything and everything becomes possible.

You see then how you can gradually slip quite outrageous things past people if they are equated with prosaic and simple things, especially if you throw in a little distraction. I know this may sound complicated, especially if the idea is new to you, but it is much easier than you might expect in practice. It is something we do almost intuitively, particularly when we are working co-operatively with the associative mode in our own minds to construct the imagery path.

54. Direct & Indirect Routes

Images can be evoked through either of two very different approaches. Traditional hypnosis *commands* relaxation: your eyelids are getting heavier and heavier, they are so heavy you cannot hold them open any longer. This often is called the 'direct' approach. Some years ago Milton Erickson developed another form of induction and therapy, which he called indirect hypnosis. In this, associative images are used extensively. The client is not told things directly, but concepts are suggested, through metaphor and double meanings, to the associative twin and thence into the unconscious.

Many people do not respond well to the direct techniques. 'No, it isn't!' is often their immediate reaction to direct suggestions. This reaction may be conscious (and therefore they are aware of their resistance) or it may be unconscious (and they only know that the imagery didn't work). For people who do respond well to direct suggestion, it is a simple, straightforward way to work. For the many people who don't, we have to be a bit tricky.

We have used both types of suggestion in the outlined relaxation exercise in Chapter 57. The first part of it, the induction, is direct, but the main body of the imagery is indirect suggestion, so you can clearly see the contrast between the two. This is probably a reasonable approach for use in relaxation imagery because it then works well for both types of people. By using the direct approach first, we give those for whom it does not work well a chance to defy something. With the rebellious part of themselves then up in arms watching for more commands, the indirect suggestions which follow may slip by even more easily.

Another technique of the indirect approach is to give a choice that is not as much of a choice as it seems. For example, in *Journey to the Waterfall*, the imager is given a choice of *where* to put the globe of healing, but he is not actually given a choice about whether or not to use it at all. He is distracted from that ungiven choice by thinking about where and how he might want to use it. The globe goes along with his choice, and then adds its own as well. In the end, the imager's analytic mode has been kept busy thinking about something that does not really matter, while the important choice of whether or not to use the globe and the issue of whether or not it might really work are bypassed without conscious notice or resistance.

What I am trying to say here is that, if you want to get someone to do something which might cause the rebel within them to balk, follow the suggestion immediately by a choice. This choice should be one where both options take the imager where you want her to go. For an example of this, see the part about getting the imager in the carriage in the *Emerald City* outline in Chapter 57.

The indirect technique may sound difficult, especially if you are accustomed to using primarily analytical thinking in your problem-solving. If you look back over the imagery we have done already, you will see how it has been used again and again, both in the main body of the journey, and in the inductions. This is a natural thing for the associative twin to do, being merely a specific application of the use of metaphor. If you have been doing the paintings and interpretations as suggested, as well as frequently using the imagery journeys them-selves, you may well find you have learned to use indirect suggestion almost by osmosis. If not, well, practice makes perfect — or at least, better and better.

55. Beginnings

The start of an imagery journey does much to determine its quality. This part of the journey is called the *induction,* and we use it to induce a relaxed, cooperative ASC in the imager. If the beginning is inappropri-ate or badly timed, people will have great difficulty in adjusting to and becoming involved with the journey itself. If the beginning is right, the whole thing is much easier for everyone.

In *Winnie-the-Pooh*, A. A. Milne wrote, "Here is Edward Bear, coming downstairs now, bump, bump, bump, on the back of his head, behind Christopher Robin. It is, as far as he knows, the only way of coming downstairs, but sometimes he feels that there really is another way, if only he could stop bumping for a moment and think of it."[15] This is a terrifyingly accurate description of the human condition much of the time.

Bumping down the stairs hurts, and this pain is, of course, the reason we keep looking for a 'better way'. As Pooh recognised, we need to stop bumping in order to think. We need to find a way to be still. This is why all of the imagery journeys begin with a process of stilling the mind and body.

It is very helpful for the imager if the guide begins each journey with a time for relaxing and focusing. When working with a group this can be a bit of a problem. Some people relax quickly and fall asleep (or shall we be polite and say 'into a deep ASC') if the induction is very long. On the other hand, others may just be starting to slow their mental merry-go-round. All we can do is try for a happy medium somewhere in between. It seems to be a law of nature that every group will contain extremes of both types. As people become more practised in imagery work, it usually also becomes easier for them to relax into it at the beginning, and if you are doing on-going work with a group, they probably will gradually grow more in harmony with one another in timing.

One group I worked with for quite a while included a young woman who had great difficulty with imagery. One night several members of the group complained of feeling unusually tense, and they asked for a full relaxation exercise as an introduction to the imagery journey. I did it, and to their chagrin, they all fell asleep (no nonsense about deep ASCs here — several of them were snoring). All, that is, except the young woman who usually found it so unfruitful. She had a wonderful, intense, emotional, rich journey filled with creative, magical images. She was so excited and overwhelmed by it, in fact, that she never came to the group again. These things happen.

Before beginning

It is sometimes helpful — and sometimes not — when you are leading others through an imagery journey that is new to them, to start by explaining something about its purpose. This explanation should not be enough to confuse, but enough to give them the idea that you do have an objective in mind. Keep this explanation as simple as possible. Just say something like 'this is an exercise in earthing and centering' or 'we'll be talking to your heart to find out what it needs from you' — don't get bogged down in long-winded explanations. You don't want to give the imagers time to decide that they know all about what is going to happen and what they will learn from the imagery before you even start.

Where the imagery is about a process — that is, an experience of something new and/or different in ourselves — healing, relaxation, stress reduction, or consciousness expansion, for example — it is usually best to let each step come as a surprise, and to give the very minimum of advance information about the journey to come.

It is also important at the beginning to remind everyone that they are in control of the journey, they can quit wherever and whenever they like. This is especially important for beginners. Let them know that continuing is always their choice.

The beginning

There are several suggestion below about beginning an inner journey. Use them with discretion and common sense. Some you may want to use often, others you probably will only need when working with beginners.

Remind people at the beginning that they are to accept the first thing that comes into their minds when you ask a question (if it is that sort of imagery journey). At the same time remind them that, if they miss something or if an image doesn't come, they should to allow themselves to go on to the next thing and to stay with you rather than struggling and falling behind.

Try to judge the mood of the group when you start your imagery. A group that is excited, tense, or inexperienced will need a longer induction than one that is relaxed and experienced. With practice, a guide begins to have a feeling for the length of relaxation process needed, and he can sense when his imagers are more or less ready to go on with main body of the imagery. This simply comes with practice and observation.

When working one to one, it's a good idea to ask an experienced imager whether he feels he needs a longer or shorter induction to the imagery.

You probably have noticed that I've used different beginnings and endings to each journey throughout this book. I could have used the same one each time, but I wanted to give you a variety of inductions and endings. I also want you to invent your own. Look at the different inductions given in the imagery journeys. As you consider them, note the types of images associated with relaxing and focusing on the imagery. The breath is used often because it is an excellent way of centering and relaxing at the same time. Notice that all the breath exercises centre on the natural breath, not on a rigid, counted kind of breathing pattern. Such formulated breathing patterns have their uses and are quite powerful for certain things, but they are not conducive to relaxation for someone who is inexperienced in using them.

56. Endings

The first thing we need, as we come to the end of an imagery journey, is to give the imager a sense of completion. A journey is not really over until we are home again and our bags unpacked. If you check back through the imagery journeys we have done, you will find some where we actually retraced our steps back to the beginning, but in others, we have come out through another path. It doesn't matter which you do, but it is important to have that sense of completion, of leaving the inner world and returning to the outer world.

As we leave the inner world, we may want to remind the imager of the points he particularly needs to remember — promises made, gifts given or received, et cetera. This makes a kind of mental bridge that helps him to bring the memory from the ASC to ordinary consciousness, rather than leaving it in the state-specific memory. At this point we may also want to reaffirm whatever benefits (healing, relaxation, re-energising) the imager might have received on the journey. Or we may just want to say something like, 'Now think back over the journey and consider what it may mean for you.' It's rather like getting back the photos we took on holiday, which, with luck, remind us of what a good time we had. It extends the benefit of the journey into our everyday world.

Once back in the outer world, we focus attention first on the physical body. We do this through having the imager pay attention to her breath and to other physical sensations, such as flexing the fingers and toes and stretching. We may also ask that she notice the environment around her. These are all ways we help the imager to become really earthed and centered in her body.

The deeper the ASC the imager has been in, the more attention and time needs to be given to the return.

57. Creating a New Path

Once we have clearly decided our objective and chosen the most suitable symbols to work with, creating the actual journey is relatively easy and fun. First, we need to help the imager to reach a relaxed, receptive, cooperative state.

Next, we need a path into a suitable environment for the journey, and a way to move from the relaxed state to that environment. This should be simple and not ask for too many leaps of faith at first. It also should have its own internal logical consistency. For example, we would not ask someone to go up in an elevator to reach the source of their depression — they would naturally need to go down. Nor would we start out by asking them to fly or to do some other 'impossible' thing — these things work best if they are reached gradually. The ability to fly, for instance, needs to be bestowed in some magical way before the imager is expected to do it. It is also usually helpful if the first steps are safe and not too risky seeming.

The next step depends on your objective. If we want information, we need an appropriate symbolic source and a set of questions to elicit the desired information.

If the object is transformation, we require a symbolic representation of what we want to be transformed into and a way to move from the imager-now to the imager-to-be. For transformation, we need to start where we are now, as in *Pool of Water* and *Meta-Mind*, move beyond that, and then come back to our (hopefully) altered self.

If we want healing or relaxation, we need either a direct or a symbolic way of moving the imager into that state.

Last of all, you need a way to bring the imager back to the ordinary world. Simple, isn't it? The fun and magic and effectiveness of the journey depends on how creative, imaginative, and intuitive we are about taking these simple steps. And we get a great deal better with practice.

I'd like us to work with a couple of examples. First, we have not done any imagery where the entire journey is specifically for relaxation, so let's do a structured one where the induction is direct imagery and the main body is indirect. We will just make an outline here, and you can write out a complete journey based on this outline.

THE LAKE

Suggest to imager that she sits comfortably and breathes.

Briefly state purpose of imagery and remind imager that she is in control.

Go through parts of the body, working up from the feet, and have the imager silently tell each part that it is warm and relaxed.

Imager standing beside a wide, slow river.

Imager walks along path by river, finds small boat, gets in.

At first imager rows, but then realises she does not need to work so hard, and puts oars in boat where they will be handy if needed.

Imager just floats along watching the banks and looking in the water.

After a while imager lies down in the boat, watches the sky and the drifting clouds. Imager sees images in the clouds (guide provides relaxing symbols for these images).

Boat drifts out onto large lake. The lake is completely calm, no wind, no current. The boat's own momentum carries it to the centre of the lake, where it drifts to a stop. The imager lies in the boat at the centre of the lake.

The imager sees a vision in the clouds — an archetypal image of peace and beauty. This 'something' may — or may not — interact directly with the imager in some way. The guide can choose the image or find a creative way to allow the imager to provide it.

A gentle breeze carries the imager's boat to the shore.

Imager gets out, feeling calm, rested, relaxed.

Bring imager back to ordinary consciousness.

The logic of the imagery

Here are a few things for you to think about. Why is the imager rowing at first? What are we metaphorically suggesting to her by having her put down her oars? What does the centre of the lake symbolise? What are we suggesting by having the special vision at the centre of the lake? How can you use the cloud images over the river to prepare people for the special vision later on? Which do you personally find more effective — the direct suggestions at the beginning or the indirect suggestions later on? Which is more fun?

For our second practice exercise, I'll give you an outline for an interactive imagery journey to visit the heart, the personification of our ability to love, to learn what our heart wishes to give us. From this outline you can create a full interactive journey.

EMERALD CITY

Suggest to imager that he sits comfortably and breathes.

Briefly state purpose of imagery and remind imager that he is in control.

Take imager through suitable induction procedure.

Imager is standing on a yellow brick road. Walks up road, finds a fountain, with beautiful water.

Drinks water, washes, plays in fountain.

Comes out, dries in air, and finds new clothes beside fountain — the most beautiful and comfortable clothes he has ever had. Old clothes have disappeared. Dresses, continues on road.

Road goes uphill. Finds carriage at the top, gets in. Imager tells driver how fast he wants to go. Driver agrees, starts out that way, but speed increases as carriage races down the hill.

Carriage goes faster, out of control, hits a bump, begins to fly, very high, still out of control.

Imager falls out of carriage, falls and falls, discovers new clothing acts as wings, can control flight.

Imager sees Emerald City, lands at the gate of the city.

Guard demands payment for entry, imager gives guard something that really matters to the imager.

Imager goes into city, everything is shades of green. Wanders around looking at buildings and people.

Does imager recognise any place or anyone?

Finds fountain at centre of the city. Is thirsty again, and is given a drink by the guardian (heart energy personification) of the fountain.

The guardian asks imager what is imager's heart's desire. Imager answers with first thing that comes into his mind.

Guardian listens and asks imager what he is currently doing to attain that desire.

Imager answers. Guardian offers to help. Imager chooses whether to accept help or not. They decide how guardian can best help.

Guardian gives imager a symbolic gift, explains meaning of gift.

Then guardian gives imager a pair of ruby slippers, which bring him back to starting place in ordinary world.

Bring imager back to ordinary consciousness.

The logic of the imagery

Once again we are using the idea of going to the centre and finding what we need there. To get there we had to wash and drink in the fountain and change our clothes (purification and ritual entry into magical world). To enter our own hearts we must take risks, become vulnerable, risk a fall. When we take risks for our hearts' desires, we discover unknown and unexpected capacities and abilities in ourselves (flying). The guardian of the fountain is, of course, our heart and the fountain is the energy of love and compassion, which the heart gives freely. The guardian offers to help, but we must let it know what we really want, and what kind of help we need.

The interpretation

How difficult is it to get past the guard at the gate (to enter our hearts)? Who and what do we find in the heart (Emerald City)? What is the heart's desire that arises spontaneously? The imager intentionally was not forewarned that he would be asked this. What is he doing to bring it about? What kind of help does he ask for? What gift is he given and what does it symbolise?

You see? It really is easy, and becomes much easier with practice. After practising with the above outlines, I suggest you create an outline of your own and use it. The first few times, you may want to write out a fairly complete journey in advance. However, you will probably want to move to using a briefer outline as soon as you can, especially on interactive journeys. This will give you an opportunity, as well as almost forcing you, to think more holistically as you go.

Let me also mention that the suggestions given here are suggestions only — not rules. Whatever *works* is right.

Treat the creation of an imagery journey as fun, and the journey will become a source of joy, knowledge and transformation. If you have a good time making it, others will have a good (and probably a more productive time) following it.

Review

Have there been any changes in your Elder Self since you first met it? If so, how do you feel about these changes? Is there anything about the Elder Self now that you would especially like to change? If so, which aspect(s) of your self could help work on that change?

How is your understanding of your dreams progressing? Have your dreams themselves changed in any way since you seriously began working with imagery?

How do you look to yourself now in the *Walk in the Forest* and how has that changed since the first time you did it?

Has freeform imagery become a tool you automatically use when you need insight?

Has working with healing imagery had any noticeable affect upon your health? Has your inner Healer changed since you first met it?

Part XV

Serving as a Guide

"He landed this morning. He might have met a great hero, or the cunningest of thieves, or some wise and great sage. He met you. He has employed you as a guide. You will be a guide, Rincewind, to this looker, this Twoflower. You will see that he returns home with a good report of our little homeland. What do you say to that?"

"Er. Thank you, Lord," said Rincewind miserably.

— Terry Pratchett
in The Colour of Magic

58. Leadership Skills

The leader of a journey has a great deal of responsibility. The plan of the journey has to be well thought out, with points of interest appropriately interspersed with places for rest and refreshment. Balance between education and fun, and balance between necessity and pleasure are required. It helps if the guide is a practical poet, as well as being knowledgeable both about the territory and the travellers.

Not only does she have to work out the itinerary, but she also has to deal with the problems that come up along the way, including the ones posed by the personalities of her group of travellers. Ingenuity, tact, and an ability to think on her feet are essential.

There are skills and techniques we can learn to become better leaders, but most of what we learn will come from experience. Our imagers are our best teachers. If we give one another honest feedback (tactfully so, when possible) on our leadership, we learn faster. If we can actually listen to and act upon constructive criticism without feeling hurt and becoming defensive, we learn fastest of all.

Leadership is not a privilege, but a rather burdensome responsibility — and anyone who thinks differently probably has some false ideas about what the job entails.

But it has its rewards.

From guiding others, we not only develop skills, but we also practise looking at things objectively. It is always easier to see what may be going on in someone else's imagery than in our own. The same is true of dream work, which is simply another form of inner imagery work. How often has someone told you a dream that baffled them, and you were immediately able to see some of its relevance to their life? Or the other way around? Being uninvolved helps clarity immensely, but there is also a kind of skill in the way we learn to question and look at things. As we practise with others, it becomes easier to apply to our own inner world.

Helping others also forces us to think in more holistic terms ourselves.

And of course, it is immensely rewarding to see others break through old patterns and release themselves from old constraints into new, more creative and fulfilling ways of being.

59. Group Tours

We have already discussed some of the difficulties we may have in finding the best pace for guiding a group through an imagery journey. In addition to that, some people will come back to ordinary consciousness after the imagery more quickly than others. Don't rush them, and don't pounce on them to find out what interesting things happened in their inner world. Give them a few moments to get themselves back together. If you suggest that they make notes about their imagery, it gives them a chance to focus back into ordinary consciousness before a general discussion is begun.

When everyone is more or less back together, you can start around the circle, one by one, in an orderly fashion, asking each person to share their imagery. Several things are important here:

1) Each person should take his proper turn, listening courteously and attentively to others when it is their turn.

2) It is the job of the guide to ask questions that will help the imager clarify the meaning of his symbolic imagery, and others in the circle can and should help with this — BUT it is not the job of either the guide or of other members of the circle to say what they think the imager's imagery is about! Nor should they make comments about its value or validity. The basic rule is: Questions are fine, comments are out. And comments thinly disguised as questions are very much out.

3) If an imager is having a great deal of difficulty expressing herself, it is often a good idea to ask if she would like you to go on around the circle and come back to her later.

4) If the imager seems to have had a very emotional experience, give him the time and attention he needs to assimilate and work through the experience (more about this in Chapter 61).

One of the first steps when leading a group through an imagery journey is to tell them that they can and should bring themselves out of the imagery if they become really uncomfortable or distressed. Discuss this before beginning, and explain that they may leave the room or do whatever they need to do to help themselves. They should, if at all possible, avoid disturbing the other group members *during* the imagery, but do give them an opportunity to talk their feelings through in the discussion following the journey, if possible.

60. Individual Journeys

One of the great advantages in working one-to-one is that the imager can respond verbally to your questions. In such a case, listen carefully to what he says so that you can ask any additional questions needed to aid him to clarify his experiences. Feel free to ask whatever questions are needed to help him learn more about what is happening, but if he does not seem to get something clear fairly readily, just pass on to the next step in the journey. Do not insist on getting each image clear. To persist when the image does not come readily may be digging into something that the imager is not yet ready to face and he will unconsciously resist you, perhaps even coming completely out of the relaxed ASC necessary for imagery work. Don't push him, just go with the flow, moving on with the journey outline and perhaps expanding on any areas that seem open for exploration or of special interest.

Sometimes people are so relaxed and turned inward that they speak very softly or slur their words together. If this is a problem, simply gently ask them to speak a little more loudly or to speak more clearly.

In guided imagery work, it is important that the imager understands what she is seeing and experiencing, but it is less important that the guide does. Sometimes, when the imager is having difficulty in expressing herself, all the guide needs to do is to ask if she clearly understands what is happening. If she does, go on. The guide can find out what happened later, if he needs to know.

If you are doing a structured imagery journey and there is no verbal feedback from the imager, watch for signs of discomfort. Wiggles, itches, frowns, moving into a more closed or tense posture — all these and more may be signs of distress. Before you begin such a journey, you may want to instruct the imager to lift his hand (or make some other agreed signal) if he is having trouble or feeling discomfort or distress. You may be able to quietly question the imager without losing the relaxed state, but if not, it might be best to terminate the imagery, discuss the problem, and if appropriate, start again.

61. Breakdown Or Breakthrough?

Although most imagery journeys are either enjoyable or neutral, occasionally we may hit a rough spot — or perhaps several of them in a row. Assuming you have paid attention to Chapter 32 and are working with people with a fair degree of emotional maturity and reasonably good psychological health, there will still be times when we encounter monsters in the inner world. These monsters may even have infected the inner world around them, turning it into a loathsome and nightmare place. There are many, many ways and circumstances in which these inner monsters can manifest themselves. These may be difficult for us to cope with because ours is such an emotionally repressed society.

First, there is the simple emotional release of old distress or anxiety, or other feelings. Perhaps this most often is experienced in difficulty with particular parts of structured relaxation or in healing imagery. We store our tensions, anxieties, and distresses in different parts of our bodies, and when we release the physical tension, we may become aware of the unreleased emotions behind it.

When we experience an emotion in the world and, for some reason feel unable to express it, we often suppress it by tightening up a particular group of muscles. Those muscles then stay tense to 'lock in' that emotion. We may, if the same distress occurs again, add it to the tension of the initial distress, which then becomes more solid, the muscles more rock-like. Masseurs and other bodyworkers often find that a client will begin to cry or to express anger or some other strong emotion when a locked muscle group relaxes during treatment. The same thing may occur in imagery work. These locked-in, old muscle tensions are called 'artifacts' and we tend to experience emotional release as they let go physically.

This works the other way around, too, of course. Imagery work may find and release a particular locked-in emotion, and the imager may realise later that there has been a release of muscular tension or pain as well. Their right shoulder may no longer hurt; the pain in the lower back may have gone, the tense, easily-upset stomach may become more peaceful.

The important thing to remember about these kind of releases is that they are old stuff, and they are not relevant to the present. If we look for 'reasons' for them in the present, we will become confused.

Once an exceptionally good masseuse, Judy Dean, was giving me a lovely massage, but there was one muscle in my right upper arm that just would not let go. She soothed it and coaxed it, she pushed it, prodded it, and stroked it, she worked at the release points around it, and it just stayed stone-like. Finally, Judy simply held my arm between her hands, and patting the muscle gently with one hand, said, "There, there, little muscle — everyone gets to relax *sometimes*." I burst into noisy tears, and sobbed for about five minutes, while Judy continued to hold the muscle, and to give me paper handkerchiefs. When I stopped crying the muscle was completely relaxed. I didn't know — and didn't need to know — what the tears were about. They were old stuff, an artifact from some experience long gone.

These artifacts may also show up in interactive or freeform imagery. Usually the best way to handle this is to just go through the experience, allowing the emotional release to take place without interference or reaction from the guide. *The guide does not need to sympathise, to fix anything, or to try to make the imager feel better.* In fact, trying to do so will usually hinder the release. The imager will let go of as much as he needs to — if he feels that he is being allowed the space to do so — and find his own balance. If we say something like 'there, there, it's all over now' or anything else that denies him the opportunity to simply express and release his old feelings, what we are really saying is that he is making us uncomfortable (possibly because of our own unreleased old stuff) and we want him to stop it.

This is a tricky balancing act that a guide needs to perform — trying to help the imager recognise when an emotion being released is actually relevant to present circumstances (and something may need to be done about it) and when it is just old stuff, an artifact, which only needs to be released. The thing that makes it so tricky is that we can always find something to be angry or distressed about, if we look for it. If the emotion really is a current issue, it will probably be obvious to the imager, but if she is saying things like 'it might be because . . .' or 'I *think* that it's . . .' we may be talking about an artifact. If we get it wrong on this, thinking that something is an artifact when it is not, it is not usually a major problem. Current issues have a way of returning again and again, until they have been properly dealt with.

This kind of old, locked-in emotion is something we frequently encounter in imagery. Also, it is usually the easiest to deal with, in that the imager actually does all the work and needs nothing from the guide but gentle, quiet support and non-interference. The only problems with this come when the imager doesn't allow himself to release the emotion and suppresses it again, because he doesn't feel ready to or doesn't know how to let go yet. I don't think we need to worry about this. After all, it is up to the imager to decide when he is ready, and if he needs help in letting go, it is his responsibility to ask for it. If we, as guides, try to push him, we will probably simply stiffen his resistance. If and when an imager *does* ask for help, if you have any doubts about your own competence to cope with another's heavy stuff, he should be referred to a competent and appropriate professional.

A less easy situation to deal with is when the imager is faced with a current issue that is painful and challenging. The thing that makes it difficult for the guide is that we seem, in general, to hold the mistaken idea that it is our responsibility to straighten out others' lives. It is not. Good therapists know this, and they don't tell their clients what to do or try to fix them. We have already looked at the idea that *we all know exactly what our problem is and we know exactly what to do about it — the guide's job is simply to help us to hear that information.* This means that the guide does not need to tell anyone how to cope or what to do, but simply that the guide should ask open-ended, non-judgmental questions, patiently, until the imager solves her own problem. This is often what interactive imagery journeys are all about, and they and freeform imagery are some of the best tools we have for this kind of personal problem-solving.

Generally speaking, we tend to think that unhappiness and 'negative' emotions are to be avoided — and that, of course, is how they come to be locked up in our muscles or upsetting our physiological systems in the first place. If we believe that we are not allowed to feel certain things (denial) or that we must not express them (repression), we certainly will find it almost impossible to allow others to do so. There are no 'bad' emotions — only ones that feel good and ones that hurt or exhaust us. All emotions are part of the human process, and they have their place in our development. All of them need to be acknowledged and faced with honesty, integrity, and compassion.

There is a particularly 'new age' problem with all this. Many people confuse *acknowledging* and *appropriately expressing* emotion with bombarding everyone in their environment with it. Suppression is not always a bad idea — especially if we want to keep the job or the relationship. All the world is neither prepared nor obligated to act as our therapist, non-judgmatically and objectively listening to us without reaction. We cannot always expect a detached, objective, compassionate attitude from others, especially when we are busy demonstrating our inability and/or unwillingness to give that to them. What we say and do will be remembered — even when it is forgiven, it is still remembered. We want to be reasonably certain that what we are saying and doing is what we really want to have remembered and that it is what we really mean — not just some passion of the moment, perhaps caused by something entirely unrelated. This kind of self indulgence can get us into much worse trouble than a bit of suppression.

What *is* bad, in the long run, is to just leave the feelings suppressed and pretend they are not there. We need to take them out, honestly face them, examine and clarify them, work through them, and *then*, if appropriate, talk to the people involved and/or take the action needed. In other words, in the real world, it is still important to think before we speak or act.

These things are all 'common sense' — it's just that they often don't seem to be remembered, and we may need to remind ourselves from time to time.

When you are working in a group, of course, you may not immediately know when someone has a problem. If someone begins to fidget or scowl or cry, these are rather obvious clues that they are having some kind of difficulty. There is little you can do about this, except to ask a few questions about the environment or something you hope will be neutral, and see if that seems to calm the imager. In this situation, the imager herself must take responsibility for her responses and for taking care of her own needs. She must decide whether to continue with the imagery or to bring herself out of it.

Perhaps the most difficult thing for the guide — apart from facing his own emotional stuff — is when an imager resists or is distressed or upset by the emotional content of her inner work and blames the guide. This happens a lot — you went too fast (too slowly), your voice was too loud (too abrupt, too quiet), you asked the wrong questions (didn't ask the right questions), you just didn't do it right. These criticisms may be expressed quite strongly. Such accusations tell us, especially when accompanied by tears or anger, that the imager may well have *displaced* her feelings from her own inner world and *transferred* them to the guide. *Don't argue with her.* If you do, she will just become even more certain it is all your fault. This is not a rational process, but it is a fairly common one, being a programme that many people have.

What the guide needs to do in such circumstances is, first, to breathe, and then to consider whether there may not be some validity to the criticism, even if the imager is obviously in a state of resistance and over-reactivity. Stay centered and earthed. This is the real test of how good a guide you are: can you let someone else vent their feelings without leaping immediately to your own defense and trying to prove them wrong and you right?

None of us is perfect, but we can at least try to get it right. When you are acting as a guide for someone else, there is an unspoken agreement that this is his time for dealing with his problems, not yours.

This is one of the most important things in this entire book. If we let someone freely express such feelings, listen with consideration, offer cooperation where we can (as in going slower, faster, et cetera), sooner or later he will either realise *for* himself that the problem is *in* himself, or he will reach a point where we can gently suggest that he may be experiencing some resistance or encountering an emotional block. It is only when he can truly accept that this is happening that he is going to be able to move on through the resistance. If we suggest it before he is ready to hear it, the resistance is usually strengthened.

It is usually at times like this, when resistance has been overcome, and emotions have been released that we find a new clarity, and break*down* becomes break*through* into a new way of seeing and responding to life.

62. The Qualities of a Good Guide

As you can see from the foregoing chapters, certain characteristics are especially valuable for the aspiring guide — patience, alertness, flexibility, and emotional clarity and balance, for a start. We need to have the patience to listen carefully, to move at a relaxing and comfortable speed, to give people ample time to explore one thing before going on to the next, to allow them to feel unhurried and unpressured as they grope through difficult patches where they encounter their own resistance, to deal with that resistance gently and lovingly, and perhaps most of all, to give them time to discover for themselves what may, if we have been really alert, have been obvious to us all along. We need a lot of patience.

We also need the flexibility to adjust to the imager's immediate needs instead of insisting on a set pattern, the ingenuity to find new ways to ask an old question without sounding as if we were nagging, the quickness to find gentle (perhaps even sneaky) ways around resistance, and the adaptability to adjust our ideas about the imager's needs as new information comes to light.

We need the emotional clarity and realism in ourselves that allow us to cope with our own emotions when they come up, without suppression or denial. If we can do this, we can usually accept other people's need to express emotion and allow them to do it in a healthy way, without overcompensating for our own denial by encouraging them to wallow excessively in their stuff — a fine line to balance upon.

We must try to listen with alertness and intelligence. We need to cultivate the much-neglected art of really hearing what someone else is saying, instead of giving most of our thoughts to our reply to what we *think* they are about to say — which is one of humanity's great communication problems.

And we need to remember that all of this is especially applicable when the person we are guiding is ourselves.

Above all, the good guide will continue to learn about the territory, and will invite comments and heed constructive criticism from her travellers.

Remember: We are being admitted to others' private worlds, to their most vulnerable places. We must respond to this honour and privilege with the integrity, tact, and compassion it deserves. If we don't, a kind and loving, generous universe will teach us why we should have done so. This is what ethics is all about.

Review

What do you feel, at this moment, is the most important thing that you have learned from working with this book?

Looking back through your journal, you may want to do an assessment of what you have learned, and how you think you may have changed.

Do you feel that you use imagery and associative thinking more fluently now than when you began this journey?

Once again, if you are sharing the journeys with others, it is time to review and reassess your skills in leading imagery journeys. If several or all of the members of the group share the task, you may want to have a discussion about the way that leadership has functioned for you. What can each of you do, both as individuals and collectively, to improve?

If you are working with a group, this is also a good time to review

Appendix A: Working Together. How would you assess your group's performance on the various points? Is there room for improvement? And if so, what commitment do each of you, as individuals, need to make to enhancing the functioning of the group? Do you want to continue to work together after you finish this book? If so, you may find it helpful to begin now to consider new objectives and goals for the group.

Part XVI

Encounter with a Magician

"You know what the greatest tragedy is in the whole world?"
said Ginger, not paying him the least attention. "It's all the
sons who become blacksmiths because their fathers were black-
smiths. It's all the people who could be really fantastic flute
players who grow old and die without ever seeing a musical
instrument, so they become bad ploughmen instead. It's all the
people with talents who never even find out. Maybe they are
never even born *in a time when it's even possible to find out."*

She took a deep breath. "It's all the people who never get to
know what it is they can really be. It's all the wasted
chances. Well, Holy Wood is my *chance, do you understand?*
This is my time for getting!"

Victor didn't. "Yes," he said. Magic for ordinary people,
Silverfish had called it.

— *Terry Pratchett*
in Moving Pictures

63. Meet The Magician

This is Real Magic — our creative energies acting in us and in the world constructively, compassionately, fruitfully, and with style and grace. We have to remember that in our anti-magical, analytical culture of the moment (fashions in cultures *do* change) Merlin, the great magician, is still bound in a cave, under the enchantment of another. The magic of inner creativity is bound by the limitations of the analytic twin and the suppression of the associative mode.

It may be that your own creativity is not fully free. It may be that your inner magician, like Merlin, is held in an enchanted cave somewhere in the recesses of your own mind — hidden by illusion and delusion. We do sometimes delude ourselves that we have no magic and that we are not creative.

Where is your unfulfilled potential concealed? And how is it disguised?

It doesn't have to remain this way.

Approximate travel time: 25 minutes.

THE CRYSTAL CAVE

Please be seated comfortably. This is an imagery journey to contact your inner magician, Merlin. It is best to sit with your spine erect and relaxed but properly aligned. If you are seated on the floor with your legs crossed, place your hands on your lap. If you are seated on a chair, please place your feet flat on the floor. Let your shoulders and neck relax, but keep your head erect during the exercise so that your entire spine remains in proper alignment. This will help you to stay awake and focused on the imagery. Allow yourself to relax into this position, your body balanced in an effortlessly relaxed yet erect posture.

First, just close your eyes and take a couple of deep breaths. As you inhale, breathe in relaxation and peace. As you exhale, breathe out all of the tensions and distractions of the day.

As you sit there, being aware of your body letting go, relaxing, I'd like you to become aware of movement of your breath, of the movement of your diaphragm. Be aware of the sensation as you inhale, as you exhale. Breathing in, breathing out. Be aware of your breath in your abdomen and chest. And be aware of your breath as it passes through your nostrils.

As you breathe, you may notice that some of your breaths are longer, some shorter, some more shallow, some more deep. The natural breath changes from moment to moment, the movement of air becoming easier as you relax, as you become more still. Be aware of the natural breath and its movement within you, and allow yourself to let go of any need to control, to *do*, and just *be* with your breath for a moment.

Imagine to yourself that you are inhaling through your navel, and as you inhale through your navel, your breath rises, rises up to your throat, and then as you exhale, your breath falls back down to your abdomen, and out through your navel. Imagine each breath, inhaling through your navel, the breath rising up to your throat, and descending again, exhaling through your navel, like a wave, washing in and up the shore and back out to sea.

Don't try to do anything special with your breath — just allow your breath to be free and natural. Some breaths will be faster, some will be slower, some may be shallow, some may be deep. It doesn't matter — just allow them to be whatever they are. Just imagine with each breath that the breath comes in through the navel, up to the throat, and back down to the navel. All through this journey you can allow yourself to continue allowing your breath come in waves, waves washing in and up, and down and out.

As each breath washes in, it brings a surge of warmth and energy. And as it washes out it washes away any tension or fatigue that may be in your body. Be aware of this in your breath; be aware of the life force flowing in with each breath and anything in your body that you don't need or want flowing out with the outgoing breath.

And as you continue to be aware of each breath, flowing in, flowing out, you are ready to begin your journey. As we begin travelling through your inner world, I'd like you to flow easily with all the things you see and all the things that happen. Just accept each image as it comes to you, flowing with the first thing that comes into your mind. Each image, no matter how strange, no matter how unusual, has something important to say to you. Let each thing be what it is, without trying to change it, and let it show you its true self.

And remember, that you are in charge here — you can quit or continue, just as you wish, at all times.

I'd like you to imagine that you are standing in the entrance of a cave. The cave seems filled with sparkling light, and even before your eyes become fully accustomed to it, you can see that the walls of the cave are covered with myriads of natural crystals.

As you enter the cave, the crystals seem alive with energy. What colour or colours do you particularly notice in the crystals? How big are the largest crystals? How small are the smallest? Touch them with your fingers.

What kind of texture does the surface have? Do the crystals or the cave have any scent?

As you continue to be aware of the colours and nature of the crystals, notice the air around you. How does it feel — warm or cool, moving or still, damp or dry?

In this cave, the light is dazzling and the walls and ceiling glitter brightly. Long ago and far away, so long and so far that you have almost forgotten it, you were told that Merlin is imprisoned in a cave like this. When you were told this, you were given a tiny key, and you find that you have this key with you now, hanging on a fine golden chain around your neck. Perhaps this is the cave where Merlin is trapped.

When you begin to explore the cave to see if you can discover a hidden door, you realise that you may have to use more than just your eyes, as it may be concealed by illusion. How is the door hidden?

When you find the secret of the door, go through it into the inner chamber of the cave. At first you may not be able to see in this chamber, your eyes still dazzled by the crystals, but you can still explore.

What is the floor of the inner chamber like? How does it feel to your feet? What is it made of?

If you touch the wall nearest you, what does it feel like to your fingers?

When your eyes adjust enough to tell, where is the light coming from?

As you are looking around, you discover Merlin himself. How is he kept imprisoned here?

Is Merlin old or young or in between? What colour are his eyes? And what one word best described the expression you see in them?

How do you feel as you look at him, and how does he seem to feel as he looks at you?

What is Merlin wearing? How can you tell, by what sign or mark, that he is a magician? And how is he different from ordinary people?

If you feel it would be all right to do so, ask Merlin to show you around the chamber. Perhaps he will show you his most prized possession.

What colours or sounds or scents do you especially notice here?

How do you feel about Merlin being imprisoned here? Would you like to begin taking steps to free him? If not, just leave now, locking the door behind you, and go outside and sit in front of the cave.

If you do want to help him, ask him what is needed for the next step in achieving his liberation. What does he ask of you?

Think carefully. Is this something you are willing to do? Is it something you *can* do? If not, ask Merlin for something else you can do, and reach a compromise agreement.

When you have reached an agreement, clearly state your pledge to Merlin.

Now ask Merlin what he will do for you as you keep your covenant with him. Ask him to clearly state his pledge to you.

This pact that the two of you have made is in itself magical, and Merlin immediately begins to change, becoming more of what he has the potential to be. How does he change?

Can you also feel any change in yourself?

It's time to leave now, so say goodbye to Merlin for the moment. If you want to, ask him when he wishes you to return to him.

When you leave the inner chamber, think carefully — do you want to leave the door open or do you want to lock it behind you?

As you pass back through the crystal cave, notice whether or not there has been any change in it. Is the door to Merlin's chamber any different? Are the colours of the crystals and the light in the cave the same or have they altered in any way?

As you pass outside of the cave, into the outer world, take a couple of deep breaths.

Notice the seat you are sitting in and the environment around you. And take another deep breath.

When you are ready, flex your fingers and toes, open your eyes, and stretch.

Think back to what you promised Merlin and what he promised you. You may want to write that down just now.

The logic of the imagery

It seems pretty plain. You must know all that by now. There is just one thing I would remind you of: what you do in your inner world is *real*. The actions you take there change who you are. Such change may be a little, or it may be a lot. You are changing yourself in several ways.

First, when we change the way we think about ourselves, we change the way we behave. The knock-on effect of this is to influence the way others treat us and the way they function in our presence. This may affect them so that they modify the way they behave in general, and this, in turn, influences others. It's like a pebble tossed in a pond; the ripples go out, bounce back from the edge, crossing and recrossing indefinitely. The first gentle breeze that blew on the ocean is still reverberating through it — and through the rest of the world.

It's like that great writer, Anonymous, said: The lifting of a finger disturbs the farthest star.

Secondly, by making an inner contract, you are giving parts of yourself permission to act on your behalf. You are awakening and empowering latent potential. In the imagery, Merlin became more of what he has the potential of being, and he is left that way. In essence, you are accepting this potential as an active, living, functioning part of yourself.

Just as we usually find it difficult to continue doing something after we see how invalid — perhaps even silly — our reason for doing it is, we also find it less easy to make excuses and *not* do the wonderful something we really want to do once we have seen that we have the creative potential to do it.

This is pretty powerful stuff.

The interpretation

You can learn a lot about your creative potential if you consider the symbolic form of the magician. I suggest you paint the magician, and then carefully consider the painting.

What was in the inner chamber with the magician? Were there any tools of the trade — books, musical instruments, painting equipment, or perhaps something else altogether? Are these symbols of your present expression of creativity, or are they just potentials? Each time you go back to visit the magician, notice the environment carefully. What does it and the condition of the magician tell you about the present state of your creative energies?

Possibilities for expansion

This is a specialist imagery journey for a specific purpose and not really suitable for other intentions. It was developed, using the principles in Part XIV, for a group that contained artists, some of whom were feeling that their creativity was blocked. They found it useful then, and so have many others from all walks of life. The possibility for expansion here comes in another way. If you do as you promised, and then go back and ask for the next step, and then do that, and continue this process indefinitely, you will find that your own creative potential, your own magic will become more and more powerful, more expressed and fulfilled. You only need to keep at it.

Is any of this real? Does it actually matter what we do in our heads? Remember:

> If it affects you, it's real enough.

In coming to the end of our journey together, I would like to give you one more game to play with your images, a game that combines analysis and association, logic and fantasy, reason and archetypal energies, to reach creative insights.

64. Imagic

This game is the opposite of name magic, which we considered back in Chapter 13. We use name magic to give ourselves an illusion of understanding and control. Image magic, imagic, does just the reverse, in that it starts with the names of images and restores some of their mystery and richness.

Go back over the imagery journeys that you have done and choose one in particular to work with. It might be one that you felt a bit unsatisfied about, particularly as far as your interpretation was concerned, or it might be one that stood out for some special quality of intensity or for some other reason. In any case, it should be one you *want* to work with now.

Choose three simple images from that journey. These images should be primary ones, images that are especially vivid in your mind, that particularly impressed or puzzled you, even though they might not sound special to someone else.

When you have chosen your three images, make up a very short story in which all three of the images appear. You may bring any other images and ideas into the story as it unfolds when they are needed by the story. Tell the story quickly, using the first ideas that come to your mind. Don't fiddle around with it, trying to be clever. If you aren't sure how this should be done, find a four or five year old child. Give the child three images — a cat, a tall tree, and a small dog would do — and ask the child to tell you a story about them. Almost any child can do it, unless it has been severely deprived of stories in its life. Now, you might think a story about a cat, dog, and tree would obviously have the cat chased up the tree by the dog, but a young child may surprise you, because children have not yet learned to avoid creativity by the use of cliches. This is the kind of story you want — spontaneous and free of preconceptions about what a story should have in the way of plot, beginnings and endings, logic, et cetera.

I wanted an example of this, so I just stopped writing for a bit and went for a *Walk in the Forest*. I find it a useful exercise to do every once in a while anyway. In this particular *Walk*, I encountered three things I don't understand very well. There was a bear flying above the trees. He just appeared of his own accord, without being looked for. The container was a little varnished oak keg, which seemed to be empty, but perhaps wasn't. The water was a fountain with a wren playing in it. So, I have a bear that flies, a rather nice little oak keg, and a wren. I shall tell you a story about them, just as it comes, and I promise not to cheat by rewriting and 'improving' it.

Once upon a time, a young bear lived in an ancient forest. He liked honey and stories and honey, in that order. He liked to read fantasies and myths and tales of faraway places, and he believed them all, every word, because even though he was young, he understood that believing is more fun than not believing. He was the only bear in the forest, but he had made friends with the rabbits, the squirrels, and the birds. He never managed to make friends with the bees because he kept stealing their honey and then they would sting him. It's very hard to be friends with people if you steal from them, or if they sting you.

One day the bear was sitting in a sunny meadow in the forest, reading an especially exciting story to his friends. It was about some gods and goddesses and their problems, which they solved by magic.

"I wish I could do magic", sighed the bear, when the story was over.

"I'd make meself invisible!" exclaimed an old rabbit.

"I'd magic an oak tree so that it always had bunches and bunches of ripe acorns, all lovely and luscious and ready to eat," said a young squirrel.

"What would you do, if you could do magic, Only Bear?" asked the wren.

"I'd make myself able to fly," answered the bear decidedly.

"Not an endless supply of honey?" asked the wren.

"I don't think honey would mean much if I had an endless supply of it," the bear responded thoughtfully. "It's probably the better for a few stings."

"You're a wiser bear than you look," said the wren, and he flew away, his wing tip just brushing the crown of the bear's head as he flew past.

A little while later, when the bear was walking alone, thinking about magic, a very strange feeling came over him. He felt like he had bubbles inside himself. He felt like giggling. He felt bouncy. He bounced once and then twice for the fun of it. On the third bounce he found himself soaring over the treetops.

"Oh, my!" said the bear. "Oh, dear!" said the bear. "Oh, wheeee!" said the bear. "Oh, ouch!" exclaimed the bear as he blundered through the upper

branches of a particularly tall tree. And he flew and he flew, dizzy with excitement, blundering and soaring, enchanted, delighted, and frightened nearly out of his wits. At last he came to a giant sequoia, and he managed to grab one of its huge, high branches. He clung to it, panting. "Oh, dear! Oh, my! Oh, oh, oh!" he gasped. "'Swonderful! How did I do it?" he wondered. "Will I be able to do it again? What if I can't? I'm miles in the air — what if I never get down again? Oh, dear. Oh, my."

Looking around him, he saw a small golden oak keg sitting on the branch a few feet away. He crept carefully over to the keg and picked it up and sniffed at it. "Smells of honey," he muttered. "Sealed tight, can't open it." He shook it experimentally. "Feels empty." He shook it again. "Or maybe it's full." He thought and he thought. Finally he said, "Either it's honey or it isn't — I can't tell. Either I can fly or I can't. Only one way to find out!" And, clutching his keg, he jumped.

And the last I saw of him, he seemed to be flying — or maybe he was just falling slowly. I can't be sure which.

The next step is to think about the story and what it tells us.

In this case, the wren, which was associated with my energy in the original *Walk In The Forest*, can do magic, and it does it with discrimination and great discretion. I really like that.

The keg, which represents the way in which I unconsciously feel others see me, either contains honey or it doesn't. No one can tell because it's sealed shut. I don't like that, because it tells me that I am feeling that I've shut myself off from others. I may contain sweetness or I may not — no one can tell. I need to take steps to connect more with friends, to be more companionable, to open myself to others.

The bear, the wonderful bear! Whenever an image appears without being invited, as this one did in my *Walk In The Forest*, it usually has something especially interesting, perhaps even important to tell us. These spontaneous images are often hard to interpret, partly because we don't have a ready-made context for them. From the unfolding of the story, I recognise this bear. It's me whenever I do something new, especially something I doubt I can do, where I question the actual possibility of doing whatever it is I'm attempting. I have plans for some big changes in the next few months, amounting to a major restructuring of my life. Can I pull it off? If my ideas get off the ground, will they continue to fly? Or will I strand myself out on a limb?

The story doesn't answer this, doesn't give me any assurances that it will all work, but it does give me some hope. It tells me that my own energy is capable of magic, of making dreams come true — discreetly and with discrimination, even without my noticing that it is happening. And it tells me that I am going to need to open up more to others if I want my wishes to magically come true. The bear was sharing himself with others when the wren decided to help. On another level, it would seem to imply that I need to pay more attention to my own desires — both the wren and the bear are, after all, aspects of myself. And there is the bear/bare sound-alike — is this in some sense my naked self? A more real self than people often see?

There are some other interesting things in the story — the difficult relationship of the bear and the bees, for example. I'm not certain what that is trying to tell me, but it may have something to do with that closed keg. Later on, when I have mulled this one over a bit longer, it might be useful to tell myself a story about bees, a bear, and a closed keg.

It also comes out in the story that the bear is wiser than he looks. He has a quality of childlike wisdom that I quite like. Perhaps it is the part of me that has that quality — that understands that honey is the better for a *few* stings and that belief is more fun than disbelief — perhaps that is the part of me that will actually achieve my plans and dreams in the future. This is also the part of me that is willing to hope and trust and jump. The doubter in me wouldn't even try.

Do you see how this all works? By making up a story (just any and every story will be the right one), we evoke our unconscious imagic to give us a deeper view. We are letting our imagery tell us another story, a bit further in. We are going further down the mountain, the Sun God with his light at our side, learning more secrets, bringing the light of insight to bear (an unintentional, probably not very significant pun) on the things we don't let ourselves see, and the Earth Goddess guiding our steps. We are using a kind of freeform imagery to enhance and clarify information given in our interactive imagery journeys.

This technique improves rapidly with practice. The more stories you tell yourself, the more meaningful and powerful they become. The more your creative energy/impulse/magic is used, the more creative you become. Creativity is like a muscle — if it is never used, it becomes weak and feeble. One of the wonderful things about these little stories is that they are just for us. We are not setting them up for judgment by others, although we sometimes might want to share them with someone who can be trusted to treat them with respect and love.

These stories don't have to follow any rules. They don't have to be logical or to have proper endings or beginnings or plots. They enhance our spontaneity as well as our creativity. *Anything* can happen in one of these stories — magic, jokes, tragedy — anything is possible. There are no limits. We learn best when we are having fun. We are most spontaneous when we are playing. Creativity arises from play and joy. It also arises from sorrow and grief. Basically, though, it comes from being alive.

The whole world tells us stories about our images and gives us messages about them, if we listen. I was playing this imagic game recently, working with three symbols — sand, eye, wind. The story that immediately came to mind was very short. It was:

Once upon a time there was a woman lost on the desert. The wind came up, and it blew and it blew. It blew sand in her hair, it got in her clothes, and in spite of everything she could do, it got in her eyes. And so she wept and she wept.

I got stuck there and couldn't go any farther — but the story didn't really end there, although I found it so distressing that I didn't want to think any more about it just then. I switched on the radio. At that very moment, a man's voice was saying, "It's like the poet says — when the wind blows the sand in your eyes until you cannot see for weeping, you must simply endure. For the wind will die and the sand will settle, and you will see a new world with new eyes."

And that, my dear, is what inner work is all about — discovering a new and living world, seen through new eyes by one who has endured and creatively transcended old limits and darkness, one who has discovered the divinity in all that is. In the end, of course, the only thing you can truly create is yourself, and whatever self you create, manifests in the world through everything you do.

So what do the gifts you received in the first journey, *Light into Darkness*, mean to you now?

Appendix A

On Working Together

There are several things that may make working together as a group easier.

Choosing the group

The first to consider is the choice of members for the group. They need to be comfortable with each other, although it usually works best if they are not close friends, relatives, or spouses. Close personal relationships, even good ones, can inhibit group processes in all sorts of ways.

Members of the group don't need to be alike, but they do need to have a certain kind of compatibility. I went to a hypnotist once to work on a particular problem that I thought hypnotherapy might help. The poor man, with his flashy diamond ring and little black mustache, reminded me strongly of the archetypical villain of an old-fashioned melodrama. I couldn't relax, I couldn't trust him. My inner ectype of Wicked Man plastered itself all over him, and I couldn't see the person for the ectype — and all my resistance attached itself to this. Needless to say, the hypnosis didn't work. It wasn't his fault and it wasn't my fault — it was just the way things were. There are people we are comfortable with, people we are uncomfortable with, and in this kind of group work, it is important to be clear about this. That intangible thing called *rapport* is of inestimable value here.

This doesn't mean we should all be alike, mirror images of one another. A diversity of backgrounds, a variety of ages, a mixture of sexes can all add to the richness of the group. It also does not mean that everyone will agree with everyone else all the time. Again, differences of opinion and different world views can enrich the process, enabling us to see things in ways that may never have occurred to us before.

In a compatible group the level of trust and openness will build and build, creating a special kind of personal yet objective bonding between members. I have been involved in groups of this kind that went on for years and years, with people hardly ever dropping out.

New people might join once in a while, but they either dropped out after a week or two, or they stayed forever.

Don't worry too much about getting this perfectly right to start with. A person who is incompatible with the group will usually be uncomfortable enough to drop out after a few sessions — often after one. If they don't, it may be necessary to ask them to leave. These things can only be worked out by trial and error. Sometimes the only solution is to disband the group and reform later, differently structured. Don't be afraid to try — mistakes are a part of our learning process.

For a group of this nature, I recommend a membership of six — too small for anyone to disappear into the wallpaper and large enough to offer a reasonable variety of viewpoints. I don't think that I, personally, would want to work with less than four or more than eight — and that's stretching it a bit both ways.

Regularity & commitment

Regular meetings are important. If we work together on a regular, scheduled basis, we build up a momentum that helps us over the barren or difficult parts of our own inner journey. Regular attendance by all the group members is also important. The members of the group need to be committed, both to the work and to each other. They need to respect the importance of being there for each other, as well as for themselves.

It is also helpful to have a set time to begin and to finish each session. Once these times are set, it is important to stick to them. Otherwise, the one or two people who are always a few minutes late get later and later, knowing that the group will wait for them. At the other end, there is always 'one more' thing to say or do — and it really can wait until next time.

People who come in late should avoid interrupting and calling attention to themselves by apologising to the group. They should simply enter quietly and join in with the work in progress.

Listening

One of the most important aspects of inner work is *listening*. On the whole, we don't listen to others or even to ourselves. Working in a group is one way to cultivate the difficult art of listening with openness and without prejudging someone's intention. What we normally do in a conversation is to partly listen, to jump to a conclusion about what the person is about to say, and to concentrate on what we are going to answer. We hear very little of their actual statements.

It is important to listen while another is talking in the group. Good listening requires the following minimum conditions:

a) don't interrupt while another is speaking,

b) don't whisper or talk privately with the person sitting next to you while the group is working as a whole,

c) don't leave the room while someone is speaking, unless it is absolutely necessary,

d) don't look bored — listen and be seen to be listening, and

e) don't busy yourself writing your notes or doodling while others are speaking.

In other words, the ordinary rules of common courtesy are applicable. All of the above rules concern things that are visible to others, but there are also aspects of listening that are entirely internal. Listening is just listening — it is not analysis, nor is it thinking about what clever thing you are going to say next. It is simply attending to the speaker and giving him your undivided attention. People can tell when your attention is actually elsewhere. Although they may continue to speak, not knowing what else to do, they know that they are not being heard, that what they say is not of interest or importance to you. They feel that they, along with their experiences and feelings, are being devalued and rejected. This is just as rude as interrupting. People have enough difficulty sharing their inner feelings and images without having to face this kind of discourtesy and rejection.

And of course, if you are not listening you are not learning. The experiences and images of others expand and clarify your understanding not only of them, but of yourself and your own images — if you really listen and if you really think about what they have to say.

Scapegoats

It is best not to get into blaming other members of the group for your own discomfort. Unless you have chosen, as a group, to be an encounter-type group with everyone being ruthlessly blunt about all their feelings — and I do NOT recommend mixing that sort of work with imagery work and the opening up of ourselves facilitated by this course — remember that the ordinary rules of tact, consideration, and politeness prevail. In fact, you probably need them even more in this work than in ordinary life.

There is a world of difference in the attitude behind a statement like 'you really hate your mother — in fact, you're quite a bitch' and 'what do you think this may say about your relationship with your mother and what you might do to improve it?' Instead of being negative and condemning, evoking defensiveness (and possibly anger), we need to be supportive, asking open-ended questions intended to invoke positive, constructive, perhaps even creative responses. But you shouldn't agree with her that it is all her mother's fault, either. Integrity with compassion is required.

One of the horrible things that happens if criticism and blaming become the order of the day is that the group begins to find one or two members that bear the brunt of the most of the resistance to the process by individual group members. They also are blamed for any pressures that may build up in the group as it works together. In that sort of situation people tend to go for the most vulnerable and leave the tougher well alone. These members then become the scapegoats for other's problems, and people do not take responsibility for their own feelings.

This kind of thing is totally out of line in a group where people are supposed to be focusing on healing themselves, becoming more open, and taking more responsibility for themselves. If unconditional regard is essential in this work — and I believe it is — then criticism, confrontation, and blame are completely out of place.

Unconditional regard

Unconditional regard means to listen without judging, to offer support without dominating, manipulating, or directing, and to be honest with compassion. It does not mean telling people what you think they want to hear, but it does require that we show integrity combined with tact and gentleness.

In such an atmosphere, trust develops, and we feel that we can open ourselves to one another, sharing things we may never before have admitted to feeling, even to ourselves. In such an ambience, miracles of healing may take place.

Confidentiality

Any working group of this nature should be a closed group in the sense that *nothing anyone says is* ever *repeated or revealed or used in any way outside of the group*. Everyone must be quite clear about this. A member may discuss his own images and insights and feelings with family or friends, but must *never* comment on other members outside of the group itself.

This is necessary in order to maintain the confidentiality needed to create an atmosphere of trust in which members can honestly and compassionately look at themselves. Obviously, this means that someone who is notoriously gossipy is not a suitable member for such a group. You may discuss your own processes outside, but not those of others. You can't even hint. The law of karma is that, when we make a mistake, the universe will help us to learn why we shouldn't have done it and what we should have done instead. Learning 'why we shouldn't have done it' can range from mildly embarrassing to completely humiliating, from merely difficult to thoroughly devastating. The longer we take in learning such a lesson, the tougher the lessons seem to get. You have been warned, she said in sepulchral tones.

This is not a competition

One of the problems in our linear-thinking, hierarchical society is that we get into the habit of judging everything — whether judgment is appropriate or not.

One of the saddest things we do is to invalidate our experiences in our inner world by judging them by some kind of inappropriate standard of excitement, drama, and extravagance. Other people's images often sound more creative, more magical than our own — and they usually think the same thing about ours. Whenever you hear yourself saying or thinking that someone's images are 'more' anything than yours, press your lips firmly together, acknowledge that you have temporarily slipped into being judgmental, stop it, and do what you are actually supposed to be doing at this moment instead.

I had one student long ago who always had incredible, sparkling, flashy, over-the-top images. Not for him the little house in the woods — his buildings were all palaces, his guides great masters, his grass greener and his creatures more amazing than anyone else's. One day he made a sudden shift into a quite ordinary inner world, and he seemed to gain more *practical* insight through this one journey than all of his preceding ones. Not surprising when you consider the amount of energy he must have been using to stage-manage his huge production numbers. The competitive spirit is entirely out of place in this kind of work.

Not only are we not competing for the title of Best Imager, we are also not in competition for the titles Most Profound, Most Emotionally Shattered, Most Sensitive, or Most High Anything-Else. We need to just take our journeys as they come — exciting moments and dull ones, little insights and important revelations are all grist for the mill of growth.

If a group's members get into dramatising themselves and their journeys and insights, the group is doomed. How is that for a bit of gratuitous drama?

Emotional reactions

Having said all that, there are times when we do have dramatic reactions in our inner journeys. We may cry, become distressed, feel anger, or experience an overwhelming joy. If we are not in the habit of crying 'Wolf!' every time we see a mouse, we are more apt to be encouraged to work through it by the group.

When this does happen, the person involved needs to be encouraged to talk it through. They may need to be asked questions in a sensitive and non-invasive way.

They do not need to be told what you think it all means.

They do not need to be told what you think they feel or ought to be feeling.

They do not need to be told what you think they think.

They do not need to be patted and hushed and told that it's all right.

They do not need to hear what other people are thinking or feeling about themselves at this time.

The is the moment when giving good quality attention is the greatest thing the other members of the group can do.

Leadership

If you are working with a teacher, fine — the leadership question is all taken care of. If you are working without one as a group of equal partners in this journey, there are some things you need to bear in mind.

First, analytic mode thinking is comfortable with hierarchies;

associative mode thinking is comfortable with circles. The trouble with hierarchical structures is that someone is always on the bottom — and this is not the kind of structure you want between equals. The trouble with circular structures is that no one takes responsibility for steering, and the group tends to wander at random. In our search for inner balance and integration, it might be useful to have the group structure mirror the holistic pattern we would like to see operating between these two modes in our own minds. Let's see if we can't find a balance between these two.

If the group is to operate efficiently, it needs someone to take responsibility for keeping everyone on track. One good solution is to rotate the leadership through all the members of the group. Since the book itself acts as a path, the guide only needs to remind people when they are diverging into other areas. The other duties of the guide are to get the group working on the session's activities, to talk the group through any imagery journeys in that session, to suggest a break and then to call the group back to work, and to bring the session to a close.

I don't recommend appointing two people as co-leaders — this tends to result either in a situation where they are either competing for the group's attention, or where they both defer so politely to each other that neither actually leads, or a situation where the more outgoing of the two takes over. It is much simpler just to have one person do it.

If a member of the group does not want to take a turn as guide, you may want to consider a couple of things. Is he saying that he feels inferior to the others in the group? Is she asking to be 'carried' by the group without sharing the responsibilities? Is he going to sit back and be critical or judgmental about the efforts of others without exposing himself to any risk? Is this a person who won't take responsibility for herself and will want to blame others when she has difficulties?

However the leadership question is handled, the leader of the next meeting should always know well in advance that it will be his responsibility. For one thing, he or she will need to study the material in advance of the meeting. All members of the group who are going to act as facilitators might find it helpful to read *Appendix B: For the Teacher*. It is also a good idea for the leader to review it when it is their turn in the leader's chair if they are inexperienced in leading groups.

If the leader thinks of herself as the person who is helping others get the most out of being there instead of the Person In Charge, she will make a much better job of it.

The lesson plan

This book is not divided into sections that I think should make a session. The rate at which you travel through these experiences will vary greatly from person to person and group to group. Simple things like the fact that it takes longer to go through the individual discussions of the imagery journeys as the group becomes larger make it impossible to estimate suitable times. For a group working together as partners, I recommend making this an open–ended course which finishes whenever you finish. Just do what you can each evening, and don't worry about reaching a predetermined target.

It probably would be helpful if all of the group members read the relevant theoretical chapters before the next meeting, so that you could go directly into a discussion of the material (making certain that you all think it means more or less the same thing), and then settle down to the imagery, paintings, and interpretation.

Take your time with this. In order to achieve what I really hope you will gain from all this, the imagery journeys should be used extensively, both in the group and privately. They and the interpretive techniques (including the paintings) need to become a tool that you automatically reach for in time of need.

Besides, if you are not hurrying, it will be a lot more fun, and I hope you will enjoy it very much.

Appendix B

For the Teacher

There are two intentions behind this book. One, the explicit one, is to teach the use of imagery for personal growth and healing. The other, not so explicit (until Chapter 43), is to help many people to develop a new way of thinking. There are various splits in the mind — conscious-unconscious, analytic-associative, and the 'why not? versus the 'play it safe' urge. There are three things we are trying to do here.

1. Develop a natural and individually appropriate balance between the analytic and associative modes of thinking to eventually produce an integrated holistic mode.
2. Teach the conscious mind to listen to the messages of the unconscious, and the unconscious to send clear signals to consciousness.
3. Become skilled in finding a creative, constructive, reasonable and realistic balance between the 'why not?' and the play it 'safe' urges.

At this point you may want to read Chapter 43, *Two Travellers*, which is an explanation of the analytic and associative modes and the differences between them.

The imagery journeys, paintings, and interpretive techniques are designed to teach people to not only listen to both modes of thinking, but in time, to get them engaged in active cooperation. The holistic mind is not an either/or place, but is an integrated, creative, intuitive place, open to insight and inspiration. This probably will not be achieved right away. To reach the fullest flower of holistic thinking may take years of practice with these techniques, but the benefits of using them will be felt almost immediately. One of the most important things the teacher can do to enhance this process is to continually encourage the students to use these techniques and tools for problem-solving and clarification in their daily lives.

There may be a temptation, especially if you are not 'artistic' yourself, to leave out the paintings as unnecessary and time-consuming, but the paintings and the techniques for working with them are absolutely essential to developing a good associative-analytic balance. Most of us learned analytical techniques in school. In fact, such techniques are usually the primary scholastic emphasis, especially for older children. We need to start with some simple techniques for learning to consciously use associative thinking, and the paintings provide much of the scope for that. The attention given to feeling, to colour, to form and line and space are all a part of reclaiming the wisdom of the associative mode, and integrating it into our thinking and into the interpretations of our spontaneous images, the messages of the unconscious.

Even the use of stories is a part of the pattern. They give the associative thinkers an image to help them to get the point, but they also encourage the analytic thinker to put an image in their minds along with the words, making it more memorable. I recommend adding your own teaching stories that illustrate the points as well. Preferably, these stories should not be heavy-handed moralistic tales. Humour, like Mary Poppins' spoonful of sugar, (there is a nice little associative image to stick the point in your mind) make the implicit, perhaps even unspoken moral of the story go down painlessly. Stories add feeling and life, and stick in the memory better than dry theory.

There is no right or wrong balance between the analytic and associative modes. In some people the analytic is dominant, in others the associative, and most of us will find ourselves tending toward one side or the other. It is vitally important for each of us to develop the right individual balance for ourselves. We need to be able to move back and forth freely between these modes, and we need to be able to combine them appropriately for the different activities in which we might engage, if we are to do so creatively and effectively.

Going on automatic

Learning the various techniques for using the associative mode and for bringing it into co-operation with the analytic mode is only an intermediate step to something else. We are using these techniques to retrain our conscious thinking, and this will eventually filter down to our automatic, unconscious process of thinking. When we learn a new skill, like driving or handwriting or sewing, we begin by learning bite-sized bits in logical, sequential steps. The process is taken apart for us so that we can deal with one piece at a time. Dealing with all those pieces is often very complex. However, at some point in this learning process, we make a quantum leap. We learn the process so well that it becomes automatic and unconscious — we just do it.

This will happen with the imagery analysis techniques, if they are practised sufficiently. We take that quantum leap as they become automatic and unconscious. We then have a richer and more productive way of processing information, without consciously and laboriously thinking about it. This also allows the unconscious to contribute directly to the analysing and integrating process. The information is then presented to consciousness as a developed whole, a creative insight.

To get to that point, we must go through the slow steps of learning the skills, one by one, or we will be unable to see and understand. With practice, insight and intuition will present themselves to consciousness without all those slow, arduous steps. We will be able to ask for a symbolic image and just *know* what it means; we will better understand the meaning of our dreams; our lives will be filled with a sense of meaningful purpose — and from that, creativity flows. And when we get stuck, we have our step by step techniques to fall back on.

A small warning

It should also be emphasised that the preferred and primary mode of thinking is not expected to change from one to the other when we learn to use the other mode more freely and effectively — although it might move more toward the balance point between them. Such a change can be expected only if someone has been forcing himself to value and operate in a mode that is not his natural mode, while strongly suppressing his natural way of functioning.

If someone has been doing that, driving everywhere in reverse, there may be fairly deep psychological problems. Helping such a person find a more appropriate balance might require both a high level of skill and extensive undivided, individual attention — assuming that person *really* wants to make such deep level changes. This amounts to changing *who* we are.

Because the different modes have different values and priorities, it also means establishing new values as well as different ways of functioning. This is extremely difficult to do. Not impossible, but so challenging as to often seem both impossible as well as undesirable to the person involved. To want to change our system of values, essentially to become someone else, is almost unthinkable — and often frightening.

Such a person may experience great resistance to learning and using the techniques which develop the suppressed mode. And they may need professional help if they are to succeed — assuming that they want to. Extreme analytic mode users are more apt to make this choice, because repression of the associative, feeling mode may result in severe physical disorder. The extreme associative thinker usually suffers from believing they cannot cope with ordinary life. Chaos reigns, and sadly, they tend to resign themselves to this.

Which is which?

As teachers, it is useful to recognise the associative-analytic balance in our students and ourselves. In Chapter 44 there is an exercise in right brain-left brain integration. In the process of doing this exercise, we often experience a noticeable difference between one side of the brain and the other, and this is one way of observing and assessing the degree of balance and of blockage individuals experience.

We can also look at the information given on the signs and symptoms of the two modes, their abilities and difficulties, and maintain an ongoing assessment of students and self — although it is, of course, much easier to see in others than in ourselves.

We need to know how our students function most strongly so that we can present information in the way most likely to be understood, especially when we are trying to answer individual questions.

I have found it interesting and challenging to try to put into written form balancing techniques that I use intuitively, on the wing, in classes and with individuals. I hope you find it rewarding to use.

Appendix C

Taping an Imagery Journey

The imagery journeys in this book are copyright. You have permission to make tapes of these journeys for your own use, but you may not sell or use them commercially, nor may you make tapes of them for others, whether you intend to sell them or not.

Many people find it helpful to make themselves a tape of an imagery journey. I recommend it highly. Guiding a journey that you don't know by heart while simultaneously doing the journey is rather like trying to read a map while you drive. Driving is easier with a good navigator in the passenger seat, and your tape-recorder can be an excellent navigator. That way we can relax and concentrate on the images instead of worrying about what comes next. If you do (or are planning to do) a lot of personal growth work, it is a good idea to get in the habit of taping meditations, guided imagery, and some exercises — it encourages us to use them more frequently. Making tapes for your own use also gives you practice in guiding the imagery, which will be useful if you want to guide someone else.

Most of us are embarrassed (or even appalled) at first by our own voices on tape. They sound so unlike ourselves — which is curious, because other people sound like themselves, at least to us, on the same tape. This is just something we have to get used to. If we don't like what we hear, we can always work on changing it.

In taping guided imagery it is important to go slowly enough to allow time for the images to arise and complete themselves in our (hopefully) relaxed state — but not so much time that we go to sleep or wander off to greener mental pastures. Be certain to leave adequate pauses after each question or statement for the images and feelings to rise to the surface of the mind from the deep unconscious. Also allow plenty of time at the beginning for the initial relaxation and centering. The 'best' pace is something that each of us needs to find for ourselves. This matter of timing is difficult for the beginner. People usually make several tapes that are too fast before they get the speed right.

Taping a live session when you are the guide and someone else is the imager is also useful. In replaying it, you may well hear things you missed during the actual journey. These things could be fruitful topics of discussion with the imager. Also, listening again to the imagery may stimulate the imager to tell you something that happened that she didn't mention during the journey. Such repressed information may give you an entirely new slant on what is really going on and/or what you might want to try with that imager in a future imagery journey.

If you have two tape decks there is another thing you can do when you are working on your own. When you are actually going through the journey, make your replies out loud and tape the whole session, both the original imagery recording and your comments. If you need to, you can keep your hand on the pause button of the recorder playing the original tape and give yourself time to make your replies. This may seem a bit awkward at first, but it usually becomes automatic in a fairly short time and doesn't interfere with the imagery. The advantage is that you don't have to try to remember what is happening to think about it later — it is all there for you. As in working with another person, you may hear things in the second tape that you didn't notice at the time or you may be reminded of things that seemed 'not worth mentioning' at the time, but which may seem quite significant later on. This technique takes a bit of practice, but is well worth developing, especially if you don't have anyone else to work with you as you go through the journeys.

There are a couple of chapters which contain information that might be especially useful in making tapes. They are Chapters 8 and 59.

For a catalogue of imagery tapes by Jessica Macbeth, please write to:

Gateway Books
The Hollies
Wellow
Bath
BA2 8QJ

or

Atrium Publishers Group
11270 Clayton Creek Road
Lower Lake, CA 95457

Notes

1. *The Pocket I Ching: The Richard Wilhelm Translation*. translated into English by Cary F. Baynes and simplified (abridged) by W. S. Boardman. London: Arkana, 1984.
2. If you want to know more about these two modes, and why they are important in imagery work, please read *AppendixB: For the Teacher*.
3. These are simple one-pointed meditation techniques. If you want to know more about thme or to try others, I suggest you read *Moon Over Water* by Jessica Macbeth, Gateway Books, 1990.
4. *The Magical Child* by Joseph Chilton Pearce. New York: Bantam, 1977.
5. C. G. Jung in *Dreams*, p. 9. London: Ark Paperbacks, 1985.
6. John Donne in *Sermons*, i, p. 820, No. lxxx. At the Funeral of Sir William Cokayne.
7. C. G. Jung in *Dreams*, p. 9. London: Ark Paperbacks, 1985.
8. Muz Murray in the letter column of *Link Up*, December 1989, *41* p. 18.
9. Jean Houston, PhD, in *The Possible Human*. Los Angeles, J. P. Tarcher, Inc., 1982, p. 135.
10. Ibid.
11. Alan Bleakley in *Earth's Embrace*. Bath: Gateway Books, 1989, p. 27.
12. In *The Thirteen Clocks* by James Thurber. Puffin (Penguin), New York & London.
14. For a more technical discussion in academic language of the experiential criteria for recognising an ASC, see *States of Consciousness* by Charles T. Tart. New York: E. P. Dutton & Co., 1975, pp. 12–13.
15. A. A. Milne in *Winnie-the-Pooh*. Methuen, London.

Recommended Reading

Edwards, Betty, *Drawing on the Right Side of the Brain*. Fontana/Collins, 1979.

Feinstein, David, & Krippner, Stanley. *Personal Mythology*. London: Unwin Paperbacks, 1989.

Houston, Jean. *The Possible Human*. Los Angeles: J. P. Tarcher, Inc., 1982.

— *The Search for the Beloved: Journeys in Sacred Psychology*. Los Angeles: J. P. Tarcher, Inc., 1990.

Macbeth, Jessica. *Moon Over Water*. Bath: Gateway Books, 1990.
888